Contents

THE WELCOMING CONGREGATION HANDBOOK

Resources for Affirming Bisexual,
Gay, Lesbian, and/or Transgender People

Second Edition

Unitarian Universalist Association
Office of Bisexual, Gay, Lesbian, and Transgender Concerns

Contributing Editors
Scott W. Alexander, Meg Riley, and Keith Kron

Assistant Editor: Barb Greve
Production Editor: Brenda Wong
Text Designer: Suzanne Morgan
Cover Designer: Bruce Jones

ISBN 1-55896-190-9
Printed in the United States.

10 9 8 7 6 5 4 3 2
05 04 03 02 01 00

Contributors

Terry Burke
F. Jay Deacon
Lucinda S. Duncan
Ann Fields
Wendy Fitting
Harry H. Hoehler
David Miller
Barbara Pescan
Marianne McCarthy Power
James Robinson
Douglas Morgan Strong

Acknowledgments

Dr. Roberta Harro and Dr. Patricia Griffin, who developed the entire Workshop Series, acknowledge their gratitude to Diversity Works.

We are grateful to many individuals, publishers, and gay rights organizations for the use of their material in this handbook.

"Definitions of Oppressions" is from "The Common Elements of Oppression" by Suzanne Pharr in *Homophobia as a Weapon of Sexism* (Iverness, CA: Chardon Press, 1988). Used by permission.

"Twenty Questions About Homosexuality" is used by permission of the National Gay and Lesbian Task Force, 1517 U Street, NW, Washington, DC 20009, (202) 332-6483. (The National Gay and Lesbian Task Force is the oldest and largest national civil rights organization dedicated to building a movement to promote freedom and full equality for lesbians and gay men.)

"What Does the Bible Say About Homosexuality" by the Reverend Dr. F. Jay Deacon is used by permission of the author.

"Inclusive Liturgy and Preaching" by Chris Glaser is from *Breaking the Silence, Overcoming the Fear* (The Program Agency, Presbyterian Church, 1984). Used by permission.

"Biblical Perspectives on Homosexuality" by Walter Wink is from *The Christian Century*, November 7, 1979, no. 46A. Used by permission.

"Klein Scales" is adapted from "The Klein Sexual Orientation Grid" by Fritz Klein in *The Bisexual Option,* 2d ed. (New York, NY: Haworth Press, 1993). Used by permission.

"Homosexual" and "Sex" are from *Whistling in the Dark* by Frederick Buechner. Copyright 1988 by Frederick Buechner. Reprinted by permission of Harper & Row, Publishers, Inc.

Responsive reading by John Fortunato is excerpted from *Embracing the Exile.* Copyright 1982 by John E. Fortunato. Reprinted by permission of Harper & Row, Publishers, Inc.

Responsive reading by Carter Heyward is reprinted with permission as published in *Our Passion for Justice: Images of Power, Sexuality and Liberation* by Carter Heyward. Copyright 1984, The Pilgrim Press, New York, NY.

INTRODUCTION

Second Edition

Oppression changes.

Homophobia and heterosexism are alive and well, yet the oppression has become more sophisticated. For example, it used to be that gay and lesbian people were seen as being child molesters and were dangerous to children. Now it is said that children need two parents of different genders to be healthy and that having openly gay or lesbian teachers is confusing to children and they are not ready for this. The message is the same: Bisexual, gay, lesbian, and/or transgender people are second-class citizens, less important than heterosexual people, and less valuable to society. Only the way that it is presented has changed.

The way we work to dismantle oppression needs to change as well. This work is a process, and our strategies must be constantly monitored and evaluated. Change is an important piece in this process. In 10 years, who knows what changes we'll need to make? The world will be different then.

It took two years of revising the *Welcoming Congregation Handbook* for me to figure out the real reasons for doing these revisions. That is not to say that the original reasons were not adequate. I originally decided to revise the handbook because it seemed out of date and was missing several components. Lip service was given to bisexual issues, and transgender concerns did not appear at all. The second edition is more inclusive of bisexual and transgender concerns. Admittedly, there is still less material on these areas than on gay and lesbian concerns, and the material is far more basic and introductory. What our eight-year history with the Welcoming Congregation Program and our thirty-year history around dismantling homophobia tells us is that as people work through their understanding of homophobia, biphobia, transphobia, and heterosexism, they progress in predictable ways. People deal with homophobia first, then biphobia, and finally transphobia in that order. The quandary is how to end oppression against all people in the most expedient way. While the hope is that someday this will change, for now, this truth guides the selection and amount of materials for this handbook.

If your congregation has different needs about these issues than what is presented here, please contact the Office of Bisexual, Gay, Lesbian, and Transgender Concerns at the Unitarian Universalist Association for more information or referrals to more information.

My second reason for wanting to revise the handbook was that it seemed to be designed solely to educate heterosexual people. However, many bisexual, gay, lesbian, and/or transgender people take this program. My hope is that all people will gain something both for their congregations and for themselves from the series. Bisexual, gay, lesbian, and/or transgender people should have the same opportunity for personal depth work as heterosexual participants.

Also, the handbook had not been looked at through an intentional anti-racist, anti-sexist, anti-oppressive lens. Additionally, this book seemed to have little connection with Unitarian Universalism or religion—at least directly. Dismantling homophobia and heterosexism is religious work. Why not have more of a connection to this throughout the manual?

Lastly, as a teacher and minister, I—perhaps arrogantly—felt the actual sessions themselves could be more varied, up-to-date, and interesting. I felt strongly that a program that teaches there is more than one way to be in the world should utilize a design and practice that model more than one way of learning. While the Welcoming Congregation Program is flexible, its original design did not take into account congregational size or location. It seemed designed for mid-sized, suburban, middle-America congregations. The program operates slightly differently in other kinds of congregations. Feel free to make adjustments based on what you need to do.

Large Congregations. Often, the program reaches some folks in larger congregations, but it is hard to reach everyone. Offer the program several times. Make use of the bulletin board and newsletter to relay information. Consider ways to "infiltrate" the entire congregation. One suggestion is to have every committee in the congregation do shorter versions of two of the sessions. Think about milling time—letting people know there are folks who are willing to talk about Welcoming Congregation during coffee hour and have them stand and be recognized in the Sunday service. Create formal and informal opportunities for people to talk to you and each other about it.

Mid-sized Congregations. The program is designed for these groups. Offering it more than once is still a good idea. Keep influential people in the loop of information.

Smaller Congregations. Most smaller congregations scramble through the program because of the human power needed to undertake this project. Do less, but be more deliberate and intentional. You might want to do the program as a retreat over a weekend. In less traditional settings, you might think about doing a series of four sessions as Sunday services, adapting them to make them more of a worship service. Consider modifying the sessions to do an adult religious education series for an hour before or after the service. Make the program work for you.

Geography. You know best the political terrain of your community and congregation. Keep these things in mind and adapt the program accordingly. Various parts of the continent are in different places around bisexual, gay, lesbian, and transgender issues. In a place where there is a lot of hostility toward bisexual, gay, lesbian, and/or transgender people, there may be either fear or excitement (or both) about doing the curriculum. In very liberal places, passivity is common and people wonder why you are attempting the program. If you are unclear about how you might answer these questions, you may wish to contact the Office of Bisexual, Gay, Lesbian, and Transgender Concerns and explore possible answers.

Time Frame. Most congregations can expect to complete this program within 18 months. The program may take longer in a congregation with an openly bisexual, gay, lesbian, and/or transgender minister. Often many people deal with their homophobia quietly and first speak to the minister of their congregation with their concerns. If the minister is bisexual, gay, lesbian, and/or transgender, this resistance and work may take longer to surface. Whenever you start hearing resistance in your congregation, this is often a sign of progress—even though it may not feel like it. Open concern and resistance are steps beyond silent resistance.

I must confess to being pleased with the results of this second edition. Some of you have experienced these revisions and your feedback has been both useful and affirming.

Yet not until I began to write this Introduction did I really understand why I have revised this handbook. My experiences and my training around anti-oppression work have led me to some interesting conclusions. The most significant conclusion is if we are not intentional about dismantling oppression as well as stopping it, oppression will change into a new form.

I want to thank Barb Greve, Susan Gershwin, Carol Johnson, and Paige Getty for their input, feedback, and listening ears. I also want to thank all of the people who contributed through writing or revising their work and those who were guinea pigs as this manual developed. There is more I could have done, more I wished I had done, best laid plans that went awry, deadlines that came and went too quickly. But, remember, *you* will make more of a difference than this handbook will. People will look at your convictions, your style, your openness to change as a model for themselves. A manual will not change the world. People will—if they choose to do so.

Good luck as you undertake this important religious work. Be careful though. You may change the world a little by doing so. You risk changing yourself as well. I know I did.

Rev. Keith Kron
Director
UUA Office of Bisexual, Gay, Lesbian,
and Transgender Concerns
January 1999

First Edition

How the Welcoming Congregation Program Came to Be

In 1987 the Unitarian Universalist Association, sensing that there was a great deal of unexamined and hurtful homophobia in local congregations, established the Common Vision Planning Committee (CVPC). It was the task of this diverse committee of clergy and laity from across North America to assess the degree to which bisexual, gay, and lesbian persons felt welcomed and accepted in their own congregations, so that if necessary, a remedial program could be developed. No one was quite prepared for the painful stories that emerged.

Although the Unitarian Universalist Association (UUA) had been on record since 1970 as supporting the rights and worth of bisexual, gay, and lesbian persons, the CVPC heard from many individuals who felt profoundly unwelcomed, unaffirmed, and unsupported in their local congregations. Anonymous surveys of thousands of individual Unitarian Universalists further revealed many negative attitudes, deep prejudices, and profound ignorance about bisexual, gay, and lesbian life and persons. The hurtful exclusion that resulted (much of it subtle, polite, and unintentional) made many bisexual, gay, and lesbian Unitarian Universalists feel that they did not have a safe or comfortable place in their home churches. This lack of an accepting and affirming environment led many of them to either drift away from their congregation, or stay deep "in the closet," hiding this fundamental fact about who they were from other church members.

The reality and pervasiveness of this homophobia and exclusion troubled the many in our faith tradition committed to making our congregations welcoming and inclusive places for *all* people, especially minorities that are despised and dismissed in our society. Citing the first principle of our Unitarian Universalist faith—that we "covenant to affirm and promote the inherent worth and dignity of all persons"—the delegates of our denominational General Assembly voted in 1989 to initiate the Welcoming Congregation Program recommended by the Common Vision Planning Committee. It was a call to make our congregations truly welcoming places for people of all sexual orientations.

This manual is designed as a practical resource for any congregation or faith group interested in becoming more welcoming of bisexual, gay, lesbian, and/or transgender persons. The problem of homophobia, which is so pervasive in our society, also runs deeply in all kinds of religious communities. The materials and workshops we have developed will help people of any faith tradition examine their homophobia, biphobia, transphobia, and heterosexism (conscious and unconscious) and move toward new and more inclusive attitudes and behaviors that will make bisexual, gay, lesbian, and/or transgender people in congregations feel genuinely safe and at home.

Take the Time to Allow Dialogue and Build Consensus

This manual is not a blueprint for how to build a perfectly welcoming congregation. It is an artist's sketch of what an inclusive and accepting church might look like, and how your congregation might get there by following an array of user-friendly materials. We hope you will not let the sheer volume of these materials overwhelm or intimidate you! We encourage each unique congregation to select, adapt, and employ this smorgasbord of resources to best fit their own particular situation, needs, problems, and concerns. This program will work, look, and feel different in every congregational setting. When preparing to participate in the Welcoming Congregation Program, each congregation's leadership should decide the content, pace, and style that will work best in their unique situation.

A congregation that is interested in becoming more welcoming of bisexual, gay, lesbian, and/or transgender persons will need to take the time to involve as many people as is possible in the decision-making process. The more listening, consultation, dialogue, and consensus that occur at the beginning between the professional staff, trustees, boards, committees, and members of the congregation, the more likely the program is to succeed once the congregation as a whole is invited to participate.

Once the leadership of the congregation has laid this groundwork required for a successful beginning, they will need to focus their attention on the program's Guidelines, found on pages 13 and 14. Both the Commitments and Actions need to be carefully studied so that the premises, parameters, and possibilities of the program are clearly understood. Please keep in mind that these are guidelines, not dogmatic absolutes. You may decide to adapt them for your congregation's particular circumstances.

Unitarian Universalist congregations beginning this program have Welcoming Congregation Program Trainers in every UUA District, who are available to lend support and advice as needed at any step along the way. To establish contact with the consultants in your area, contact your District Executive, or the UUA Office of Bisexual, Gay, Lesbian, and Transgender Concerns at 25 Beacon Street, Boston, MA 02108, (617) 742-2100, obgltc@uua.org.

Form a Diverse and Committed Committee

Early in the process, a Welcoming Congregation committee will need to be formed. This committee should represent the diverse makeup of your congregation—members of all genders, sexual orientations, ages, and cultural and racial groups—and each member should be thoroughly committed to the goals of the program. It is especially important that bisexual, gay, lesbian, and/or transgender members of the congregation (if there are any who are comfortable enough to be open about who they are) not be expected to provide all the energy and leadership required by this program. People who are "heterosexual allies" of bisexual, gay, lesbian, and/or transgender persons seeking a safe and affirming place in our congregations and society need to assume a major leadership role. Having many heterosexual persons visibly and actively involved in this program makes other heterosexual members of the congregation, who might not otherwise feel entirely comfortable with or welcoming of bisexual, gay, lesbian, and/or transgender members, feel "safer" when attending Welcoming Congregation events.

Begin by Offering Events and Programs, Not Voting

Some congregations interested in beginning this program have formally put the question of participation to a congregational vote. This can be done, and has worked in some settings, but we frankly do not recommend this approach. In many congregations, a formal vote at the beginning of the process (before people who are still uncomfortable with or judgmental about homosexuality, bisexuality, and transgender identity have had the chance to learn and grow from the various components of the program) can create an atmosphere of conflict, entrenchment, and polarization. We suggest that the only consensus required at the start in most congregational settings is the agreement of the lay and professional leadership to form a Welcoming Congregation committee and to offer educational workshops and other events. In this way, the Welcoming Congregation Program can function like so many other groups in a typical congregation—a program energized by a core of interested persons offering voluntary events and opportunities to the congregation as a whole.

Time Frame

Each congregation will want to use this program at a pace that works for their own particular situation. Some congregations, ready to aggressively confront their homophobia and begin extending a warm welcome to sexual orientation minorities, dive enthusiastically into the program, moving quickly on the particulars found in the Guidelines. Other congregations move more cautiously, building consensus and spending years processing the materials. Keeping these possible variations in mind, most congregations can reasonably expect to complete this program within 18 months. Of course, no congregation becomes completely welcoming "once and for all" within such a short time period, but most congregations are able to make substantive progress in a year or two.

Monitoring Your Progress

As you work with the program, your congregation should monitor its progress using the specific Commitments and Actions found in the Guidelines. There is a Measuring Your Progress form at the end of this handbook that can be photocopied and used to track which program Actions you have completed. It is helpful to keep the congregation informed as to what has been accomplished.

Obtaining Recognition as a Welcoming Congregation

Unitarian Universalist congregations that have worked with this program may obtain formal recognition as a Welcoming Congregation from the Unitarian Universalist Association (other faith groups adopting this model could establish a similar procedure). When your Welcoming Congregation committee feels that the suggested Actions have been sufficiently addressed, it should fill out a Measuring Your Progress form. If some of the suggested Actions have not been necessary in your congregation, simply indicate why no action was necessary. The form and a record of the congregational vote to become a Welcoming Congregation, along with a cover letter requesting formal recognition as a Welcoming Congregation, should be sent to the Office of Bisexual, Gay, Lesbian, and Transgender Concerns at the Unitarian Universalist Association, 25 Beacon Street, Boston, MA 02108. For further information, write or call (617) 742-2100 during normal business hours.

Don't Get Discouraged!

Some congregational leaders committed to this program become discouraged by how long it can take to change homophobic attitudes and unwelcoming behaviors in both individuals and the church as a whole. They also become disheartened when they feel that the more homophobic members of the congregation may be staying away from Welcoming Congregation workshops and events. We urge you to remember that most enduring human changes occur *over time,* not (as we sometimes idealistically dream) as a *revolution.* Homophobia is entrenched, pervasive, and complex in our society, and both individuals and institutions will require time to genuinely integrate new, more accepting and welcoming attitudes and behaviors. It is also important not to assume that the program can change the attitudes and behaviors of *everyone* in the congregation—it cannot! It is vital that we remain realistic about the variable pace of change and uneven acceptance of new attitudes and ideas, but never lose hope that even the most homophobic individual or institution will someday become more welcoming!

Above all else, this program requires gentleness and patience! In working with hundreds of congregations on the issue of homophobia, we have learned that establishing an atmosphere of gentleness and patience is crucial if the program is to be effective in bringing about real, sustained, and positive transformation. As Dr. Roberta Harro, co-creator of the Workshop Series, points out, people are most open to new insight and understanding when the program is engaged with a spirit of respect, civility, non-judgmental listening, and caring. Many people, regardless of sexual orientation, experience intense feelings when grappling with the substance of this program, and so it is

vitally important that your congregational leadership for this program maintain a keen sensitivity to and respect for each individual's emotions, ideas, and experiences. Dr. Harro writes:

> Our intention is to create a climate of growth and learning, to have the program be a laboratory for talking openly in a setting that is respectful, forgiving, truthful, and understanding. This means:

- helping participants feel comfortable with their own experience and knowledge levels,
- acknowledging their discomfort if it exists,
- taking time to establish trust in working groups,
- avoiding "right" and "wrong" responses to comments and questions,
- refraining from judging people or their views regardless of how homophobic they may be,
- creating and enforcing "discussion safety guidelines," and
- welcoming all questions.

The congregations that have experienced difficulties realizing lasting and positive results from this program are those in which people (of all sexual orientations and gender identifications) have been made to feel judged, defensive, or dismissed.

While not losing our sense of urgency to end the painful homophobia under which bisexual, gay, lesbian, and/or transgender persons suffer, we need also to remember that our society (and congregations whose members are immersed in that society) did not become homophobic overnight. Bisexual, gay, lesbian, and/or transgender persons have had hostility and condemnation directed at them for hundreds of years, and heterosexual people have been exposed to homophobic attitudes and actions their entire lives. The process of both individuals and congregations becoming more welcoming and inclusive is, in most ways, an evolutionary one. Congregations, like all enduring human institutions, tend to change slowly and awkwardly. If we are to learn and grow together, everyone (bisexual, heterosexual, homosexual, and transgender people) will need to be gentle and patient with one another.

In working with members of congregations wrestling with their own personal homophobia, I have coined the phrase "heart-lag" to describe a commonly experienced problem. Heart-lag is what we religious people experience when our *hearts* lag behind what our *heads* already tell us.

Let me give two examples of heart-lag. A Caucasian friend (who has been a very active supporter of African American civil rights for decades) recently experienced heart-lag when his daughter announced her engagement to an African American man. While his *head* told him the impending marriage was fine, in his *heart*, deep in his "guts," he just could not get used to the idea of having black grandchildren! Similarly, an ardent feminist friend (who has long worked for equal job opportunities for women) described with embarrassment the heart-lag she recently experienced when, while sitting on a jetliner ready to take off, a woman's voice identifying herself as the pilot came on the intercom, and my friend involuntarily got sweaty palms!

While we are often hesitant to admit it, most of us have some level of involuntary heart-lag toward some human group or minority. To be human is to often be uncomfortable when confronted by "strangers," despite our religious aspirations and ideals. Understanding and working with one another's heart-lags is crucial to setting that tone of gentleness and patience that we believe is so necessary to the process of a congregation becoming genuinely more welcoming. When I introduce this program to a congregation I often say, "It's O.K. to be nervous or uncomfortable the first time you see two lesbians holding hands in church, or encounter some other aspect of what it means for people to be bisexual, gay, lesbian, and/or transgender. Being a Unitarian Universalist (or a member of some other caring religious group) doesn't mean you're instantly and perfectly comfortable with human differences or lifestyles that seem foreign to you. What it does mean is that you are willing to honestly work on your discomforts, ignorance, and prejudices as you move toward being a more generous and welcoming person."

We must resist the self-righteous temptation to "beat up" on one another for our heart-lags. If people feel defensive or ashamed of their natural feelings of discomfort, they may go into either a resistance mode (Don't tell me how to feel!) or a denial mode (I don't have any problem with these gay people being around church!).

Keeping Focused . . .
Widening the Welcome

Although bisexual, gay, lesbian, and/or transgender persons are not the only individuals who may feel unwelcomed in your church, we believe it is very important for congregations engaging in this program to resist the temptation of devising some generalized program designed to tackle all human exclusions and prejudices. We say this not be-cause we believe that the oppression and exclusion experienced by sexual orientation minorities are any greater or deeper than those experienced by racial and ethnic minorities or the physically challenged, but because homophobia does have different dynamic and context that lead to people feeling excluded from a religious community—dynamic and context that need to be specifically and aggressively confronted.

Once a congregation works on its homophobic exclusions through this program (or begins with a program specifically designed to help a congregation look at its racism), it quite naturally begins to see (and wants to eliminate) other exclusions it allows to be experienced by other minority groups. A congregation can become truly welcoming of all minority populations only when it intentionally and separately "unpacks" the ignorance, prejudice, and exclusions that each group must endure. The problem human communities have with "strangers" is a universal one, but the welcoming solution lies only in confronting the particular dynamics of each prejudice. So keep focused, even as you look ahead to the work that will be required to eventually expand your welcome to all!

Even though the workshops and other materials of the Welcoming Congregation Program deal with many issues that are controversial, personal, and sometimes painful, this manual has been designed to be enjoyable, educational, and transformational for your congregation. Congregations that have used the various resources provided here report a great deal of excitement, growth, and enjoyment generated in and among members. The issues are serious, but that does not mean that you cannot have fun while wrestling with them!

Use by Other Denominations

Congregations of faith traditions other than Unitarian Universalist may want to adapt, re-write, or enhance this program to fit their own social, theological, and ecclesiastical context. In fact, several denominations have already adapted this program for themselves. Three years after initial publication, many congregations of other denominations have become Welcoming Congregations.

The Reverend Scott W. Alexander
July 1993

COMMON QUESTIONS

As a heterosexual, I am afraid to lead this program! What if I accidentally say something homophobic and offend someone?

In this culture, we are all trained to be homophobic, regardless of our sexual orientation. Unfortunately, we hurt and offend each other all the time. The spiritual gift of doing anti-oppression work is that it helps us to learn that we can make mistakes, sometimes terrible ones, and still be valued and loved as we begin to take responsibility for them. The Welcoming Congregation Program urges each of us to explore and value our own feelings when we are confronting homophobia. Your fear is part of the cost of homophobia. Acknowledge it, live with it, and live through it. There is a lot of energy on its other side.

Why are we singling out homosexual people to welcome to our congregations? Isn't it the job of our membership committee to welcome everyone?

Churches are the most anti-homosexual institution in America, and much of the justification used to promote anti-homosexual feelings, legislation, and violence is couched in "religious" language. One researcher discovered, for instance, that 95 percent of convicted gay-bashers interviewed in prison cited "religious" motivations for their crimes. So, it is particularly hard for bisexual, gay, lesbian, and and/or transgender people to feel safe bringing their whole selves into churches. Even in Unitarian Universalist congregations, many bisexual, gay, lesbian, and/or transgender people are afraid that revealing the gender of their partner means being asked, directly or indirectly, to leave. When the congregation indicates a commitment to the hard work necessary to welcome bisexual, gay, lesbian, and/or transgender people, it heightens their sense of safety to be open and involved in congregational life.

But one of the people who resists the program is our president/minister/largest donor!

Say you have one hundred people in your congregation. Perhaps ten people are excited to get started, ten people think it's the worst idea they have ever heard, and the other 80 simply do not care—they would rather watch TV. Begin with the ten excited people. Each of them is probably friendly with at least one of the TV watchers. Some night when they are watching TV together, the enthusiast mentions that the film series at the church is the most exciting thing that's happened in a while. The TV viewer is curious and decides to attend. After most of the indifferent 80 have switched off their TVs and headed for church, the last ten people are going to feel left out and come to check it out. If your minister is truly non-supportive, talk to your district Welcoming Congregation trainers to find supportive ministers in the area.

We feel so isolated out here! How can we find support?

Every Unitarian Universalist regional district has trained people to help you through difficulties. A list of those people is available by calling or writing the UUA Office of Bisexual, Gay, Lesbian, and Transgender Concerns. If there is a gay newspaper in your area, look through it for references to other congregations that are "Open and Affirming" (United Church of Christ), "Reconciling" (United Methodist), "More Light" (Presbyterian), etc. You may want to co-sponsor events with these congregations. Another group with many local chapters is Parents and Friends of Lesbians and Gays (P-FLAG). They can be reached at (202) 638-4200 or you can visit their Web site at http://www.pflag.org. If you are in a remote area, call a big city nearby and speak with a bisexual, gay, lesbian, or transgender speakers' bureau, hotline, information line, or community center. You may want to join Interweave (Unitarian Universalists for Lesbian, Gay, Bisexual, and Transgender Concerns), a grassroots member organization with many local chapters.

Does our entire membership have to vote to become a Welcoming Congregation, or could our Board vote?

Each congregation decides the best way to proceed toward its vote. Voting at a congregational meeting brings everyone into the decision, and while it may be more challenging, it also brings more ownership of the decision. On the other hand, some congregations find that to be an unnecessarily cumbersome process. The Office of Bisexual, Gay, Lesbian, and Transgender Concerns does, however, need a record of a vote to send out certification.

Ongoing consultation and support are available from the Office of Bisexual, Gay, Lesbian, and Transgender Concerns at the Unitarian Universalist Association, 25 Beacon Street, Boston, MA 02108, (617) 742-2100, obgltc@uua.org. Supplemental materials are available on the Web site, http://www.uua.org/obgltc.

GUIDELINES

In 1988, the UUA Board of Trustees formed the Common Vision Planning Committee to create a program for congregations interested in becoming more inclusive. No set of guidelines can address the diverse needs of the wide range of Unitarian Universalist congregations, but the following Commitments to inclusiveness and Actions for achieving those Commitments were adopted by the delegates of the 1989 General Assembly as the outline for the Welcoming Congregation Program. Please remember that these guidelines are not a precise blueprint, but rather a suggestive road map for congregations beginning the journey toward becoming truly welcoming.

Commitments

1. A Welcoming Congregation is inclusive and expressive of the concerns of bisexual, gay, lesbian, and/or transgender persons at every level of congregational life—in worship, in program, and in social occasions, welcoming not only their presence but the unique gifts and particularities of their lives as well.

2. A Welcoming Congregation does not assume anyone's affectional/sexual orientation and/or gender identity. Vocabulary of worship reflects this perception; worship celebrates diversity by inclusivity of language and content.

3. An understanding of the experience of bisexual, gay, lesbian, and/or transgender persons will be fully incorporated throughout all programs, including religious education.

4. The bylaws and other official documents of a Welcoming Congregation include an affirmation and non-discrimination clause affecting all dimensions of congregational life, including membership, hiring practices, and the calling of religious professionals.

5. A Welcoming Congregation engages in outreach into the bisexual, gay, lesbian, and transgender communities, both through its advertising and by actively supporting other bisexual, gay, lesbian, and transgender affirmative groups.

6. A Welcoming Congregation offers congregational and ministerial support for services of union and memorial services for bisexual, gay, lesbian, and/or transgender persons, and celebrations of evolving definitions of family.

7. A Welcoming Congregation celebrates the lives of all people and welcomes same-gender couples, recognizing their committed relationships, and equally affirms displays of caring and affection without regard for sexual orientation.

8. A Welcoming Congregation seeks to nurture ongoing dialogue between people of different affectional/sexual orientations and gender identifications, and to create deeper trust and sharing.

9. A Welcoming Congregation encourages the presence of a chapter of Interweave (Unitarian Universalists for Lesbian, Gay, Bisexual, and Transgender concerns).

10. A Welcoming Congregation affirms and celebrates bisexual, gay, lesbian, and transgender issues and history during the church year (possibly including Gay Pride Week, which is in June).

11. A Welcoming Congregation, as an advocate for bisexual, gay, lesbian, and/or transgender people, attends to legislative developments and works to promote justice, freedom, and equality in the larger society. It speaks out when the rights and dignity of bisexual, gay, lesbian, and/or transgender people are at stake.

12. A Welcoming Congregation celebrates the lives of all people and their ways of expressing their love for each other.

Actions

Education

1. Offer religious education that incorporates bisexual, gay, lesbian, and transgender life issues, including the workshop series from the Welcoming Congregation Program.

2. Promote participation by the congregation's minister, religious education minister or director, president, and/or moderator in the Welcoming Congregation Program.

3. Offer a congregation-wide workshop program(s), with follow-up opportunities for study and reflection.

4. Use the Unitarian Universalist Association's sexuality education program, *Our Whole Lives*.

Congregational Life

5. Form a broad-based Welcoming Congregation committee to offer programs and monitor progress.

6. Adjust congregational bylaws and other relevant documents to include an affirmative non-discrimination clause concerning membership, hiring practices, and the calling of religious professionals.

7. Use inclusive language and content as a regular part of worship services, and provide worship coordinators and speakers with guidelines on inclusive language.

8. Provide main worship space and ministerial services for bisexual, gay, lesbian, and transgender rites of passage, such as services of union and dedications of children.

9. Welcome bisexual, gay, lesbian, and/or transgender persons in the congregation's brochure.

10. Ensure that publications, public information, and programming reflect the requested status of any individual as she or he sees appropriate; recognize same-gender couples in directories and other publications as they desire.

Community Outreach

11. Celebrate and affirm bisexual, gay, lesbian, and transgender issues and history during the church year (possibly including Gay Pride Week in June or National Coming Out Day in October).

12. Participate in and/or support efforts to create justice, freedom, and equality for bisexual, gay, lesbian, and/or transgender people in the larger society.

13. (again) Provide main worship space and ministerial services for bisexual, gay, lesbian, and transgender rites of passage, such as services of union and dedications of children. (This guideline is also listed as number 8 under Congregational Life.)

14. Establish and maintain contact with local bisexual, gay, lesbian, and/or transgender groups to offer support and promote dialogue and interaction.

15. Advertise in the local press and/or other media that reach the bisexual, gay, lesbian, and transgender communities.

16. Provide use of building space on an equivalent basis with other Unitarian Universalist organizations when requested by members for programs and meetings of an Interweave (Unitarian Universalists for Lesbian, Gay, Bisexual, and Transgender Concerns) chapter.

PROGRAM FOUNDATIONS

Attitude Questionnaire

This simple questionnaire can help to determine a group's attitude toward bisexual, gay, lesbian, and/or transgender people and the issues that affect their lives. It can be used in a number of ways.

- The leadership of the congregation, the staff, or members of your Welcoming Congregation committee can complete it and discuss the results.

- It can be passed out at a worship service devoted to the subject of the Welcoming Congregation, and the results compiled and later shared.

- A small group participating in one of the programs can complete and discuss the questionnaire.

Keeping the individual results anonymous will help to reveal true feelings—information that should be valuable to a congregation involved in or considering the Welcoming Congregation Program. Many congregations are surprised by the level of discomfort and distrust that exists. Only by being honest can a congregation hope to make progress toward inclusion and acceptance.

This questionnaire is designed to measure the way you feel about bisexual, gay, lesbian, and/or transgender people. It is not a test, and there are no right or wrong answers. It is also an educational tool. Please answer each item as carefully and accurately as you can by circling the appropriate number:

1—yes   2—somewhat   3—don't know   4—probably not   5—no

1. Would you be uncomfortable learning that your neighbor was a . . .

gay man?	1	2	3	4	5
lesbian?	1	2	3	4	5
bisexual person?	1	2	3	4	5
transgender person?	1	2	3	4	5
heterosexual person?	1	2	3	4	5

2. Would you be uncomfortable learning that your best friend was a . . .

gay man?	1	2	3	4	5
lesbian?	1	2	3	4	5
bisexual person?	1	2	3	4	5
transgender person?	1	2	3	4	5
heterosexual person?	1	2	3	4	5

3. Would you be nervous being in a group of . . .

gay men?	1	2	3	4	5
lesbians?	1	2	3	4	5
bisexual people?	1	2	3	4	5
transgender people?	1	2	3	4	5
heterosexual people?	1	2	3	4	5

4. Would you be uncomfortable in a gay or lesbian bar, restaurant, or business?

1	2	3	4	5

5. At a party, would you be uneasy talking with a . . .

gay man?	1	2	3	4	5
lesbian?	1	2	3	4	5
bisexual person?	1	2	3	4	5
transgender person?	1	2	3	4	5
heterosexual person?	1	2	3	4	5

6. Would you avoid social events at which . . .

one bisexual, gay, lesbian, and/or transgender person was present?	1	2	3	4	5
some bisexual, gay, lesbian, and/or transgender people were present?	1	2	3	4	5
bisexual, gay, lesbian, and/or transgender people were more than half the people present?	1	2	3	4	5
bisexual, gay, lesbian, and/or transgender people were the overwhelming majority of those present?	1	2	3	4	5
one heterosexual person was present?	1	2	3	4	5
some heterosexual people were present?	1	2	3	4	5
heterosexual people were more than half the people present?	1	2	3	4	5
heterosexual people were the overwhelming majority of those present?	1	2	3	4	5

7. Would you be uncomfortable walking through a predominantly gay or lesbian section of town?

1	2	3	4	5

Is there one in your area?   yes   no   I don't know

Would you be uncomfortable walking through a predominantly heterosexual section of town?

1	2	3	4	5

Is there one in your area?   yes   no   I don't know

8. Would you be upset if you learned that your
brother or sister was gay, lesbian, or bisexual?   1   2   3   4   5

Would you be upset if you learned that your
brother or sister identified as transgender?   1   2   3   4   5

Would you be upset if you learned that your
brother or sister was heterosexual?   1   2   3   4   5

9. Would you be disappointed if you learned that
your child was gay, lesbian, or bisexual?   1   2   3   4   5

Would you be disappointed if you learned that
your child was transgender?   1   2   3   4   5

Would you be disappointed if you learned that
your child was heterosexual?   1   2   3   4   5

10. Would you feel that you had failed as a parent if you
learned that your child was gay, lesbian, or bisexual?   1   2   3   4   5

Would you feel that you had failed as a parent if you
learned that your child was transgender?   1   2   3   4   5

Would you feel that you had failed as a parent if you
learned that your child was heterosexual?   1   2   3   4   5

11. Would you be uneasy learning that your spouse or
partner was attracted to members of his or her gender?   1   2   3   4   5
of another gender?   1   2   3   4   5

12. Would you be uncomfortable knowing that your
son's male teacher was gay or bisexual?   1   2   3   4   5

Would you be uncomfortable knowing that your
son's male teacher was heterosexual?   1   2   3   4   5

13. Would you be uncomfortable knowing that your
daughter's teacher was a lesbian or bisexual?   1   2   3   4   5

Would you be uncomfortable knowing that your
daughter's teacher was heterosexual?   1   2   3   4   5

14. Would you be shocked to learn that your minister
was a bisexual, gay, lesbian, and/or transgender person?   1   2   3   4   5

15. Would you be uncomfortable seeing . . .

two women holding hands?   1   2   3   4   5

two men holding hands?   1   2   3   4   5

a man and a woman holding hands?   1   2   3   4   5

16. Would you be uncomfortable working closely with a . . .

bisexual person?	1	2	3	4	5
gay man?	1	2	3	4	5
lesbian?	1	2	3	4	5
transgender person?	1	2	3	4	5
heterosexual person?	1	2	3	4	5

17. Would you be uncomfortable learning that your boss was a . . .

bisexual person?	1	2	3	4	5
gay man?	1	2	3	4	5
lesbian?	1	2	3	4	5
transgender person?	1	2	3	4	5
heterosexual person?	1	2	3	4	5

18. Would you be uneasy learning that your doctor was a . . .

bisexual person?	1	2	3	4	5
gay man?	1	2	3	4	5
lesbian?	1	2	3	4	5
transgender person?	1	2	3	4	5
heterosexual person?	1	2	3	4	5

19. Would you be uncomfortable knowing that
you attracted members of your gender?   1   2   3   4   5

Would you be uncomfortable knowing that
you attracted members of another gender?   1   2   3   4   5

20. Would you be upset if you found yourself
attracted to a person of your gender?   1   2   3   4   5

Would you be upset if you found yourself
attracted to a person of another gender?   1   2   3   4   5

21. Would you avoid identifying yourself as a
bisexual, gay, lesbian, and/or transgender person?
(Answering this question is optional.)   1   2   3   4   5

Thank you for your honesty and openness!

Toward Inclusive Language

Names
Reverend Barbara Pescan

What we call ourselves—what we wish to be named, all us human beings—is very important. Sticks and stones will break your bones, but names will hurt you, too. It is crucial to remember that the language used to label you might say more about the user of those words than about your worth or being.

People who love people of the same gender have been called names. Sometimes these words have been offensive slang, sometimes clinical, official-sounding terms. Most of us are sensitive to these words. Bisexual, gay, lesbian, and/or transgender people nowadays often use all those words to refer to themselves. Saying the words helps desensitize us to their awesome power, and represents an ongoing effort to reclaim our language from those who hate us and would kill us, first, with their words.

Silence may also maim and kill. If you are part of the dominant culture, you have language ready-made to define you much of the time (which may be a mixed blessing). You may not have had to search for and create language that names you with care and accuracy. Perhaps those easy words do not fit you all that well, even if, at first glance, they appear to. People who do not fit the mold have to work at language.

Imagine a world in which your life appears only as a negative. Imagine that whenever you hear your life mentioned it is with a laugh or a sneer, in a whisper or an apologetic tone of voice. Imagine that you have lived with the person you love for years and have never heard—in school, on television, in popular films, in your family, in your religious community—your life and circumstances addressed, affirmed, or positively reflected back to you. That this is changing, even slightly, is due to 25 years of work in bisexual, gay, lesbian, and transgender communities and with the understanding of non-gay people.

Imagine having to become bilingual in the language of families, because loving whom you love is seen as not legitimate love or life, like everyone else's. Imagine having to scour the language of your birth to create a language you can use with self-respect, because most of your culture denies—and you are not certain, either—that you have a right to the language. The language ascribes all the values, living skills, terms of affection, and descriptions of intimacy as belonging to someone else. Imagine having to call your life partner, your lover and husband, your helpmeet and mate, the passionate companion of your days with whom you make love and fight and negotiate and make plans and create a life—imagine having to introduce this person as "my friend."

One of the essential movements of the Welcoming Congregation Program is toward a language that is inclusive and expressive of the concerns of *all* its members, including bisexual, gay, lesbian, and/or transgender people. It strives to ensure that worship and program leaders not only welcome their presence in general, but address the particularities of their lives as well. For example, worship leaders can give examples of family life that speak of two men or two women, and whatever children live with the couple, as well as examples of a man and a woman and children, a woman and her children, a man and his, a woman on her own, a man on his own, and families with children chosen and adopted by one or two people. In addition, they can routinely use lesbian and gay people, as well as heterosexual people, to illustrate discussions of committed relationships, business practices, grief, or love.

Bisexual, gay, lesbian, and/or transgender people are able to acknowledge their lives and partners with varying degrees of openness. Many people cannot be "out of the closet" for reasons of homophobia, biphobia, or transphobia in their workplace or families. But welcoming congregations can give support to those who wish to acknowledge their lives with their partners by acknowledging their relationship in as many ways as the religious community acknowledges heterosexual couples.

With each individual's assent, and with respect for the wishes of each, a congregation's directory can list and cross-reference each member with his or her partner and children. For example:

Barrett, Betty	(Bob Browning)
Browning, Bob	(Betty Barrett)
Stein, Gertrude	(Alice Toklas)
Toklas, Alice	(Gertrude Stein)
Windsor, Liz and Phil	(Chuck, Annie)

A welcoming congregation also makes sure that examples of bisexual, gay, lesbian, and transgender existence are sprinkled throughout the religious education curricula, not just as special units such as *Our Whole Lives*. The point is to teach our children that there are many ways to be human, just as there are many ways to be religious, and that being fully human as we are and being religious as our spirits guide us are inextricably bound. What better place than our congregations for our youth to find models for affirmation of their lives—whether our children turn out to be gay or straight. A Welcoming Congregation can make certain that its bylaws affirm bisexual, gay, lesbian, and/or transgender people with non-discrimination/inclusion clauses. (See the Revising Congregational Bylaws section of this manual.)

A standard criticism of gay-rights efforts is "Why do they have to flaunt it?" This really means, "Please don't mention 'it' at all." It means don't make me take account of the facts of your life; don't push me; it's not time; don't use those words and make me look at my own prejudices, fears, and unsettled issues about my own sexuality. A Welcoming Congregation says those exact words and ideas that have been forced into silence for so long, to give them fresh air and heart room. The intentional use of inclusive language asks that we look at not only who comes to join us but also what kind of people we are. Examining and extending our language gives us a chance to broaden our definition of the word *we*.

Myths
Reverend James Robinson

After having been ordained for five years, I had written and delivered five years' worth of sermons without worrying about how my language would affect people who were homosexual, bisexual, or transgender. I had a blind spot. Then Kim Crawford Harvie arrived as our student minister. Kim and her partner were open about their lesbian relationship. Kim was comfortable speaking about it from the pulpit. Other lesbian couples began joining the church.

I soon discovered my blind spot—actually, I found that I had a lot of them. Here is a partial list:

Blind Spot

The typical UU congregation does not have many bisexual, gay, lesbian, and/or transgender people.

In sermons, I used words such as "marriage," "spouse," "nuclear family," "husband," and "wife."

In sermon illustrations or stories, it is not necessary to regularly include stories with a homosexual orientation.

People with a homosexual or bisexual orientation will not join my church because we are mostly heterosexual.

It is enough to accept that homosexuality and bisexuality are natural and normal.

My congregation might get upset if same-gender couples hold hands and hug at church.

I am not homophobic. After all, I have close personal friends who are bisexual, gay, or lesbian.

Now I See

If a Unitarian Universalist congregation has 200 members, it probably has more than 20 members who are bisexual, gay, lesbian, and/or transgender. If it doesn't, then people with a bisexual or homosexual orientation and/or transgender identity have not felt welcomed.

It is also important to use words such as "union services," "partner," "lover," "gay or lesbian couple," and "committed relationship." Some committed same-gender couples choose the word "spouse" (which means "to promise solemnly") to describe the person with whom they share their life. While the classic definition suggests "wife" or "husband," this word can be used inclusively.

It is important to include sermon illustrations and stories with a homosexual orientation, and to do so on a regular basis.

Bisexual, gay, lesbian, and/or transgender people are searching for spiritual community and once they feel truly welcomed will join a church that is predominantly heterosexual.

It is important not only to accept that homosexuality is natural and normal, but to publicly celebrate it as a joyful expression of love.

My congregation is happier because same-gender couples feel free to hold hands and hug at church.

Everyone in this culture is homophobic, to one degree or another. People who have a homosexual or bisexual orientation and/or transgender identity internalize this oppression.

When I began to see my own homophobia, I could see more clearly how my church community as a whole was not truly welcoming to bisexual, gay, lesbian, and/or transgender people. I could see how morally important it was to implement a Welcoming Congregation Program. As we have studied and taken action, the sense of love has deepened within the church. Gay and lesbian people who were in the closet have come out publicly. They were always members of the church, but now they are more truly themselves in community. Gay and lesbian people have begun dropping by for services, and some have joined the church. It has been a wonderful experience.

Now, as I prepare a sermon or write a newsletter article, I watch my language. I use words that are inclusive. I am careful to make sure that people of all sexual orientations will feel represented in the words which I write or speak. I tell stories, or use examples, from both homosexual and heterosexual orientations. After a short while, this approach becomes second nature and requires no extra preparation time.

I am not as blind as I used to be; the truth has set me free.

Imagination
Reverend David Miller

Bisexual, gay, lesbian, and/or transgender people have been oppressed for centuries and from time to time are still publicly harassed, beaten, and even killed because of their identity. They often live in danger of losing their jobs, being evicted from their homes, and being shunned by their families. Most religious institutions reject them publicly. Many bisexual, gay, lesbian, and/or transgender people assume they will be no more welcome in Unitarian Universalist congregations, unless we actively show them that they are welcome. Nowhere is this more important than on Sunday mornings, when the whole church gathers to explore and affirm our Unitarian Universalist faith and to welcome newcomers.

Confucius taught that the "rectification" of language is the beginning of wisdom and is essential to putting human relationships on a proper footing. Just as we have been challenged to rectify our language to make it include women, we now face the challenge of making it include bisexual, gay, lesbian, and/or transgender people.

I have come to realize that my thinking and preaching about relationships have reflected biased assumptions. Some terms such as "husband" and "wife" are not inclusive and can be used only when referring specifically to heterosexual relationships; other terms such as "spouse," "couples," "partners," and "marriage" can be used inclusively, but only if I make it clear that I mean to use them as applying to gay and lesbian people as well as to heterosexual people. To avoid misunderstanding and constant defining of terms, I try to speak of "committed relationships" rather than "marriages"; of our "intimates," "living companions," and "life partners"; and I refer to "those who are near and dear to us" rather than to our "families." Same-gender couples may consider themselves united as spouses, in marriage, and hence may think of each other as family; but, given the linguistic traditions of our culture, they cannot assume I share their perspective. It is my responsibility as worship leader to make it clear that I am being inclusive.

There are other ways to communicate inclusiveness in services. Bisexual, gay, lesbian, and/or transgender people and their concerns may be mentioned in sermons and services in which they are not the main focus, as in services that focus on social justice, relationships, child care, aging, and so on. Readings and prayers or meditations may be chosen to reflect gay and lesbian concerns, or because they reflect universal human concerns and are written by bisexual, gay, lesbian, and/or transgender authors. For example, in a recent sermon I focused on the theme that heaven and hell are in this life. For one of the readings I selected a passage from Oscar Wilde's poem *Ballad of Reading Gaol*, which spoke movingly of guilt and of the hellishness of imprisonment. I asked, "How could Wilde write so powerfully of the prison experience? He had spent two years in jail after being convicted of the 'crime' of homosexuality."

Inclusiveness also can be reflected in the minister's choice of a sermon topic, or by inviting a bisexual, gay, lesbian, and/or transgender minister to preach. When the church is accustomed to inviting laypeople to present whole services, participation by bisexual, gay, lesbian, and/or transgender members of the congregation conveys a powerful message of inclusiveness.

The announcements may also reflect an inclusive approach in the life of the church. At our church we have grown accustomed to hearing announcements of meetings of the local Interweave (Unitarian Universalists for Lesbian, Gay, Bisexual, and Transgender Concerns). We have learned that church suppers or other activities billed as "family" events may seem to exclude both single members and gay and lesbian members of our congregation. We have also learned that, for some people, just hearing the words "lesbian," "gay," "bisexual," or "transgender" spoken aloud in the church in an accepting way can be a liberating experience.

We stand just at the beginning of this newest rectification of the language of our common life and worship. My colleagues are an inventive lot, and I look forward to seeing what the individual and collective exercise of our imaginations will bring forth.

Inclusive Congregational Bylaws

One fairly simple step a congregation can take to become more welcoming is including in its official bylaws and other relevant documents a non-discrimination or welcoming clause. Although such an action is largely symbolic, publicly proclaiming the congregation's commitment to inclusiveness can be a very significant and meaningful step.

All congregations participating in a Welcoming Congregation Program should examine their bylaws to make sure they include such a clause. Here are several examples that might be helpful to congregations drafting such clauses:

Non-discrimination

We affirm and promote the full participation of persons in all our activities, including membership, programming, hiring practices, and the calling of religious professionals, without regard to race, color, gender, gender expression, physical ability, affectional or sexual orientation, age, or national origin. We also affirm the practice of affirmative action to remedy the results of historical discrimination.

From the bylaws of the First Parish (Unitarian Universalist) of Brewster, MA.

Membership

No test of creed, of faith, or national origin, of race or color, of gender, of sexual or affectional orientation, of physical ability, or other similar test shall be imposed as a condition of membership. . . . Eligibility for minister of the church shall not be restricted on the basis of age, national origin, race or color, gender, sexual or affectional orientation, or physical challenge.

From the bylaws of the Unitarian Universalist Church of Worcester, MA.

You might want to extend this non-discrimination pledge to all persons employed by the congregation, not just the minister.

Non-discrimination

The Association declares and affirms its special responsibility, and that of its member societies and organizations, to promote the full participation of persons in all of its and their activities and in the full range of human endeavor without regard to race, color, sex, disability, affectional or sexual orientation, age, or national origin and without requiring adherence to any particular interpretation of religion or to any particular religious belief or creed.

From the bylaws of the Unitarian Universalist Association.

Some may prefer the use of "gender" in place of "sex" and "physical abilities" in place of "disability."

Inclusion

This congregation affirms and promotes the full participation of persons in all our activities and endeavors; including membership, programming, hiring practices, and the calling of religious professionals; without regard to race, color, gender, physical or mental challenge, affectional or sexual orientation, age, class, or national origin.

By the Reverend Scott W. Alexander

Other examples are available from the Office of Bisexual, Gay, Lesbian, and Transgender Concerns of the Unitarian Universalist Association, 25 Beacon St., Boston, MA 02108, (617) 742-2100, obgltc@uua.org.

Ministering to Bisexual, Gay, Lesbian, and/or Transgender People

(An Open Letter to My Colleagues)
Reverend Douglas Morgan Strong

One of the gifts we, as ministers, bring to our people is our ability to be authentic and present. We have a wealth of resources we draw on to provide counseling, support, affirmation, challenge, and assistance to someone in need of pastoral counseling. But many of my colleagues have confessed to feeling very uncomfortable in working with bisexual, gay, lesbian, and/or transgender people. A wide gulf separates most clergy from the sexual minority community. Confusion, misunderstanding, judgments, and fear prevail. We may well feel neither authentic nor able to be emotionally supportive of homosexuals and homosexuality.

Many bisexual, gay, lesbian, and/or transgender people feel equally uncomfortable seeking assistance from a member of the religious community. For centuries, the Church has been a leading force against sexual minorities. It encourages prejudice against anyone whose sexual truth falls beyond the conventional. It is not surprising that gay people are reluctant to reach out to the very institution that oppresses them.

Yet bisexual, gay, lesbian, and/or transgender people have no less need for warmth, caring, and affirmation than anyone else who calls the liberal church their religious home. In fact, as a subculture in society, bisexual, gay, lesbian, and/or transgender people may need our support more than does the general population.

Look Inward First

Before we can minister to our bisexual, gay, lesbian, and/or transgender neighbors, we must first take an inventory of our own attitudes, feelings, and prejudices about homosexuality. This is especially true for white, straight, male ministers, who have historically been the most hostile to pluralism in sexuality. I think women ministers tend to be more empathetic, perhaps because all women share a common bond of oppression.

Years ago, as I struggled with my own sexual truth, I read a book called *Loving Someone Gay* by Don Clark. I read about gay people "celebrating" their sexuality and felt sure it was a misprint.

"How," I wondered, "could anyone celebrate such a painful, pitiful, perverted truth?" Many of my colleagues ask the same question.

Perhaps a starting point for self-evaluation can be to ask yourself:

- How many bisexual, gay, lesbian, and/or transgender people do I have as friends?

- What is my gut reaction when I think about . . .

  two people of the same gender living together?

  a same-gender couple raising children?

  openly bisexual, gay, lesbian, and/or transgender people working in my church?

  political equality for homosexuals, bisexuals, and transgender people?

- Do I immediately think of gay men when I read or hear something about AIDS?

- What is my greatest fear around the concept of same-gender affection?

- How would I feel if a family member (spouse, child, sibling, parent) told me he or she was bisexual, lesbian, gay, and/or transgender?

- How comfortable would I feel having lunch (dinner, going to a movie, etc.) with someone who is bisexual, gay, lesbian, and/or transgender?

Stages of Understanding

Understanding the variety of ways people express their sexuality occurs on several levels. Ministers who wish to work beyond their categorical thinking about bisexual, gay, lesbian, and/or transgender people often pass through several stages of personal growth.

Repugnancy. We feel physically nauseous at the mere thought of homosexuality. Thinking of two men or women being together triggers intense discomfort. We see gays and lesbians not as people, but as sick, perverted, and loathsome. We are hostile and may participate in anti-gay slurs. We see nothing wrong with discriminating against these people; they are out to molest our children and deserve to be beaten.

Toleration. We know a few of "them" and feel that, as long as they don't flaunt their dirty perversion, we can live with it. We avoid saying the word "gay" or "lesbian" and enjoy a good laugh at their expense, but feel a little guilty for doing it. But everyone knows "they" are ruining the traditional fabric of the family.

Acceptance. "Live and let live" is the theme during acceptance. We have friends who know people who are "that way" and may even socialize with some bisexual, gay, lesbian, and/or transgender people. We welcome them in our churches but hope that not too many show up, lest we become known as "the gay church." We intellectually realize that they can teach in our religious education program but privately hope they don't make an issue of their "lifestyle." We may have read a book on the subject, but probably don't own one.

Affirmation. We embrace and celebrate the unique gifts that bisexual, gay, lesbian, and/or transgender people bring to our midst. We often use the words "lesbian" and "gay" in conversation and freely speak of our gay friends to non-gay people. If political activism is our model, we work for equality of sexual minorities. We find the sexual truth of people essentially irrelevant. We have close relationships with gay men, lesbians, bisexuals, and/or transgender people and welcome them into our lives as equals.

Starting the Process of Understanding

An important part of understanding involves learning more about the bisexual, gay, lesbian, and transgender cultures that exist in most communities. It is discouraging to realize that virtually none of our ministers regularly see or read the gay/lesbian press and have few books on homosexuality or same-gender coupling in their libraries. Many of our colleagues know more about the mating habits of humpback whales than the lives of 10 percent of their congregations!

Before we can offer quality ministry to bisexual, gay, lesbian, and/or transgender people, we need to remember four aspects of their community that will affect our role as pastoral counselors.

Handle with Care. Like other oppressed groups, bisexual, gay, lesbian, and/or transgender people understand that the institution capable of providing support and affirmation is the institution that promotes homophobia and perpetuates self-hate. It is natural that they will be cautious. As ministers we should provide assurances that we have worked through and accepted our own homophobia. We will want to open ourselves to listening to their needs without becoming judgmental.

Death and Healing. The gay community is a grieving community that has been devastated by death and ignored by society. No population has been so devastated by AIDS. Most gay men know people who have died from the disease. The general population seems unable to grasp the profundity of this loss. Most people live their entire lifetime knowing fewer than 10 or 12 friends who have died. Many gay men now lose 10 or 12 friends to AIDS each year. My lover and I can count more than 100 deaths in three years! The impact of this tragedy is obvious. During times of grieving, people turn to their community of faith for comfort, strength, hope, and healing. We must be prepared to provide it.

A New Sense of Family. Everyone wants and needs to be loved. But society forbids lesbian and gay people from seeking, forming, and nurturing loving relationships. Same-gender couples face incredible barriers. Many couples find the heterosexual model inadequate. They need tender counselors who understand the unique stresses and pains faced by same-gender couples. They need the support of their minister in working through couple problems. Many ministers draw on their own training and experience in counseling, so non-gay clergy should familiarize themselves with the unique qualities and dilemmas that face same-gender couples before extending a counseling hand to them.

Being Lovable and Capable. Building self-esteem within the bisexual, gay, lesbian, and transgender community is a huge struggle. Most bisexual, gay, lesbian, and/or transgender people have internalized the societal values that teach only negative attitudes toward homosexuality (internalized homophobia). Many transgender people have internalized rigid and dualistic notions applied to gender. We all need positive role models to help us shape and strengthen the delicate strands of self-assurance. Precious few such role models exist for bisexual, gay, lesbian and/or transgender people. You can be one.

Awareness of Substance Abuse. One of the ways internalized homophobia painfully expresses itself in the lives of many bisexual, gay, lesbian, and/or transgender persons is in substance abuse or other forms of addiction. Drug and alcohol dependence are quite common in sexual minority communities, and may be issues for some of the bisexual, gay, lesbian, and/or transgender persons active in your congregation. To whatever extent you can be understanding of the underlying self-esteem issues and supportive of their efforts to start or stay in recovery, your ministry will be invaluable.

The First Step

Many of us in our ministry tend to avoid things that make us uncomfortable. We yearn for harmony, and therefore may find ourselves easily slipping into quiet acceptance of our bisexual, gay, lesbian, and/or transgender members—hoping that our silence will not offend them, but fearful that speaking out will upset some in the congregation. We aim for passive support, praying that it will placate everyone.

That approach ultimately does not work. We must risk going beyond the convention, and actively let it be known that we not only acknowledge bisexual, gay, lesbian, and/or transgender people, but truly welcome them—by using the words "gay," "lesbian," "bisexual," and "transgender" from the pulpit; by assuring that bisexual, gay, lesbian, and transgender literature is available in the church and that our library contains resources to help us minister to bisexual, gay, lesbian, and/or transgender people; by availing ourselves of special training to help us better understand and appreciate the gifts these people bring to our church community.

The Unitarian Universalist Association's Office of Bisexual, Gay, Lesbian, and Transgender Concerns is an excellent resource. It offers materials highlighting our denominational efforts on behalf of equality, sample services of union, a video and print library that includes many AIDS education materials, and friendly people who are willing and trained to help.

The Lambda Minister's Guild, Unitarian Universalist, is a gathering of our bisexual, gay, lesbian, and/or transgender clergy. The guild welcomes inquiries and stands ready to help colleagues better understand their feelings toward homosexuality in general and toward bisexual, gay, lesbian, and/or transgender Unitarian Universalists.

Interweave (Unitarian Universalists for Lesbian, Gay, Bisexual, and Transgender Concerns) is another excellent ministerial resource. This continent-wide organization has, for 15 years, provided support to bisexual, gay, lesbian, and/or transgender people. It holds a convocation each February and publishes *The Interweave World* quarterly. It also sponsors programs, workshops, and a worship celebration at each General Assembly.

The Reverend James J. Reeb once commented, "Life is full of inequities, and it is our job to bring them to an end." The Welcoming Congregation Program is a wondrous way to get your congregation started in bringing to an end the long-standing discomfort and misunderstandings that surround our feelings toward bisexual, gay, lesbian, and/or transgender people. It is a worthy ministry.

For Religious Educators

Setting an Example
Reverend Ann Fields

Religious education is a vital part of the Welcoming Congregation Program. If you have been asked to help your church become a Welcoming Congregation, you'll probably want to consult at length with your minister and other congregation leaders. Talk with your church board and your religious education committee to explore appropriate educational goals. For most of us, new information and new understandings will be needed to move beyond the homophobia that we have been taught. There are many ways to begin a program, but it is important to allow plenty of time for everyone to move through their doubts and fears.

Teachers and other religious education staff will have concerns that may best be handled in an early staff meeting. At such a meeting, staff members can discuss issues, answer questions, and prepare for situations that may arise. For instance, will religious education greeters be unflustered by the arrival of a same-gender couple with a child to be enrolled? If a teacher overhears one child say to another, "You're a fag" or "You're a dyke," how might he or she respond? Will family groups be spoken about and portrayed on bulletin boards in a variety of colors, genders, and ethnicity? Will teachers use inclusive language—for example, rather than saying, "When you go home to your mother and father," saying "When you go home to your family . . ."?

Your congregation may consider forming groups such as Parents of Gays, Lesbians, and Bisexuals; Gay and Lesbian Parents; Families and Friends of AIDS Patients; and Older Singles. Many groups in the church begin with a social agenda and gradually come to function as friendship and support groups; members soon begin to minister to one another.

"Religious education," says John Westerhoff, "is the sum total of all that a child experiences in the church." In all that our congregations do and say, there are messages. Our buildings often tell the story of what it is we care about, or fail to care about. You may want to consider the following ideas for showing your congregation's welcoming attitude toward bisexual, gay, lesbian, and/or transgender people.

- Unitarian Universalist Association pamphlets that support bisexual, gay, lesbian, and/or transgender people prominently displayed in the pamphlet rack.

- Sign-up sheets for car pools to attend a concert of a gay men's chorus or similar group.

- A bulletin board of children's art that includes a picture of a family with two mothers.

- A poster announcing a dance for lesbian and gay people on Friday nights.

- An appeal for help for your local AIDS service organization in the Sunday order of service.

- A notice inviting the entire congregation to attend a same-gender service of union for two of its members.

Think of the socializing impact on children, youth, and adults of any of these ideas or similar ones. Think of the affirmation these messages would give to any bisexual, gay, lesbian and /or transgender newcomer. This would indeed be a Welcoming Congregation!

Creating a Welcoming Youth Group
Reverend Meg A. Riley,
with special thanks to Christine Murphy

Providing safe, nurturing places for all youth is not only a good idea—it may literally save their lives! Bisexual, gay, lesbian, and/or transgender youth are two to three times more likely to attempt suicide than other young people. They comprise one quarter to one third of all completed youth suicides annually. As ever, the worst casualties of oppression are our young people. Creating support for bisexual, gay, lesbian, and/or transgender youth is an urgent task for all congregations, schools, and communities.

Where to Start

Step 1. Assume that there are bisexual, gay, lesbian, and/or transgender youth in your group. In addition, assume that members of your group have parents, siblings, and friends who are bisexual, gay, lesbian, and/or transgender. Few people will self-identify unless it feels safe for them to do so, so don't assume that you know anyone's sexual orientation or gender idenity, regardless of what they say or how they act. Many youths are not yet sure how to identify themselves, and need plenty of time and space to wonder and question in a nurturing environment.

Step 2. Inform your adult advisors and youth leaders about the realities of bisexual, gay, lesbian, and/or transgender people's lives. They may benefit from the adult education series in the Welcoming Congregation Program, or from presentations made in other settings. Leaders need time to work through some of their own issues before presenting before a group.

Step 3. Always use language, examples, and activities that include reference to people of all lifestyles, genders, and races. For example, when your youth group talks about "Life after High School," and discusses how to choose a college or living environment, include in the discussion how various colleges respond to bisexual, gay, lesbian, and/or transgender youth. If you're doing a unit on career choices, talk about how homophobia impacts the career choices of bisexual, gay, lesbian, and/or transgender people. Obviously, any unit on relationships or sexuality should project an inclusive bias.

More important than a specific six-week focus on homosexuality is your awareness of bisexual, gay, lesbian, and/or transgender youth present at all times in the group.

Step 4. Always confront any heterosexist language, even jokes. These jokes are hurtful and create an unsafe environment. Use "I" statements and a vision of a safe and inclusive youth group to confront such language. Don't shame the people who use it.

Step 5. Acknowledge the special gifts and contributions of bisexual, gay, lesbian, and/or transgender members of the group. The presence of people who are open about their sexuality and gender identity creates an environment of trust and safety where everyone can be more honest.

What to Do

Programming at youth conferences and youth group meetings can be an effective way to inform youth about homophobia, heterosexism, and the realities of bisexual, gay, lesbian, and/or transgender life. It is important to remember, however, that it is not the bisexual, gay, lesbian, and/or transgender people's responsibility to educate heterosexual people. Make sure that any programming is led by people of all sexual orientations and

gender identities. In other words, do not plunk a bisexual, gay, lesbian, and/or transgender person in front of the group and abandon them to the task of transforming it. To be effectively addressed, these issues must be owned by the whole group.

Program Ideas

The first trick in deciding your programming is identifying for whom you are doing it. How much understanding of bisexual, gay, lesbian, and/or transgender issues exists in the group? How willing are the members to discuss controversial or emotional issues? Have there been incidents in the group with homophobic language? Are there openly bisexual, gay, lesbian, and/or transgender youth in the group? Children of bisexual, gay, lesbian, and/or transgender parents?

Once you determine who your group is and how it works, consider some of the following options:

- Bring in a panel of bisexual, gay, lesbian, and/or transgender people, and have the group write anonymous questions on index cards for the panel to address. Nearby colleges may provide a speakers' bureau; some larger cities have bisexual, gay, lesbian, and/or transgender youth centers, programs, or speakers' bureaus. Generally, younger speakers are more relevant for the youth in the group, though adult role models are also important.

- At conferences, hold a workshop on homophobia. Encourage all youth—including heterosexually identified ones—to talk about the ways in which homophobia has been used as a rationale for their physical, verbal, or emotional harassment. Almost every youth has experienced homophobic name calling or taunting. Talk about how it feels, what it means, and the impact of such harassment.

- Show movies and follow up with a discussion in small groups. Use videos, such as *Torch Song Trilogy, Desert Hearts, Lianna, Longtime Companion,* and *Incredible True Story of Two Girls in Love.*

- The adult education series in this resource book may be easily adapted for high school youth. Bear in mind that many youth are impatient with long internal processing; they're more interested in the present. If the series is co-led by an older youth and an adult, the leaders will be able to tailor the series to the needs of the group and omit potentially boring sections.

- The basic learning model introduced in the *Life Issues for Teenagers* curriculum, which is available through the Unitarian Universalist Association (UUA) Bookstore, may be easily adapted to focus on issues of homophobia. Use books, films, or speakers to engage the group.

Parental Involvement

Some parents will be frightened that you are encouraging their children to take a stand on a subject which could make them unpopular or unsafe. Therefore, parent education is extremely important in this area. The more you draw the parents in, and tell them exactly what you are doing, the less fear they will have. In addition, if they learn about the high risks endured by bisexual, gay, lesbian, and/or transgender youth, they will be much more likely to come on board the project. You may want to consider a parents' night, facilitated by your director of religious education, youth advisor, minister, or a member of the Welcoming Congregation committee.

Bisexual, Gay, Lesbian, and/or Transgender Youth Outreach Projects

Many congregations, responding to the life-threatening circumstances of bisexual, gay, lesbian, and/or transgender youth, have begun outreach projects to these youth in their local communities. These include Saturday night dances, drop-in centers, rap groups, educational outreach programs to church and school leaders in the community, and fund-raising efforts to support bisexual, gay, lesbian, and/or transgender teen programs through other auspices. Your youth group should be part of the congregation's discussion as it takes on such projects. They may have fears about being identified with such programs, and they may want to help.

Other Resources

Am I Blue? Coming Out From the Silence, Marion D. Bauer, ed. (San Francisco: HarperCollins, 1994). This collection of short stories can be used to supplement *Our Whole Lives, Beyond Pink and Blue*, or other curricula. These stories can also be used to stimulate discussions in youth group settings.

The Children of Horizons: How Gay and Lesbian Teens Are Leading a New Way Out of the Closet, Gilbert Herdt and Andrew Boxer (Boston: Beacon

Press, 1993). Available from the UUA Bookstore, 25 Beacon St., Boston, MA 02108, 1-800-215-9076.

Bridges of Respect: Creating Support for Lesbian and Gay Youth, Rachel Kamel, ed. An indispensable, thorough resource guide. Available from the American Friends Service Committee, 1501 Cherry Street, Philadelphia, PA 19102.

Young, Gay and Proud, edited by Sasha Alyson, is addressed to a high school audience, and includes many writings by young people. This and a wide range of gay and lesbian literature are available from Alyson Publications, 40 Plympton Street, Boston, MA 02118.

The Respect All Youth Project at Parents and Friends of Lesbians and Gays (P-FLAG) has published a series of Issue Papers and bibliographies about youth. These are available from P-FLAG, PO Box 27605, Washington, DC 27605, for minimal cost.

The Youth Office and the Office of Bisexual, Gay, Lesbian, and Transgender Concerns at the UUA provide materials about youth issues, including contacts for workshop leadership (youth or adults), names of congregations doing community outreach projects, and trouble-shooting about your youth group's needs. Contact either office at 25 Beacon Street, Boston, MA 02108, (617) 742-2100.

Parts of this article previously appeared in Synapse, *the Young Religious Unitarian Universalists (YRUU) newspaper, and in the brochure, "Welcoming Lesbian, Bisexual, and Gay Youth into YRUU."*

Religious Education Resources

Resources of special interest to religious education leaders are available through the Unitarian Universalist Association Bookstore and/or the Office of Bisexual, Gay, Lesbian, and Transgender Concerns. Consult the Program Resources section on page 147 for more information.

Beyond Pink and Blue: Exploring Our Stereotypes of Sexuality and Gender. Developed for youth ages 13-15, this curriculum, which explores cultural and individual understandings of gender identity, is an ideal follow-up to *About Your Sexuality*.

Life Issues for Teenagers (LIFT). This curriculum

for high school youth offers further opportunities for considering sexual and lifestyle issues.

Our Whole Lives: A Lifespan Sexuality Education Series. This comprehensive sexuality education curriculum is designed for use in religious and secular educational settings. The program contains curricula for five age groups (kindergarten–1st grade; 4th–6th grade; 7th–9th grade; senior high; and adults) and addresses the following issues: human development, relationships, personal skills, sexual behavior, sexual health, and society and culture.

The Parent Trilogy: Three Programs for UU Parents and Other Adults. Contains *Being a UU Parent* (5 sessions), *Parents as Resident Theologians* (6 sessions), and *Parents as Social Justice Educators* (6 sessions). You could enhance this program by posing "tough questions" about homosexuality.

For video listings, see "Other Program Ideas" on page 127, or contact the UUA Video Loan Library at The Etc. Co., (716) 229-2857, for a free catalog.

THE WORKSHOP SERIES

If we have grown up in the mainstream of American culture, we have learned that homosexuality (as well as bisexuality and transgender issues) should be kept hidden or be condemned and that heterosexuality is the only normal form of sexual expression. We have learned not to talk about homosexuality. We have learned to fear that our children might be influenced to become gay. We have learned to accept destructive stereotypes about gay people.

Each of us responds to this learning in a different way—from feeling discomfort when discussing homosexuality or being with bisexual, gay, lesbian, and/or transgender people, to violent hatred of such people. Or we may never have thought much about homosexuality at all because we assume that everyone in our lives is heterosexual. All of these responses can be considered examples of homophobia. None of us likes to think of ourselves as homophobic and we often resist identifying our fears about homosexuality. The purpose of the Welcoming Congregation Program is not to blame ourselves for our feelings, but to help us understand how we learned our reactions to homosexuality and how we can replace old attitudes with new ones.

The Welcoming Congregation Workshop Series is an introspective and interactive educational journey into the issues surrounding the lives of bisexual, gay, lesbian, and/or transgender people. The learning goals are:

- To explore thoughts, feelings, and current knowledge about sexual orientation (homosexuality, bisexuality, heterosexuality) and gender identification (transgender).

- To probe the origins of our beliefs about sexual orientation and gender identification.

- To test attitudes toward sexual orientation and gender identification in Unitarian Universalist congregations and society, and their connections to current social issues such as AIDS, racism, sexism, ableism, ageism, and so on.

- To understand the experiences of bisexual, gay, lesbian, and/or transgender people.

- To see the effects of heterosexism and homophobia on people of all sexual orientations in Unitarian Universalist congregations.

- To uncover the biblical roots of common religious perspectives on homosexuality.

- To devise individual and institutional strategies for Unitarian Universalist congregations to become more welcoming to bisexual, gay, lesbian, and/or transgender people and their families.

Structure

This manual contains plans for 14 two-hour workshops, sequenced to promote consciousness-raising and critical thinking about attitudes toward bisexual, gay, lesbian, and/or transgender people. Its design assumes that a group of people from the participating congregation will commit to be involved in the entire workshop series, rather than dropping in occasionally.

The workshops require at least one leader, and preferably two. Weekly meetings work best, but bi-weekly meetings are a possibility. Longer gaps between workshops tend to dilute the developmental sequence, though a once per month series is not unworkable. Weekend retreats are also possible.

This manual provides suggested readings and lists other resources. Each workshop contains activities that address the learning goals, detailed directions for conducting the activities, suggested time allotted to each reading assignment, and helpful hints for the workshop leaders. Leaders should read the entire handbook before beginning the workshops, and practice doing the activities before each meeting.

Shortening the Program

Although the Welcoming Congregation Program is flexible, the sequence of workshops is important. Ideally, to accomplish the most thorough introspection, groups should participate in all 14 workshops. If you must reduce the number of workshops, the following priorities should guide your selections.

- **Workshops 1, 2, and 14** cannot be sacrificed because they provide basic information and closure. They should be conducted first, second, and last, respectively.
- **Workshops 3, 4, and 9** make up the "heart" of the program. If you can do only four or five workshops, choose your fourth and fifth from this category. We strongly recommend that you conduct at least six workshops to maintain the integrity of the program and your congregation's commitment. Schedule them in numerical sequence, because they build on one another.
- **Workshops 8, 10, and 13** focus on specific areas of interest. If you can only do seven or eight workshops, select your seventh and eighth from this category.

If you wish to conduct your program as a weekend event, set up the workshops in blocks with breaks for meals, exercise, or free time in between. Ideally, no more than three workshops should run on each day, since the material is intense and participants need time to integrate emotional and cognitive growth. This format allows for six workshops in two days, and the ideal situation would include a follow-up of several more sessions at a later time. You may have to make adjustments based on people's schedules.

No matter what form your series takes, schedule at least two hours for each workshop to allow ample discussion time.

Recommendations

Length of Program	Recommended Workshops
6 Sessions	1, 2, 3, 4, 9, 14
7 Sessions	1, 2, 3, 8, 9, 13, 14
8 Sessions	1, 2, 3, 4, 8, 9, 13, 14
9 Sessions	1, 2, 3, 4, 8, 9, 11/12,* 13, 14
10 Sessions	1, 2, 3, 4, 8, 9, 10, 11/12,* 13, 14
12 Sessions	All but 6 and 7
14 Sessions	All

* Combine materials from the two sessions.

Weekend Retreat Format

1. Kick-off weekend with follow-ups: six-session format—one session Friday night, two sessions Saturday morning, one session Saturday afternoon, Saturday evening, and Sunday morning.

2. All in one weekend: eight-session format—two sessions Friday night, four to five sessions Saturday, one to two sessions Sunday.

Enhancing the Workshops

We recommend that the workshop series be led by two people. The ideal team would consist of one bisexual, gay, lesbian, and/or transgender leader working with a heterosexual leader. This mixed approach will provide participants with different perspectives and model the belief that addressing homophobia and heterosexism is everyone's responsibility, regardless of sexual orientation. Working with a partner also gives leaders someone with whom to discuss and plan workshop activities, as well as someone with whom to share the leadership responsibilities during each workshop.

Leaders are encouraged to make the workshop series their own by using beginning and ending rituals that participants may be familiar and comfortable with, and by supplementing the materials. Often, participants feel more at ease if they have time to socialize, and food or beverages could be a regular part of the program. The workshops require about two hours each, so scheduling two and a half hours, with time before or after the workshop for conversation and refreshment, will add to the enjoyment.

Some of the workshops call for the use of a film, and several suggest inviting panels of speakers, so planning ahead is very important. The films should be reserved at least one month in advance, and most speakers need more than a month's lead time as well. Leaders should handle all the logistical planning at the beginning of the workshop series to ensure a successful program.

The Process

Becoming a Welcoming Congregation involves many phases of information gathering, congregational self-exploration, and personal consciousness raising. It will include intellectual discussions, the sharing of deeply held values and beliefs, and the expression of strong feelings. By starting this process, your congregation will embark on an arduous but rewarding journey. This manual offers concrete suggestions for a sequence of steps to assist you along this courageous path.

These suggestions originate in research from the fields of psychology, education, and consciousness raising and share several principles that underlie all of the activities in this manual. These principles include:

- The views, experience, and knowledge of every participant must be explicitly solicited and considered in the process.

- The process must provide structures for critically analyzing the content.

- The process must promote psychological development by helping people to expand the boundaries of how they see the world and to increase their options for how to act on their expanded view.

This process needs to be an active dialogue between Unitarian Universalists and their environment—their congregation, their church, their community, and the contemporary culture. Growth and clarity come not just from personal unfolding, or from just learning accurate information about the environment, but rather from interaction among all the parts mentioned above.

This kind of dialogue requires support, a high level of trust, some communication guidelines, and no surprises. People exploring strongly felt values need to feel as safe as possible in order to participate fully in the process. The activities contained in this manual are arranged to create a sequence of learning conditions that will allow participants to move toward greater awareness and feel safe enough to take risks.

These conditions are presented by Robert Kegan in *The Evolving Self* (Cambridge University Press, 1982), Gerald Weinstein and Lee Bell in an unpublished manuscript (1983), and Roberta Harro in her doctoral dissertation (1986). If created in the learning environment, these conditions are likely to promote growth, learning, and the clarification of participants' thoughts and values. The conditions are *confirmation, contradiction,* and *continuity.*

Confirmation. A feeling of acceptance and safety draws out and affirms what participants currently know and think about a topic. Every person should feel included and affirmed as she or he is now— *with absolutely no judgments* made about what they say. People who express rigidly held beliefs need to be joined, not judged. The joining and confirmation create a feeling of safety and less need to defend a position. Kegan's research indicates that the safer a person feels, the more likely he or she is to share his or her real thoughts and feelings with others, and to take the risk of considering others' views. Creating an atmosphere of confirmation opens the door to growth.

Contradiction. Kegan's research suggests that growth takes place when a person feels safe enough to acknowledge and grapple with a moderate degree of contradiction between what she or he holds to be true, and new information.

Contradictions may come from other participants ("My cousin is gay, and he wants to have children"), a lecture presented to the group (facts to refute stereotypes), a reading assignment (from a gay teacher's point of view), a video (about AIDS), research (on child sexual abuse), a structured activity (role-playing), a guest panel (lesbian and gay speakers), or personal reflection and analysis (the origins of my beliefs about gay parenting).

Some contradictions are designed into the workshops, while others will arise in discussions. Whatever the source of a contradiction, several things need to happen when it arises:

- It needs to be said out loud to someone in the group.

- It needs to be expanded and explored.

- There needs to be time to reflect, react, respond, draw conclusions (not necessarily resolve them, but "take them apart" for study), and report to the group. This is called "processing" the information and reactions, and the processing of contradictions is the core of consciousness raising.

The workshops should draw out or present as many different perspectives as possible and invite elaboration of all those perspectives in as much detail as possible. It is not a good idea to stop in the middle of a processing discussion without a sense of what will happen next (how the group will take steps toward resolution).

Since most of us are not comfortable grappling

with conflict, and growth and change are generally difficult, there is a natural drive in most groups to get resolution quickly. It is important to remember that the richest and most challenging part of this process is explaining in detail what we mean and believe, and listening to someone else do the same. These discussions are often dynamic, emotional, and hard to handle—which is why it is critical to have established confirmation before introducing contradictions. The goal of this phase of the process is to keep everyone involved, open, searching, and questioning toward resolution, whether that involves change or not. Some form of resolution is needed for a sense of continuity to emerge.

Continuity. This involves identifying new ways to think about bisexual, gay, lesbian, and/or transgender people and the church, to look at the implications of the decision to become a Welcoming Congregation, to define an ongoing support system for new ways of thinking, and to anticipate problems resulting from the shift and deal with them. These tasks will be shared through workshop activities, and it is important to give them as much validity as the content-focused activities, since they form the basis for the congregation's next step.

Kegan's three conditions may help workshop leaders understand what the learning program is trying to accomplish, and to focus on the aspects of the process that are most important.

Leadership Preparation

Effective leadership is one of the most important ingredients of a successful workshop experience. The activities provide content and process, but the leader must establish a learning climate in which participants can express their thoughts and feelings and ask questions freely. The leader has a powerful influence on how participants deal with issues and integrate new learnings. This doesn't mean that the leader must be an expert on homosexuality or homophobia. The leader needs, however, to identify her or his own struggles to understand issues raised in the workshops, and be willing to openly share this process with the group.

Whether one or two people lead the workshop series, and whether the leaders are bisexual, gay, heterosexual, lesbian, or transgender, there are several questions potential leaders should ask themselves before undertaking this responsibility.

What do I know about bisexual, gay, lesbian, and transgender oppression? Leaders should take themselves through the workshop activities before attempting to lead others through them. This process serves two purposes: you will have an opportunity to increase your understanding and knowledge of the topic, and you will be better able to identify with participants' reactions to workshop activities.

If possible, we highly recommend that potential leaders attend a homophobia workshop as participants before attempting to lead this workshop series. In addition, we recommend that you do some preparatory readings beyond those included here. This preparation will increase your ability to guide discussions, answer questions, and provide additional resources to participants.

What are my feelings about bisexual, gay, lesbian, and/or transgender people? It is important to acknowledge that we all probably feel some degree of discomfort with the topic of homosexuality, regardless of our sexual orientation. We have grown up in a culture that teaches us that homosexuality and bisexuality are deviant and unacceptable. Even those who are striving to unlearn negative images of bisexual, gay, lesbian, and/or transgender people need to understand how deeply rooted our negative feelings about homosexuality can be.

Leaders need to be willing to acknowledge their own discomfort with discussing homosexuality, bisexuality, and transgender identity, and to serve as a model for participants by sharing their feelings with the group.

The process of exploring feelings and attitudes about bisexual, gay, lesbian, and/or transgender people can raise intense feelings. You should be far enough along in your own self-exploration so that your feelings are not overwhelming. In addition, you should be comfortable with others who are expressing their feelings.

What are my motivations for wanting to lead? Be clear with yourself about why you want to lead this workshop series and what you expect to get from leading it. If you are a bisexual, gay, or lesbian person who is angry at heterosexuals and sees the workshop as an opportunity to turn the tables, vent your anger, or make others understand your personal pain, you are not ready for this role. If you are a heterosexual person who feels sorry for bisexual, gay, or lesbian people, or guilty about your own homophobia, you are not ready. If leading this workshop series interests you because you think it will be controversial, exciting, or a good way to learn something you don't know much about, please think twice.

If, however, you are a bisexual, gay, heterosexual, or lesbian person who has done some work to increase your own awareness and knowledge about homophobia and heterosexism, and if you have a sincere interest in helping others do the same and feel comfortable with your own sexual orientation, proceed with enthusiasm. The same applies for transgender people.

Am I willing to do personal sharing? Participants will be asked to talk about their feelings and attitudes toward homosexuality, bisexuality, and gender identification. A leader who is comfortable with this can provide participants with a model for sharing, and encourage a sense of mutual trust and safety.

In particular, you need to consider whether you are willing to make your sexual orientation and/or gender identification known to participants. For heterosexual leaders, this probably is not an issue, but for bisexual, gay, lesbian, and/or transgender leaders, this decision must be addressed before beginning the workshop series. A bisexual, gay, lesbian, and/or transgender leader who is afraid to "come out" will experience a great deal of anxiety and might send mixed messages to participants. Heterosexual leaders, on the other hand, might have to contend with the assumption that they are bisexual, gay, lesbian, and/or transgender because they are leading the workshop.

Regardless of your sexual orientation and gender identification, you must be clear that the reason for revealing this information is to create an authentic and open environment in which participants can learn. Personal experiences can be a powerful part of this process, but should not distract participants from their own self-examination and learning.

What kind of leadership style am I most comfortable with? This workshop series encourages a high degree of interaction among participants. Although you will, at times, present a short introduction to an activity or provide some information, most activities are designed as small and large group discussions. If you are most comfortable with a lecture format, you will need to adjust your expectations. Rather than you talking and participants listening and occasionally asking questions, you and the participants will be discussing together. The workshop leader's role is that of a guide or facilitator who creates an environment in which participants can explore their own attitudes and learn new information.

Can I establish an open and safe learning environment? Your most important task is to establish and maintain effective communication and safety. It is essential that you discuss the following Participation Guidelines with participants during the first workshop, and review them during each session.

Participation Guidelines

- **Respect anonymity.** Encourage participants to share activities, readings, and discussions with others outside the workshop, but stress the importance of keeping the content of personal sharing by participants anonymous. A participant may request that a comment be kept confidential as well and is meant only for the other class members.

- **Set own boundaries for personal sharing.** Each participant is responsible for setting her or his own boundaries for personal sharing. Invite participants to determine what and how much of their own identities, values, and history they choose to share; whatever boundaries each participant sets are to be respected by the group.

- **Speak from personal experience. Avoid generalizing.** Participants should avoid using generalizations about people or speaking for others. Encourage "I think, feel, believe, experience . . ." statements rather than "Bisexual people, gay men, heterosexual people, lesbians, transgender people do, think, feel . . ." statements.

- **Respect differences.** Help participants to hear and understand different experiences and perspectives, rather than try to convince others that they are wrong. Everyone must understand that even though the purpose of the workshop series is to change attitudes and actions, each participant must have control over his or her own change process.

- **Encourage effective communication skills.** Review the basic principles of good communication: Maintain eye contact, avoid interrupting or giving advice, use "I" statements, share speaking time, ask clarifying questions.

Finally, make it clear at the beginning that no one will be asked to share her or his sexual orientation and/or gender identification during the workshop series. Individual participants may choose to share their sexual orientation and/or gender identification but participants need to control this decision. For many bisexual, gay, lesbian, and/or transgender people, coming out is a profoundly frightening experience. Because of prejudice against bisexual, gay, and lesbian people, revealing one's orientation is not always safe. The same is true for people who understand their gender in a different way than man or woman. On the other hand, coming out can be an empowering and affirming experience.

If individual participants come out during the series, or if outside speakers do so, it can provide powerful learning experiences for all participants, but you need to be aware of two considerations. First, avoid letting participants focus their attention on those who come out or treat them as "resident experts," "specimens," or "spokespersons" for the bisexual, gay, lesbian, and trans-gender community. Each bisexual, gay, lesbian, and/or transgender person can speak only from his or her own experience and should not be expected to share more than do other participants. Each participant should be focusing on his or her own feelings and beliefs, not on those of other participants.

Second, bisexual, gay, lesbian, and/or transgender people may suffer from the same lack of knowledge and awareness that heterosexuals do. In a culture that discourages anyone from discussing homosexuality and bisexuality, homosexual and bisexual people are often as confused as heterosexuals. Bisexual, gay, lesbian, and/or transgender people have just as hard a time learning about themselves, and may have internalized many of the same myths and stereotypes about bisexual, gay, lesbian, and/or transgender people that heterosexuals have.

Communicating with the Congregation

It is important to try to reach members of the congregation who don't participate in the program. Here are some suggestions for sharing your work with them.

Bulletin Board. Place a Welcoming Congregation bulletin board in an accessible location of your building. You might post readings from the workshops, or current events pieces from the newspa-per. You might, if participants are willing, post some of the newsprint material from the workshop series to give people a feel for the workshops. Again, if you do this, get express permission from every participant to do so. You might create an interactive piece where people write responses to questions. An example might be, "When did you first learn there were gay men in the world? How? Did this make you feel good, bad, or indifferent?" You might list people to contact with concerns or questions. Make the bulletin board appealing and attractive. This simple act will send a powerful message to the congregation.

Newsletter. Use the congregational newsletter to convey information to the congregation. This might include announcements, testimonials from participants, basic tidbits of information, or thought-provoking questions. Examples of the latter two are:

- There are over 1,000 legal benefits to couples who can get legally married.
- How many congregations in our Association are officially recognized as Welcoming Congregations?
- When did the Unitarian Universalist Association pass its first resolution in support of bisexual, gay, and lesbian people?
- The word for bisexual, gay, lesbian, and/or transgender people in the West African Dagara culture is "gatekeepers." They believe that they "vibrate differently."

You can create your own questions and facts or contact the Office of Bisexual, Gay, Lesbian, and Transgender Concerns at the Unitarian Universalist Association for more.

Email. Create a distribution discussion list where people can get information and interact with others about issues raised in the Welcoming Congregation Program. You might use "Twenty Questions About Homosexuality" by the National Gay and Lesbian Task Force (see p. 44), and ask list members to respond to the questions.

Sunday Service. Use the bulletin board to make announcements. Work with the minister and/or worship committee to allow for brief testimonials of what individuals have learned as they've gone through the process.

Congregational Leadership. You might wish to ask for a series of 15-30 minute sessions with your congregation's governing board or program council and, instead of reporting progress, present an exercise from the curriculum. Examples might be "Fears and Gains" from Workshop 1, a shortened version of "Word Brain Association" from Workshop 2, or one of the religion questions from Workshop 8. This will create a different kind of dialogue than will mere reporting.

Openings and Closings At-a-Glance

All readings and hymns come from *Singing the Living Tradition* (Boston: The Unitarian Universalist Association/Beacon Press, 1993).

Workshop 1: Introductions and Expectations
Opening/Chalice Lighting
    Reading: #443 "We Arrive Out of Many
      Singular Rooms"
    Hymn: #396 "I Know This Rose Will Open"
Closing/Check Out
    Unison Reading: #689 by Paul Robeson
    Hymn: #402 "From You I Receive"

Workshop 2: What We Know and How We Learned It
Opening/Chalice Lighting
    Reading: #502 by W. E. B. DuBois
    Hymn: #127 "Can I See Another's Woe?"
Closing/Check Out
    Unison Reading: #689 by Paul Robeson
    Hymn: #402 "From You I Receive"

Workshop 3: The Common Elements of Oppression
Opening/Chalice Lighting
    Reading: #584 "A Network of Mutuality"
    Hymn: #170 "Singing For Our Lives"
Closing/Check Out
    Unison Reading: #689 by Paul Robeson
    Hymn: #402 "From You I Receive"

Workshop 4: Gender Socialization and Homophobia
Opening/Chalice Lighting
    Reading: #569 "Stand By This Faith"
    Hymn: #121 "We'll Build a Land"
Closing/Check Out
    Unison Reading: #689 by Paul Robeson
    Hymn: #402 "From You I Receive"

Workshop 5: Racism and Homophobia
Opening/Chalice Lighting
    Reading: #550 "We Belong to the Earth"
    Hymn: #305 "De Colores"
Closing/Check Out
    Unison Reading: #689 by Paul Robeson
    Hymn: #402 "From You I Receive"

Workshop 6: AIDS
Opening/Chalice Lighting
    Reading: #463 by Adrienne Rich
    Hymn: #295 "Sing Out Praises for the
      Journey"
Closing/Check Out
    Unison Reading: #689 by Paul Robeson
    Hymn: #402 "From You I Receive"

Workshop 7: The Radical Right
Opening/Chalice Lighting
    Reading: #632 "Passover Remembered"
    Hymn: #162 "Gonna Lay Down My
      Sword and Shield"
Closing/Check Out
    Unison Reading: #689 by Paul Robeson
    Hymn: #402 "From You I Receive"

Workshop 8: Religion and Homosexuality
Opening/Chalice Lighting
    Reading: #598 "Without Hate" or
      #638 "Love"
    Hymn: #392 "Hineh Mah Tov"
Closing/Check Out
    Unison Reading: #689 by Paul Robeson
    Hymn: #402 "From You I Receive"

Workshop 9: Experiences of Bisexual, Gay, Lesbian, and/or Transgender People
Opening/Chalice Lighting
    Reading: #576 "A Litany of Restoration"
    Hymn: #128 "For All That Is Our Life"
Closing/Check Out
    Unison Reading: #689 by Paul Robeson
    Hymn: #402 "From You I Receive"

Workshop 10: History
Opening/Chalice Lighting
    Reading: #447 by Albert Schweitzer
    Hymn: #348 "Guide My Feet"
Closing/Check Out
    Unison Reading: #689 by Paul Robeson
    Hymn: #402 "From You I Receive"

Workshop 11: Bisexuality and Biphobia
Opening/Chalice Lighting
    Reading: #420 by Annie Dillard
    Hymn: #298 "Wake Now My Senses"
Closing/Check Out
    Unison Reading: #689 by Paul Robeson
    Hymn: #402 "From You I Receive"

Workshop 12: Transgender Identity:
    What It Means
Opening/Chalice Lighting
    Reading: #595 "Free From Suffering"
    Hymn: #407 "We're Gonna Sit at the
        Welcome Table"
Closing/Check Out
    Unison Reading: #689 by Paul Robeson
    Hymn: #402 "From You I Receive"

Workshop 13: How Homophobia Hurts Us All
Opening/Chalice Lighting
    Reading: #561 by Margaret Mead
    Hymn: #51 "Lady of the Seasons' Laughter"
Closing/Check Out
    Unison Reading: #689 by Paul Robeson
    Hymn: #402 "From You I Receive"

Workshop 14: What Now?
Opening/Chalice Lighting
    Reading: #443 "We Arrive Out of Many
        Singular Rooms"
    Hymn: #396 "I Know This Rose Will Open"
Closing/Check Out
    Unison Reading: #689 by Paul Robeson
    Hymn: #402 "From You I Receive"

WORKSHOP 1:

Introductions and Expectations

Purpose

- To begin discovering what we know and do not know, and exploring what we will do.
- To create a worthwhile group climate by establishing guidelines, sharing fears, concerns, and expectations, and discovering common ground.

Materials

- For large group exercises: newsprint (4-5 pages), masking tape, marker, posters (if used as opposed to handouts)
- For small group exercises: none
- For individual exercises: index cards (2-3), pencils, "Definitions" handout, "Twenty Questions About Homosexuality" handout

Preparation

- Prepare newsprint posters and/or handouts listing: goals, workshop schedule, assumptions, and participation guidelines.
- Copy the "Definitions" handout for each participant. Copy "Twenty Questions About Homosexuality" to post on the bulletin board or distribute to each participant. Both handouts are printed at the end of this workshop.
- Arrange chairs in a circle or semicircle.

Workshop Plan

Opening/Chalice Lighting   (5 minutes)

(Choose *one* of these openings. If you decide to bring readings, it is suggested that participants take turns with this responsibility each week.)

- Lighting of chalice and reading.
    Reading: #443 "We Arrive Out of Many Singular Rooms"
    Hymn: #396 "I Know This Rose Will Open"
- Reading of leader's choice.
- Moment of meditation or prayer.

Beginnings: Why Are You Here?   (15 minutes)

Ask participants to take a moment to settle in, get comfortable, and think about why they are here.

After a short pause, suggest having participants introduce themselves and say what motivated them to participate. (Leaders should go first to model self-disclosure.)

Acknowledge any difficulty or struggle that people may have alluded to in making their decisions. Simply choosing to attend the workshop series may be a courageous act for many people. (You might even ask the group why this is true.)

Explain that the group is about to begin a journey that will take 14 weeks (or however you adjust it) and that each week you will address a different theme related to the goals.

Goals   (5 minutes)

Present the goals of the workshop series, using the handout or newsprint poster you've prepared. You might also wish to talk briefly about how this is the second edition of *The Welcoming Congregation Handbook*, and that changes have been made throughout to keep the process and curriculum more current and accessible to all.

The Welcoming Congregation workshop series is an introspective and interactive educational journey into the issues surrounding the lives of bisexual, gay, lesbian, and/or transgender people. The learning goals are:

- To explore thoughts, feelings, and current knowledge about sexual orientation (homosexuality, bisexuality, heterosexuality) and gender identification (transgender identity).
- To probe the origins of our beliefs about sexual orientation and gender identification.
- To test attitudes toward sexual orientation and gender identification in Unitarian Universalist congregations and society, and their connections to current social issues such as AIDS, racism, sexism, ableism, ageism, and so on.
- To understand the experiences of bisexual, gay, lesbian, and/or transgender people.
- To see the effects of heterosexism and homophobia on people of all sexual orientations and

gender identifications in Unitarian Universalist congregations.

- To explore the relationship between religion and homosexuality.
- To devise individual and institutional strategies for Unitarian Universalist congregations to become more welcoming to bisexual, gay, lesbian, and/or transgender people and their families.

Review Workshop Schedule   (5 minutes)

Explain that the curriculum is as flexible as the participants and leaders wish it to be. Each workshop is centered around a theme. Present the schedule and invite questions.

1. Introductions and Expectations
2. What We Know and How We Learned It
3. The Common Elements of Oppression
4. Gender Socialization and Homophobia
5. Racism and Homophobia
6. AIDS
7. The Radical Right
8. Religion and Homosexuality
9. Experiences of Bisexual, Gay, Lesbian, and/or Transgender People
10. History
11. Bisexuality and Biphobia
12. Transgender Identity: What It Means
13. How Homophobia Hurts Us All
14. What Now?

(Note: List only the sessions you are doing.)

Discuss Assumptions   (5 minutes)

Review the handout or newsprint poster you've prepared. Invite questions and comments if you wish.

- We have all learned homophobia, biphobia, and transphobia from our culture—stereotypes, fears, misinformation, and hatred are examples of this.
- Our culture encourages us to believe that heterosexuality is superior to homosexuality and bisexuality.
- We have very few opportunities to talk openly, ask questions, and explore feelings about sexual orientation and gender identification and our society's response.
- Blaming ourselves is not helpful or useful. Taking responsibility for learning accurate information is useful.

- We can all help each other. No one person is an expert on bisexual, gay, lesbian, and transgender issues.
- Assuming people's sexual orientation is generally not a good idea.
- Our culture is designed for us to assume a person's gender.

Participation Guidelines   (5 minutes)

Discuss and ask for group agreement about the guidelines for all participants to follow throughout the course of the workshops.

- Respect anonymity. Ask for confidentiality. (It's fine for people to process the workshop with others provided no identities are revealed. If people feel like they would like to say something that stays completely in the room, they may ask for the group to hold these remarks in confidence.)
- Set own boundaries for personal sharing.
- Speak from personal experience. Avoid generalizing.
- Respect differences between others, between yourself and others, and even inside yourself.
- Use effective communication skills. Use "I" statements. Let people finish thoughts. Allow opportunities for all to speak, particularly introverts.

Review Definitions   (10 minutes)

Pass out the "Definitions" handout. Explain that these terms are the common language of the workshop—but not necessarily the only definition for each term. Ask if there are any additional terms that participants may want to define or discuss.

Questions in Pairs   (40 minutes)

Divide participants into groups of two. Have each person in the pair answer these questions:

- When have you felt excluded?
- When did you learn about love?
- When did you learn about sex?
- How have you seen homophobia?

You may wish to explain to the group that you are not looking for "right answers" here—just their honest response. You might also acknowledge that answering these questions may be more difficult for some than others. This may be particularly true for people who are victims and/or survivors of childhood sexual abuse. Encourage participants to answer the third question as they feel comfortable, and suggest that they focus their response on the first time somebody talked to them about sex.

After the four questions are completed, take a few moments as a large group to process anything participants learned or found valuable.

Some questions you might process:

- What was it like for you to answer these questions?
- What feelings arose for you as you talked and listened?
- What was easy and difficut to answer and discuss?
- What was interesting/valuable to you in these conversations?

You may also wish to ask at what age people learned about love and sexuality. Use your judgment.

Most importantly, this is a time to get people talking.

Fears and Gains (15 minutes)

Distribute two index cards to each participant.

Ask them to reflect and then write about fears they may have concerning the Welcoming Congregation Program. Be purposefully vague, so that people have the freedom to respond personally, institutionally, or as a member of the larger community.

On the other card have the participants reflect and write about what they hope to gain from the program. Again, the vagueness of this language will produce a variety of responses.

Tell the participants that the cards will be read aloud anonymously. No one will be identified or singled out. Also, tell people that if they have no response to one or the other question they should write that on their card.

Collect all cards when done, and redistribute them so that each person has one fear and one gain. You may want to tell participants that they may get their own card but this is okay.

On newsprint, create a chart of the fears and gains, divided into three categories: personal, congregational, and community. As people read the cards aloud, record the statement succinctly in the most appropriate category. Use your judgment.

Fears		
Personal	Congre- gational	Commu- nity

Gains		
Personal	Congre- gational	Commu- nity

Take a look at where the fears and gains tend to be focused. Ask people for comments. You may also encourage them to suggest other fears and gains that now occur to them if they so choose. Look for trends, clumps, and gaps. These charts may be good to post on the Welcoming Congregation bulletin board, for the whole congregation to see.

Everything You Always Wanted to Know (5 minutes)

Distribute index cards to each participant. Ask participants to write at least one question they have that they would like answered during the course of the workshop. They may write more than one question.

Tell participants these questions will be used to shape and inform upcoming sessions. Also, these should be done anonymously as they will be shared with the entire group.

Collect the cards and read them to the entire group. You may wish to refer to the schedule to suggest when particluar questions will be answered or suggest resources for other questions.

Avoid judgments about what is on the card—even if the question is simple or merely a statement. Acknowledging statements as such is a good idea.

You may wish to post these questions for everyone to see over a period of time.

Twenty Questions and Responses   (5 minutes)

Discuss the "Twenty Questions About Homosexuality" handout. This may either be distributed as a reading or posted as part of the bulletin board (preferred). Let the participants know that the reading is from the 1980s. (There are also responses from several Unitarian Universalists, written in 1997, which are available from the Office of Bisexual, Gay, Lesbian, and Transgender Concerns at the Unitarian Universalist Association at the Web site, http://www.uua.org/obgltc or on request.) Encourage participants to do the reading and create their own answers to these questions over the course of the curriculum.

Closing/Check Out   (5 minutes)

End by asking people to share one thing they have learned, relearned, or unlearned tonight. Choose one or both of the following:

- Unison Reading (put on newsprint and keep for each session): #689 by Paul Robeson

  Sorrow will one day turn to joy. All that breaks the heart and oppresses the soul will one day give place to peace and understanding and everyone will be free.

- Hymn: #402 "From You I Receive"

Assignment/Follow-up

- Ask participants to note references they hear this week to bisexual, gay, lesbian, and/or transgender people. They will be asked to share one next week.
- Create a Welcoming Congregation bulletin board.

- Distribute "Twenty Questions About Homosexuality" as a reading if you are using it as such.

Definitions

Biphobia, n.: The fear, oppression, or mistreatment of bisexuals, either by heterosexuals or by gay men and lesbians.

Bisexual/gay/lesbian person: The preferred, self-chosen "labels" of many homosexual and bisexual people. Some lesbians refer to themselves as gay women. Most gay and lesbian people do not like the term "homosexual."

Come out: To acknowledge one's sexual orientation, often in phases from self to others and then to the public. Coming out is a process, not an event; it is a constant issue throughout the lives of all bisexual, gay, lesbian, and/or transgender people, in every new situation.

Heterosexism: Cultural, institutional, and individual beliefs and practices based on heterosexuality as the only normal, acceptable, healthy sexual orientation.

Heterosexual ally: A heterosexual person who supports bisexual, gay, lesbian, and/or transgender people in both attitude and action, and who challenges homophobia and heterosexism in self and others.

Homophobia: The irrational fear, hatred, or intolerance of gay, lesbian, bisexual, and/or transgender people. Homophobia also includes uneasiness with any behavior that does not conform to gender-role stereotypes. Homophobia can manifest itself in fear of being gay, fear of being perceived as gay, or fear of being associated with gay people. Homophobic behavior can range from laughing at "queer" jokes to engaging in violence against bisexual, gay, lesbian, and/or transgender people. Homophobia helps to maintain sexism as well as heterosexism.

In the closet: Choosing to keep one's sexual orientation a secret.

Intersexual: A person whose body deviates from the Platonic ideal of absolute sexual dimorphism. In some cases this refers to ambiguous genitalia, in others to discordance between, e.g., the organization of the sex chromosome and the internal reproductive organs or external genitalia.

Oppression: The systematic subjugation of less empowered social groups by more powerful groups.

Outing: Forcing bisexual, gay, lesbian, and/or transgender people "out of the closet."

Privilege: Access to rights and resources that are available to dominant social groups and denied to less empowered groups.

Sexism: Cultural, institutional, and individual beliefs and practices that discriminate against women and denigrate women-identified values.

Sexual orientation: A more accurate term than "sexual preference," because studies indicate that, for many people, there is no choice involved. Many people may also use "affectional orientation" to more accurately identify their understanding of themselves.

Stereotype: A set of usually negative beliefs held about an entire social group. Such beliefs are used to justify prejudice and discrimination, and also to maintain clear boundaries for domination and dehumanization of the stereotyped group.

Transgender, adj.: An umbrella term used to describe anyone who does not conform to dominant understandings of gender. It may describe a person who is transsexual, intersexual, or a cross-dresser/transvestite.

Transphobia, n.: The fear, mistreatment, and/or oppression of people perceived as being transgender.

Transsexual, n., adj.: One who changes, in any number of ways, her/hir/his biological sex to align with one's gender identity. May be of any sexual orientation. (Accompanying terms can be "pre-operative," "post-operative," or "non-operative," though surgery is not required for transsexual to be used.)

Transvestite, n.: One who cross dresses; may feel comfortable in the corresponding gender role. May be of any sexual orientation.

Twenty Questions About Homosexuality

National Gay and Lesbian Task Force,
Washington, DC

1. Who is a homosexual?

"Homosexual" is a term used to describe feelings or behavior, and it is also used to describe individuals who have feelings of love, emotional attachment, or sexual attraction toward people of their own gender.

There is no neat way of compartmentalizing people as heterosexuals or homosexuals. Human sexual behavior and orientation, it has become evident from the studies of Dr. Alfred Kinsey and other researchers, is a continuum between exclusive heterosexuality and exclusive homosexuality on which every intermediate combination may be found. People who have romantic and sexual feelings for members of the opposite sex and for members of the same sex are often termed "bisexual," although for most people one or the other orientation predominates. Furthermore, people are not limited to a set of behavior patterns or feelings which restrict them or assign them to a particular category for life.

Much evidence indicates that all human beings have the capacity to respond physically and emotionally to people of both sexes. In situations such as boarding schools, prisons, and other institutions, for example, people with strong heterosexual orientation often develop romantic attachments or temporarily engage in homosexual behavior. A great number of people whose primary orientation is heterosexual also have experimented with homosexuality. Likewise, due to social pressures, because they cannot personally identify with stereotypical images of homosexuals or simply on an experimental basis, people whose orientation is predominantly homosexual may engage in heterosexual activity, often marrying and parenting children.

Some individuals who prefer romantic attachments to members of their own gender do not use the word "homosexual" to describe themselves, since it seems to them to refer solely to sexuality, and their orientation means far more to them than that. These men and women prefer to be called "gay." There are also many women who don't like to be called "homosexual" because it has so often been used to refer exclusively to men. They prefer to be called "lesbian," a word which derives from the Greek island of Lesbos. This was the home, in the sixth century BCE, of the great poet Sappho, whose works often celebrated love between women.

The origin of the term "gay" is unclear, but it was used for many years as an "insider" term by homosexual men and women, and it gained currency as the one word which was self-chosen and not used by outsiders as a term of abuse. Some people have objected to the use of this word, because it has another meaning as well, but just as the self-chosen word "black" has gained universal acceptance, the word "gay" has now become part of common usage.

2. How is homosexuality or heterosexuality determined?

It is much easier to say what does not determine sexual orientation than to explain the apparently complex origins of a person's sexual drives and feelings. Behavioral scientists reject the notion that either heterosexual or homosexual orientation is a simple matter of choice. The vast majority also rule out constitutional, genetic, glandular, or hormonal factors, asserting that human sexuality is unfocused at birth and that the development of either homosexual or heterosexual preferences is a matter of complex learning and experience.

In this light, the proper question to be asked is: "What causes human sexuality over the whole range of the heterosexual-homosexual continuum?" But influenced by our culture's prejudices, most researchers in the past have only asked: "What causes homosexuality?" They ignored the equally significant question, "What causes heterosexuality?" and more often than not, they further limited their inquiry to the presumed causes of male homosexuality. The researchers who have pursued these questions have come up with only hypothetical answers and very little agreement. Moreover, few of them were trained in experimental methodology, and they relied upon their observation of unrepresentative samples of gay people, principally those in psychiatric treatment.

Such studies generally started from the unproven assumption that humans have a built-in blueprint for heterosexuality and that homosexual orientation indicates that something went wrong with an individual's development. Rather than admitting the possibility that homosexuality is a natural variation that develops from the same source as heterosexuality—our human capacity to love each other—this research tried to identify some flaw or failure in an individual's background and attribute homosexuality to that "cause."

Some of the alleged "causes" of homosexuality still receive wide currency, even though they have been discredited within the scientific community. The idea that homosexuality is a stage at which some people are "fixated," for example, has been discounted in most scientific quarters by evidence that there are not specific sequential stages in psychosexual development; that heterosexual and homosexual responses coexist within children at all ages; and that in many instances heterosexual interests and behavior have preceded homosexual ones.

The most popular theories about the causes of homosexuality concern patterns of family relationships, particularly the dynamics between a mother and father or parent and child. But such theories have failed to take into account the number of heterosexuals who have experienced similar family patterns and the many homosexual women and men whose family constellations did not follow such patterns.

Although most researchers now acknowledge that the causes of both homosexual and heterosexual orientation are not known, many of them believe that basic sexual orientation is set at a very early age, probably by the time a child begins school. They believe that these primary affectional inclinations may not be recognized and acknowledged by an individual for many years, but they are nevertheless established in early childhood and do not radically change.

The confusion and uncertainty sometimes expressed by teenagers and even adults about their homosexual feelings are not really doubt about how they feel. They have romantic and sexual feelings for people of the same gender, but they are aware that such feelings are not widely accepted in our society and they don't know how to cope with the pressures to conform. Teenagers seldom express "confusion" about their heterosexual feelings, because such feelings are taken for granted and socially approved.

Despite the pressures to conform, many people do acknowledge and accept their homosexual orientation, taking pride in their capacity to discover what is true and right for themselves. This has been so in virtually every time and culture, even when people have been killed, tortured, ostracized or electroshocked in punishment for their preferences. Rather than looking for the imagined weaknesses which have been called the causes of homosexuality, researchers might well begin the search for the strengths which have allowed self-acknowledged lesbians and gay men to take an independent stance in a hostile world.

3. How many homosexuals are there?

Self-acknowledged lesbians and gay men constitute a very substantial segment of American society today, but it is difficult to give a precise estimate of our numbers. In a culture in which we are subject to discrimination and harassment, it is often very necessary for us to conceal our orientation.

The only extensive surveys of adult sexuality in America were conducted by Dr. Alfred Kinsey and his associates at Indiana University's Institute for Sex Research in the 1940s and 50s. These studies focused mainly on overt sexual behavior and did not attempt to discover how many individuals were self-described as homosexual. They nonetheless represented an important contribution to the reexamination of the myths and misconceptions about homosexuality, particularly the notion that it was something which involved only an insignificant percentage of the American population.

Considering only sexual experiences after puberty, Kinsey found that 37 percent of the males and 20 percent of the females in his sample had had at least one adult experience with a person of the same gender. He also found that 13 percent of the men and 7 percent of the women were predominantly homosexual for at least three years of their lives between the ages of 16 and 55. Put another way, this meant that more than 10 percent had a very significant homosexual dimension in their adult lives.

Subsequently, Dr. Paul Gebhard, who succeeded Kinsey as head of the Institute for Sex Research, reworked the statistics, including material gathered after the initial studies were published, and determined that 9.13 percent of the sample had "extensive" or "more than incidental" homosexual experience. He has stated that, considering the low average age of the sample, and the effects of the so-called "sexual revolution," he believes that these figures would be significantly higher today. His conclusion: "It is quite evident that when one speaks of homosexuality one is talking about something which involves millions, not thousands, of US citizens, and that homosexuality is a phenomenon which, with only slight variation, appears to cross all geographic, ethnic, and socioeconomic barriers in this country."

At the time that the Kinsey studies were published, when very few gay people were revealing their homosexuality to anyone but other gay people, a 10 percent figure for those with a basic homosexual orientation fit closely into our own impressions of the situation. More recently, non-gay people seem to be agreeing with us. In national polls conducted in 1976, for example, 10 percent was the figure most often mentioned by those polled, with higher figures offered by younger members of the population.

So, assuming 10 percent to be an excellent guess as to the number of those with a homosexual orientation, this means that 20,000,000 Americans, or one child in every five American families, are gay. Considering a typical family grouping of mother, father, four grandparents, two children, an aunt, and an uncle, there is a strong likelihood that one of these family members will have a homosexual orientation. The same likelihood would be true for any ten men or women we customarily deal with in our daily life: doctor, dentist, minister, accountant, lawyer, secretary, teacher, city-council member, police officer, proprietor of the neighborhood store. Virtually everyone in America knows someone who is gay, even though most of them don't know that they do.

4. Is homosexuality healthy?

Most professionals agree that the critical test of mental health and emotional stability is whether an individual is able to maintain a more or less smoothly functioning life. An overwhelming body of evidence indicates that by this criterion, sexual orientation does not determine the quality of mental health. A number of researchers, pioneered by Dr. Evelyn Hooker in a study conducted for the National Institute of Mental Health, have administered psychological tests to groups of heterosexuals and homosexuals and have been unable to distinguish between the groups in terms of functionality, stability, and creativity.

As long ago as 1935, Sigmund Freud wrote: "Homosexuality . . . is nothing to be ashamed of, no vice, no degradation, it cannot be classified as an illness." Subsequently, some of his disciples disagreed with that view, basing their opinion entirely on studies of individuals in psychiatric treatment. But, in 1973, the Board of Trustees of the American Psychiatric Association acknowledged the research on non-patient samples and removed homosexuality from its official listing of psychiatric disorders. This decision was later ratified by the APA membership.

The APA also passed the following resolution:

Whereas homosexuality per se implies no impairment in judgement, stability, reliability, or general social or vocational capabilities, there-fore, be it resolved that the American Psychiatric Association deplores all public and private discrimination against homosexuals in such areas as employment, housing, public accommodation, and licensing, and declares that no burden of proof of such judgement, capacity, or reliability shall be placed upon homosexuals greater than that imposed on any other persons. Further, the APA supports and urges the enactment of civil rights legislation at local, state, and federal levels that would offer homosexual citizens the same protections now guaranteed to others on the basis of race, creed, color, etc. Further, the APA supports and urges the repeal of all discriminatory legislation singling out homosexual acts by consenting adults in private.

In 1975, the American Psychological Association adopted a similar resolution with this added language: "The American Psychological Association urges all mental health professionals to take the lead in removing the stigma of mental illness that has long been associated with homosexual orientation."

Many mental health professionals point out that the individual who actually needs treatment is the one who suffers from homophobia, which is a reaction of fear or rage toward homosexuality or homosexuals. Verbal abuse or physical attacks on gay people are often engaged in by persons suffering from homophobia.

5. Is homosexuality a matter of choice? Can it be changed?

Homosexual feelings—affectional, emotional, or erotic attraction to persons of one's own gender—are not a matter of choice. Neither are heterosexual feelings. And neither is the basic sexual orientation which is established in early childhood.

Choice, however, does enter into the question of what one does in response to one's feelings or basic orientation. One can decide whether and how to act upon them and how to integrate them into the context of one's life.

There is enormous social pressure for people to repress their homosexual feelings or deny their basic orientation, and to adopt a heterosexual lifestyle. Gay men and lesbians have been mocked, imprisoned, and burned at the stake in an attempt to impose conformity. We have been pressured, counseled, and prayed into heterosexual marriages. We have been told to deny or repress our true feelings at whatever cost to our psychological well-being. Some of us seem to have managed to do so.

Others of us were unable to deny our feelings, but were also unable to cope with the social pressures. These people have sometimes expressed a desire not simply to mask their orientation but to change it, and over the years there have been willing practitioners who have promised them that, by employing a variety of techniques, they could accomplish a change. As a result, a very small percentage of those subjected to these techniques did manage to change their overt behavior. But in no instance have these changes been documented for more than five years, and there is no evidence that either homosexual feelings or a person's basic sexual orientation have been or can be changed.

The question that most of us have asked ourselves is "Why should we change?" We know that it is more natural for us to explore loving, responsible attachments to people of our own gender, and we know that the quality of these relationships is no better and no worse than those of the heterosexuals around us. For most of us, the disadvantages of social non-conformity are far outweighed by the advantages of accepting and taking pride in who we are as whole human beings.

6. What causes homophobia?

Homophobia is the irrational and persistent fear of homosexuality, which often manifests itself in extreme rage reactions to homosexuals. People who are homophobic often explain their fear and rage by offering what they believe to be rational reasons: that homosexuals are "crazy" or "disgusting" or "depraved." But homophobia is not limited to people who believe these myths, and mental-health professionals have begun to look more deeply into its causes.

As they examined the character profiles of homophobic individuals, they noted that a very high proportion also had prejudicial feelings against other minority groups, or simply against those who were in any way different from themselves. It was also observed that an overwhelming number of such individuals hold rigid and traditional views about most other social issues, and are likely to be strict conformists in their own pattern of behavior, particularly as it relates to the roles of women and men.

From this profile it can be deduced that homophobia stems in part from the same dread of the different or unknown that marks racial or religious prejudice. But there is also another factor, something that is presumed by homophobic individuals to challenge their own lifestyles and lives.

For example, if a woman has spent a lifetime measuring her own worth by how closely she could conform to the stereotype of what it means to be a woman, her whole image of herself might seem to be challenged by lesbians, who say, "I am a woman, even though I have broken one of the rules for what a woman is supposed to be. There's nothing wrong with breaking one of the rules, if that's what's right for you." Anger and rage are sometimes the defense against such a presumed challenge to one's own conforming patterns. This is particularly true for men in our culture, who not only are programmed for violent reactions, but have been told that being a "man" is more important than being a woman. The majority of homophobic individuals are men.

Researchers have discovered another common trait in a majority of homophobic individuals: the importance they attach to denying or repressing their own homosexual feelings. For such people, fear and rage are an automatic reaction to gay people who say, "It's all right to have such feelings. It's possible to be a good or moral person and not repress them."

Most homophobic individuals are not looking for a cure. But those who are might start by examining the facts about homosexuality, and deciding for themselves whether fear and rage are appropriate reactions. Next, they might take time to examine the principle of cultural diversity, and ask whether it isn't possible for them to live by their own standards, without creating conflict with someone else's. And finally, they might recognize the fact that virtually everybody has had homosexual feelings, and that having such feelings isn't a sign that anything has gone wrong. There are homophobic people whose basic orientation is homosexual, and this last point particularly applies to them. But it also applies to people who may never feel any desire to express their homosexual feelings.

Homophobia in our society may persist until people are no longer afraid of their own homosexual feelings, and that time may be long in coming. But homophobia does not only take its toll on those who have it, and the oppression and persecution of homosexuals is not its only social result. It has had a significant impact on the lives of heterosexuals as well. It has barred men from showing affection to each other, and fathers have been frightened to kiss their own sons. It has severed friendships between women, who were afraid to recognize that a romantic element was involved. And it has prevented many heterosexual men and women who wished to do so from challenging the sex-role stereotypes in their own ways, and exploring new modes for heterosexual relationships. Homophobia, even in an entire society, can be cured. And not only gay people have a stake in curing it.

7. Are gay people easily identified?

We live in a culture which has set up some arbitrary rules for what it means to be a "real man" or a "real woman." These rules can change. It wasn't too long ago, for instance, that "real" women didn't wear jeans and "real" men didn't have long hair. One arbitrary idea that hasn't completely changed is that homosexuals aren't "real" men and women. There is still a tendency to think that people who are gay don't follow any of the other rules, and that everyone must be gay who doesn't conform to the "macho" or "little woman" stereotypes.

Men with high-pitched voices, delicate facial features, long slender fingers, graceful walks, a fondness for stylish clothes, or sensitive natures are often thought to be homosexual. Women with low, resonant voices, broad features, a liking for shirts and slacks, or assertive natures are often thought to be lesbians. But these characteristics have nothing to do with sexual orientation. Many non-gay people have or adopt them, and these people have often had a painful insight into anti-gay prejudice and discrimination. And most gay people don't have these characteristics; it is very easy for most of us to hide. No one can tell who is or isn't homosexual by outward appearance and behavior alone.

Transvestites, who consciously assume the clothing and mannerisms usually assigned to the opposite sex, are often perceived as what homosexuals are like. But transvestites are not all homosexual; most of them are heterosexuals who find erotic pleasure in the act of dressing up. Those who are homosexual sometimes cross-dress for dramatic or political effect: as a rebellion against the arbitrary rules for how men and women are supposed to behave and dress.

Transsexuals are men and women who do not consider themselves homosexual. Rather, they feel that they are psychologically members of the opposite sex who are trapped in the wrong body. After extensive medical and psychiatric evaluation, some of these people have undergone sex-change surgery.

Many of us who do consider ourselves homosexual once thought this couldn't be true, because our desired modes of dress or behavior did not match the stereotyped image of being gay. It often took us years to realize that acknowledging our homosexual orientation didn't require us to be somebody else or conform to any sort of stereotype. It just gave us a greater opportunity to be ourselves.

8. Is homosexuality natural?

We cook our food, put on clothes, cut our hair, transplant organs, and fight disease with chemical agents. Homosexuality requires no similar alteration of nature, and homosexual acts are possible with just the bodies we are born with.

People often think that prescribed behavior patterns of their own culture apply to humankind in general, and that everything else is "unnatural." But studies of other cultures have often disproved these theories, and an impressive number of historians, anthropologists, and ethnologists now concur that to describe homosexuality as "unnatural" is to depart from the cross-cultural facts. They have found no society in which homosexuality is completely absent, and some in which it is virtually universal. They have also found that in a majority of cultures bisexuality seems to be the norm, and that it is only in societies like ours, with strong anti-homosexual taboos, that either exclusive heterosexuality or exclusive homosexuality is common.

Anthropologists C. S. Ford and F. A. Beach surveyed 76 contemporary societies outside the West and found that, in 64 percent of their sample, "homosexual activities of one sort or another are considered normal and socially acceptable for certain members of the community." They also discovered that in a significant number of cultures, such as Africa's Siwan tribe, homosexual behavior is encouraged and expected for virtually all members of the population.

It has often been asserted that there are a number of present-day societies, such as the Soviet Union, Mainland China, or the Israeli kibbutz, which have no homosexuals. But gay *kibbutzniks* have now written about their lives, and information about gay meeting places and gay political prisoners in the Communist countries has now reached the West. Logic suggests that, in these societies, cultural oppression has simply forced gay people further underground. (An interesting sidelight is that homosexuality, in capitalist countries, is often associated with a "Communist threat," while in Communist countries it is often referred to as "bourgeois decadence.")

When some people say that homosexuality (or contraception, or any of the sexual acts outside of coitus which are practiced by the vast majority of the American population) is "unnatural," they are simply stating their belief that the "purpose" of human sexuality is procreation. But science has long ago abandoned the notion of "purpose" to explain the world, and "natural law" is not a scientific term but a theological one. Modern behavioral scientists note that sexuality serves a number of purposes for human beings, and many modern theologians believe that for homosexuals and heterosexuals alike, sexuality is a "natural" part of the total fabric of our lives, especially valued as a celebration of our love.

9. Is homosexuality moral?

Neither homosexuality nor heterosexuality in and of itself is either moral or immoral. Rather, the problem for all human beings is how to fit their sexual feelings and relational needs into the context of a responsible and moral life, and how to use their capacity to love in ways that allow both themselves and their partners to strengthen and develop their moral capacities and human potential. These problems are faced by homosexuals and heterosexuals alike. There is no single path to a moral life.

Most cultures and most religions have little to say about sexual morality, and some of these encompass homosexual behavior within their customs and religious practices. But the Judeo-Christian tradition has tended to condemn homosexual behavior on the basis of a few isolated passages in the Bible. In recent decades, however, many Christian and Jewish theologians and pastors have questioned that position in the light of new knowledge about homosexuality and within the context of a more positive religious perspective on human sexual expression in general. Many of them have concluded that sexual relationships must be appraised in terms of love, mutual support, and responsibility rather than the gender of the individuals involved.

Most scholars today point out that all biblical passages must be considered with their cultural and historical context, and they believe that contemporary morality must be informed by the knowledge which has become available to us now. They point out that just as biblical passages have been used to denounce gay men and lesbians, similar passages were used to support slavery, to maintain an inferior status for women, and to persecute Jews, blacks, and other minorities. These scholars point out that much anti-gay rhetoric is based on a kind of selective "fundamentalism" and

they observe that Jesus Christ had absolutely *nothing* to say about homosexuality in the Gospels. They point out that Jesus and the Old Testament prophets did have a lot to say about concepts such as love, truth, and justice.

It is ironic that in a nation based on the separation of church and state, and on the right of individuals to make their own private moral choices, some religious groups have insisted on imposing their sexual morality on the lives of others. The irony and injustice have been understood by an ever increasing number of religious leaders and organizations which have supported the civil rights of gay people. Among the groups which have gone on record in support of civil rights protection for gay people are the National Council of Churches, the Roman Catholic Federation of Priests Council, the Central Conference of American Rabbis, and numerous denominational bodies, bishops, and local clergy. More and more, religious leaders are asking another important question: Is it moral to oppress people because of whom they love?

10. Is homosexual love the same as heterosexual love?

Everybody understands that heterosexuality isn't just about sex; that it is also about relationships in which individuals of different genders agree to love and care for each other, and to take responsibility in each others' lives. But many heterosexuals don't understand that relationships between members of the same gender involve exactly the same involvement and commitment, the same love and caring.

The belief that homosexuals can't love each other in the same way that heterosexuals do is based on the idea, long ingrained in our culture, that there are biologically determined differences in the personalities of a man and a woman which complement each other and allow them to love each other. An increasing number of heterosexuals now realize that the majority of these differences are not inborn but culturally imposed. But gay people have always known that personality is not a function of gender, because the people we fell in love with usually had very different personalities from ours, and were members of our own sex.

This doesn't mean that there are two kinds of homosexual, one playing a "masculine" and the other a "feminine" role. It does mean that the things that make human beings love each other— homosexuals and heterosexuals alike—are not their biological equipment but aspects of their personalities which have nothing to do with gender.

Gay people have been forced to explore what each person, as an *individual*, has been able to give to the other; we haven't had the man-and-wife roles to fall back on. While the absence of a prepared script has sometimes made it more difficult for us to communicate, we have found that our need to experiment has sometimes made it easier for us to love each other in an atmosphere of genuine equality. (A study conducted by the Institute for Sex Research compared randomly selected gay couples with randomly selected heterosexual couples, and reports that more of the gay couples seemed "happy" about their relationships.)

There have also been things which have made it harder for us to love each other. Heterosexual couples were permitted to demonstrate their affection by kissing or embracing in public places. We were denied that tender privilege, because other people found our love "disgusting," and would deride or abuse us if we showed it. (Homophobic individuals seem to get more upset about demonstrations of affection than they do about sex.) Heterosexuals were encouraged to include their spouses or dates at family gatherings and social events related to their jobs. We were often required to hide even the fact of our love from our families, employers, and co-workers. As with interfaith or interracial couples in the past, prejudice and discrimination have sometimes made it harder for us to sustain our love.

There are things which make it difficult for all couples to sustain their love. Sometimes, people grow at different rates and in different directions, and loving communication is no longer possible between them. In the past, when this has happened, most heterosexual couples felt that a marriage contract or practical responsibilities required them to stay together. Most gay couples had no such formal ties, and a higher percentage of our relationships ended in separation. Today, that difference seems to be decreasing. Many more heterosexuals now believe that however much one may dream of a relationship that lasts a lifetime, longevity is not necessarily a measure of quality.

Like some heterosexuals, some homosexuals don't seek long-term relationships, attempt "open marriages," or disassociate love from the physical act of sex. But the majority of gay people are not "promiscuous." Research shows that lesbians are no more—and probably no less—promiscuous than other women, and that gay men are only slightly more so than other men. This slight difference implies no inherent connection between male homosexuality and promiscuity. Rather, it comes

from the fact that most gay men, like most other men in our culture, have been taught to think of sex as recreation or as a measure of virility, and most lesbians, like most other women, have been taught to associate it only with love.

Curiously, some of those who say that homosexuality is only about physical sex and that gay people can't love each other, also say that they can't figure out what homosexuals do in bed. Perhaps if they could understand that love and sex play the same roles in our lives that they do in theirs, they could easily imagine what homosexual sex is like; it is almost exactly like heterosexual sex. Indeed, according to such diverse sources as the Kinsey Institute and surveys conducted by *Redbook* magazine, more than two thirds of all heterosexual couples—over 90 percent below the age of 35—engage in the same sexual acts they "can't imagine" us doing.

Gay people have never denied the existence of heterosexual love. Happily, we have been allowed to see examples of it all around us. Now that heterosexuals have been given the chance to see that homosexual love is also all around us, we wonder why so many of them still refuse to acknowledge our loving relationships and to see that they include the same problems and the same joys as theirs.

11. Does homosexuality threaten the family or civilization?

The American Home Economics Association defines the family as "two or more persons who share resources, share responsibility for decisions, share values and goals, and have commitment to one another over time. The family is that climate that one 'comes home to' and it is this network of sharing and commitments that most accurately describes the family unit, regardless of blood, legal ties, adoption, or marriage."

Under this definition, it can be seen that gay couples are not a threat to the family—we *are* families.

But even if one limits the term "family" to a mother, father, and their minor children, it is important to see that gay people are a part of this nuclear structure as well—that it is homophobia, not homosexuality, which poses a threat to nuclear family life.

The lack of communication which signals a family breakup takes place between parents and children as well as adult partners, and such lack of communication has often occurred between parents and their gay children. Many of our parents, for example, refused to recognize that our search for love and caring with members of our own gender was simply another way of meeting our basic human needs, and this refusal not only caused suffering for us but for them. Indeed, our parents' relationship with each other was often jeopardized by their unreasoning guilt, and it is only when they were helped to rid themselves of this guilt that their relationship improved.

Many gay people are themselves parents, and family breakup between these parents and their children has also been the result of prejudice; of discrimination which has forcibly deprived our children of their right to be cared for—or to be visited—by their own mothers and fathers.

Most lesbian mothers or gay fathers were once part of heterosexual marriages. And many of us who entered these marriages did so solely because we were taught to believe that our need for "family" could only be fulfilled in a nuclear heterosexual structure. It was only after our marriages broke up that many of us realized that this wasn't true and that *for us*, a sense of family was possible with members of our own sex. Many family service professionals now believe that fewer nuclear families would break up if people—homosexual *and* heterosexual—weren't forced into them by pressures to conform, but were encouraged instead to choose family structures that best met their individual needs.

Some people believe that if alternative family structures, including gay families, are supported and encouraged by society, the needs of children will not be met, the human race will cease to reproduce, and civilization will decline.

It seems odd that a culture which is so concerned about overpopulation should require *everybody* to reproduce, and it seems doubly odd that people who think that heterosexuality is so much better than homosexuality should imagine that once society agrees it is acceptable to be gay, everyone will immediately prefer it. But these concerns are discounted in any case by evidence from other cultures, some of which don't have nuclear families, some of which encourage homosexuality—and all of which care for their children and continue to procreate. And despite myths to the contrary, all modern historians are agreed that attitudes toward homosexuality, whether positive or negative, have had nothing whatsoever to do with either the rise or decline of any culture. Homosexuality is *not* a threat to either the family or civilization. It has always been a part of both.

12. Do gay people molest or recruit children?

Every authoritative study on arrests for sex crimes involving children indicates that over 90 percent of such incidents involve female children and male adults, and that incidents involving adult women with children of either sex are statistically insignificant. These percentages were remarkably consistent in large-scale studies by the Institute for Sex Research and the Children's Division of the American Humane Association, and in smaller-scale surveys conducted in Oregon, Minneapolis, San Francisco, and Boise, ID. So it can be seen that even if all 10 percent of those offenders involved with male children were homosexual in their basic orientation, the percentage of gay men is no greater than the percentage of heterosexual men who are child molesters.

In addition, the studies indicate that most of the men who were involved with male children were not self-defined as homosexuals. Many of them had previously been arrested for molesting female children, and a majority were more likely to have adult relationships with females rather than males. Some offenders were exclusively interested in children, and made no distinction as to the gender of the child. It is clear that the vast majority of child molesters are not homosexuals, and that the vast majority of homosexuals are not child molesters.

The term "recruitment" is sometimes used to suggest that gay people wish to lure children into sexual activity in order to "make them into homosexuals." This charge is not only disproved by the statistics above, but by numerous authoritative studies suggesting that even if such "recruitment" were tried, it wouldn't work. Follow-up studies of male children molested by male adults indicate that no more of them become adult homosexuals than any other group of children. And broader-based studies show that childhood sexual experiences, whether homosexual or heterosexual, whether with adults or other children, are not indicators of a person's basic sexual orientation and do not determine what adult patterns will be.

For some people, what is really meant by recruitment is "proselytizing," or the imagined attempt by homosexuals to persuade children that they "ought to" be gay. Actually, "ought to" is a term which has been used exclusively by proselytizers for *heterosexuality*, and all of us who are gay have been victims of such "recruitment" many times over. In or out of the Gay Liberation movement, most gay people oppose attempted recruitment, and we don't say that anyone "ought to" be anything, except who he or she is. What we do say is that people, including young people, have the right to make decisions for themselves, and that all children have the right to know the true facts about homosexuals and homosexuality.

When all children are permitted to hear these facts, we don't think it is likely to affect their basic orientation or to increase the number of homosexuals in the next adult generation. We think that knowing the facts would simply reduce the number of adult heterosexuals who attempt to recruit children.

13. Can lesbians or gay men be good parents?

A significant number of people whose basic orientation is homosexual have been involved in heterosexual relationships and have become parents. There is absolutely no evidence their homosexuality has had any bearing on their capacity to be loving, responsible, and dependable mothers or fathers, or that their sexual orientation has played a role in the determination of their children's sexual orientation. Indeed, all studies of gay parents indicate that their children are no more likely to be homosexual than the children of heterosexuals. In fact the great majority of lesbians and gay men have had heterosexual parents.

But there continues to be fear that gay parents will adversely influence the children they have nurtured and loved. This fear stems from the myths about gay people which falsely assert that we are irresponsible or "innately bad." And because of these myths, many children have been deprived of the right to be loved and cared for—or even visited—by their own parents.

A wide range of medical and psychiatric experts, however, have testified in support of custody and visitation rights for lesbian mothers and gay fathers. Dr. Judd Marmor, a former president of the American Psychiatric Association, has written: "I know of no evidence that predominantly heterosexual parents are more loving, supportive, or stable in their parental roles than homosexual women and men." And Dr. John Money of the Department of Pediatrics at Johns Hopkins University has this to say about custody rights for divorced parents living with members of the same sex: "It is not the sameness or the difference that counts, but the quality of the relationship between them, and the quality of the relationship they establish with the child."

It is true that children also suffer from the prejudice their gay parents face. But the answer is to end this prejudice, not remove the children. In any case, as the children of interracial couples and other parents who have faced prejudice have proved, the advantages of a loving environment more than outweigh the disadvantages of social pressures. Dr. Evelyn Hooker, who headed the National Institute of Mental Health's Task Force on Homosexuality, has said: "I personally know a number of lesbian mothers and homosexual fathers. . . . In some instances, I have been able to follow the development of the children as well, and know them as young adults to be psychologically healthy, mature, responsible individuals."

The law seldom separates heterosexual mothers or fathers from their children unless they have a pronounced history of physical abuse or criminal neglect. This is not the case with homosexual parents who often have their children taken from them. But since there are absolutely no data to indicate that harm is done by gay parents, the actual harm is done by courts which separate children from the love of their parents, simply because of the anti-gay attitudes pervasive in our society.

14. Does society discriminate against gay people?

Lesbians and gay men are subjected to public and private discriminatory practices that touch upon virtually every area of our lives. We are fired or refused jobs simply for being who we are. We are denied access to federally subsidized or private housing. We are refused credit, insurance, bonding, licensing, and access to public accommodations. We are often excluded from health care, counseling, and other social services. We have been barred from entering this country, becoming citizens, and holding public office. We have been abused, beaten, and murdered by gangs of "queerbaiters"; subjected to unequal enforcement and denied equal protection of the laws; brutalized and harassed by the police. And our businesses and social, religious, community-service, and political organizations have been taxed unfairly, spied upon, threatened, and bombed.

The basis for such discrimination is in many ways exactly the same as for other victims of prejudice: a refusal to apply the same standards to one group of people that are applied to others. And the rationales for such discrimination are often identical. It is argued that teamwork on a job or neighborhood good feeling would be jeopardized by people the majority doesn't like. Parents claim the right to "protect" their children from exposure to people or ideas they don't approve of. Employers and landlords say that discrimination is "necessary" to prevent members of the majority from taking their business elsewhere. And there is the same reliance on stereotypes and myths.

But anti-gay discrimination is not quite the same as that directed against racial and ethnic minorities or women, because most gay people, like most members of religious minorities, can "pass" as members of the majority. We have not become an economic underclass and we are already integrated into the work force. Discrimination against us occurs only when we are open about our sexual orientation or are somehow "found out." Most of us live in fear that if our homosexuality becomes known, we will lose our status in the community, our livelihoods, or even our lives. The keystone of anti-gay discrimination is the conspiracy we've been forced to join, to pretend we don't exist.

Studies done by the state of Pennsylvania and the city of Tulsa have proven conclusively that massive discrimination against gay women and men does exist, and a majority of Americans, in a 1977 Louis Harris poll, believed that homosexuals face more discrimination than any other group. But only a few cases have been documented, since only a few of us can afford to protest injustice. For most of us, notoriety is the one thing we don't need if we hope to get another apartment or another job.

The gay movement is demanding an end to *all* forms of public and private discrimination, and it is working to amend all local, state, and federal civil-rights legislation to include sexual orientation—along with race, color, creed, sex, and national origin—as an illegal basis for discrimination. We are not asking for something *special*; we are demanding our right to be on a par with all other citizens, to be considered on our individual merits. We are not even asking for inclusion in "affirmative action" plans, since there's no way—without violating everybody's privacy—to take a census of employees and find out which are gay.

We value privacy. But we don't think that "privacy" can be defined differently for us. Everybody recognizes the right of tenants or employees not to talk about their race, religion, or national origin; nobody tells them they *mustn't* talk about it. But homosexuality is presumed to be about "sex," so if we choose to be open about our lives, we're told that's "flaunting."

But homosexuality is no more about sex than heterosexuality, and heterosexuals are always "flaunting." They chat about who they went out with last weekend and which members of the opposite sex they find attractive. They embrace and kiss in public places. They bring their spouses or dates to work-connected events. We are required to censor ourselves in ways that nobody who isn't gay can possibly realize.

Dr. Howard Brown, for instance, waited until he'd left his job as a New York City Health Services Administrator before making a public declaration of his homosexuality and becoming a co-founder of the National Gay Task Force. In his book, *Familiar Faces, Hidden Lives*, he wrote about the fears he faced: "As the day neared on which I was to be sworn in as the chief health officer of New York City, I found myself faced with a problem. What should I do about Thomas? We had been living together for five years. . . . I obviously passed as a heterosexual in the eyes of the Mayor and the panel; otherwise they would not have selected me."

Later, Dr. Brown discovered that some of his colleagues and supervisors knew all along that he was homosexual; that the unforgivable thing would have been to be open about it; and that it wasn't his "privacy" that caused concern, but other people's insecurities and fears.

15. Should gay men and lesbians be barred from certain jobs?

During the 1970s considerable progress was made in overcoming anti-gay discrimination. Many corporations, including such giants as AT&T, IBM, and the Bank of America, adopted non-discriminatory policies. The federal civil service and other agencies such as the Job Corps ended discrimination. More than 40 US cities passed civil rights legislation. A majority of the public came to believe that gay people deserve human rights, including the rights to housing and jobs.

But some segments of the public continue to believe that exceptions should be made for such "sensitive" jobs as teachers, foster parents, counselors, ministers, police, and members of the military. And they have particular rationales for restricting our rights. They claim to believe that we are less reliable or trustworthy than heterosexuals, and less likely to control our sexuality, even though all these allegations have been proven false. They claim that public disapproval will make it impossible for us to do our jobs, forgetting that the same argument was used by those who themselves "disapproved" of other minority groups. Most of all they claim that we will "influence impressionable children."

Most of these people know that gay people aren't child molesters, and that we aren't trying to "recruit" children to homosexuality. Many of them also know that the development of either homosexual or heterosexual orientation has nothing to do with knowing either gay or non-gay adults. What they really seem to be saying when they call our lives "unsuitable for children" is that they are made uncomfortable by homosexuals, and that they don't want their children to be any more comfortable than themselves. They forget that one out of ten children *is* gay, and that such children are forced to grow up believing there is no one like themselves to admire and respect. They forget that *all* children have the right to know the truth; there *are* gay people to admire and respect.

All that is needed to end the myths and stereotypes about gay people is for all of us who are gay to let our co-workers, neighbors, and families know we're there. But this isn't likely to happen until the discrimination ends—including discrimination in "sensitive" jobs.

Gradually, however, more and more gay people are "coming out," and prejudice, even in the "sensitive" areas, seems to be decreasing. The courts have acknowledged that openly gay people aren't subject to blackmail, and can't be discharged or denied security clearances on those grounds. All the major teachers' unions, and many school boards, supervisors, and parents' groups, have acknowledged the right of gay teachers to be honest and open on the job. Courts have recognized gay teachers' rights to champion "unpopular" views. Some denominations have ordained openly gay ministers, and most religious and professional organizations now have gay caucuses in their ranks.

Today there are many openly gay ministers, teachers, nurses, physicians, and psychiatrists. In 1972 there were hardly any. One brave psychiatrist dared appear as an "open" homosexual at an American Psychiatric Association convention. He wore a mask.

16. Should there be laws governing private sexual behavior between consenting adults?

Most Western nations, in conformity to the Code Napoleon, have no laws restricting sexual behavior between consenting adults in private. Great Britain repealed such laws in 1967, and most legal authorities in the United States, including the American Bar Association and the American Law Institute, have urged our state legislatures to do the same. They view such government regulation as an unwarranted intrusion upon an individual's right to make personal decisions about private matters, and they believe that the government has no rightful place in the nation's bedrooms. They point out that such interference involves no compelling public interest, since no one's rights are infringed upon by "victimless crimes."

From 1961 through 1978, 20 states repealed their so-called "sodomy" statutes, which criminalize private oral-genital or anal-genital activity. Of those states which retained such laws, three exempted heterosexuals, and two exempted married couples, but in all the others such acts were considered crimes for all individuals, married or unmarried, heterosexual or homosexual. Repeal efforts have been mounted in virtually all these states and, in numerous instances, attempts have been made in the courts to have the sodomy statutes declared unconstitutional.

The Supreme Court of Massachusetts has declared that the state's law does not apply to consenting adults in private, and other state courts have declared themselves prepared to rule on the constitutional issues. But the US Supreme Court refused to decide these questions in 1977, when it declined to review a lower-court decision upholding the sodomy statute in Virginia. Although this ruling has questionable value as a precedent, it came as a disappointment to civil libertarians, who saw it as inconsistent with the Supreme Court's decision in abortion and contraception cases, where it upheld the individual's right to sexual privacy and control of one's own body.

These rights are the principal grounds for continuing constitutional challenges. But also important, many legal and religious authorities believe, is the principle of separation of church and state. Additional challenges involve the doctrine of equal protection of the laws, since the sodomy statutes are inequitably applied and enforced. Sentencing, for example, has been arbitrary, sometimes involving "cruel and unusual punishment." Some states make the same acts a crime for some people and not for others. States in which the laws apply to everybody enforce them almost exclusively against homosexuals.

This selective enforcement is a major reason why gay-rights organizations make removal of the sodomy statutes a prime goal, but it is important to understand that these laws do not make *being homosexual* a crime. Under the American system of criminal law, people may be punished only for their *acts*, not for their status. Not all gay people engage in the activities proscribed under the sodomy statutes, and a majority of heterosexuals do engage in them. If status were the criterion for criminality in the states with sodomy laws, heterosexuals as well as homosexuals would be a class of criminals.

17. How does the lesbian and gay movement relate to other social movements?

The Gay Liberation Movement, which challenges traditional cultural restrictions on the degree of love and caring permitted between members of the same gender, may be viewed as part of a broader cultural trend that stresses individual self-realization rather than conformity to socially imposed patterns. This trend is evidenced in many "human potential" and self-help movements, and particularly in the Feminist Movement, which shares our emphasis on re-evaluation of the traditional roles of women and men.

It has always been clear that one of the rules for conforming to the traditional roles is that men are only supposed to love women, and that women are only supposed to love men. Some feminists, at the beginning of their movement, thought that this wasn't one of the rules that mattered, and that identifying a women's movement with lesbianism would hurt its chances for success. But gradually, an overwhelming majority of feminists have realized that a women's right to her own body and her right to make her own decisions included her right to be a lesbian. And the movement itself has recognized that all women who do not choose to play traditional roles are labelled "too strong, too aggressive, too masculine, and finally, lesbians." Passage of a sexual-preference plank at the 1977 International Women's Year Conference in Houston signalled recognition by the Feminist Movement that only when the word "lesbian" has lost its power to intimidate and oppress will women be free to abandon *any* of the traditional roles and to become strong and independent human beings.

One movement with which Gay Liberation does *not* have much in common is the so-called Sexual Revolution. It is true that both movements challenge an exclusively procreative model of human sexuality, that both are historically connected to worldwide concern for overpopulation, and that public discussion of homosexuality has accompanied freer discussion of all sexuality. But the Sexual Revolution has come to mean "sex on the loose" and a separation between sexual activity and caring or love, and this is *not* what the Gay Liberation movement is about. We are saying we have the right to be—and be open about—who we are as whole human beings, and that we have the right to love or care for whom we choose. We are saying that homosexuality, like heterosexuality, is *not* just about sex. It is about human love and responsibility, human self-realization and human rights.

Gay liberation is also related to the civil rights movements of racial, religious, and ethnic minorities. Indeed, the activist phase of the Gay Movement in the 1970s was directly influenced by the Black Movement of the 1960s, and its insistence that people have a right to be proud of their special group identity and do not have to conform to all the values, standards, or lifestyles of the majority to deserve their full and equal rights. But just as some members of religious and ethnic minorities opposed the rights of blacks, on the grounds that one form of prejudice and discrimination was "not the same thing" as another, some spokespeople for other oppressed minorities have believed the kind of myths about gay people that were told about themselves. Gradually, this too is changing, with the realization that civil rights principles require *everyone* to be judged solely on individual merit, and that when this requirement is violated in regard to *any* group of citizens, the principle is weakened for all. More and more black leaders, like Coretta Scott King and NAACP president Benjamin Hooks, have spoken out for the rights of gay people. They have been joined by a majority of groups representing the aged and the young—elements of our society which, like gay people, have yet to be granted legal guarantees of their civil rights.

18. Do gay people have special insights about the human condition?

The exploration of human truth and morality is not limited to a single culture, group, or time, but is something that all human beings share. And the insights of homosexuals, from Sappho and Plato through Walt Whitman and Gertrude Stein, have had a broadness of vision encompassing all of humankind.

Each culture, and each group in all cultures, has had a unique perspective from which to view the human condition. And gay people, in our culture, also have a special "window to the world"—something that makes it easier to see things that others might miss.

Like other groups which have faced prejudice and discrimination, for example, we have sometimes been able to cast a cold eye at the pretensions to truth and morality we have seen around us, and to challenge dogmatic ideas or rules that aren't fair. Because we know that people of the same gender could love each other, even though most people around us said they couldn't; because we knew it was right for us to refuse to deny or repress that love, even though most people said it wasn't; it was sometimes easier for us to question other conventional ways of seeing or doing things. Many of us, for instance, were at the forefront of the civil rights struggles because we knew it couldn't be "God's will" to assign inferior status to any group of human beings. And many gay men as well as lesbians have been in the vanguard of the fight for equal status for women.

As the traditional gender roles and the traditional views of human mated relationships began to change, some of us also discovered that our homosexuality gave us special insights into problems that heterosexuals were also trying to solve. Because we couldn't use the standard male-female roles in our relationships, many of us found it easier to notice that differences in basic personality structure aren't really connected to gender. We also found it easier to identify which things in our culture were really "men's problems" or "women's problems" and which were simply human problems that members of both genders share. We have been pioneers in the attempt to form relationships of real equality based on the best that each *individual* has to give.

Because our relationships were free of formal ties, some of us also pioneered the notion that good relationships don't mean "two into one" but involved the shared goals for two *independent beings*. We have pioneered a notion of "family" that stresses its *function*, as a vehicle for love and caring, rather than its structure. And many of us have long been able to understand that when shared goals are impossible and real communication no longer exists, the "family" has already broken up. Gay people have always been encouraged to share the heterosexual "window to the world," and we have learned much that has been useful to us in our own lives. Heterosexuals have not been encouraged to share our "window," but we too are willing to share.

19. Should homosexuality be publicly discussed?
We live in a nation which has prided itself on free competition in the marketplace of ideas. We have believed that freedom of speech was essential, even for views that were obnoxious to most of us, if we were to avoid becoming the sort of totalitarian society that would be obnoxious to us all. We have had faith that if *all* ideas were allowed to be expressed, those which were true would survive.

But throughout our history, there have been those who would suppress *some* ideas as too "abhorrent" or "dangerous" for our citizens to hear. Sometimes they have managed to prevent most of us from hearing them. But gradually some ideas which once could not be publicly discussed have gained currency. We no longer found them abhorrent because we discovered that they were true. And the principle of free speech was upheld.

We have also prided ourselves on our pluralism—our capacity to sustain the ideas and lifestyles of our diverse racial, ethnic, and religious groups. But throughout our history, the perspectives of *some* groups were not permitted to enter the marketplace of ideas. Because blacks were thought to be "inherently inferior" or Jews "condemned by God," it was assumed that their ideas and lifestyles did not need to be considered.

But gradually our once-despised minorities have made their voices heard. They have insisted on their right to their own choices, and their right to make their unique contributions to our society. They have cried out against oppression, and most of us were able to listen and to reconsider the morality of our own acts. The principle of pluralism has been upheld.

In the name of free speech and pluralism, homosexuality *must* be publicly discussed. We insist on entering the marketplace of ideas. And we have some ideas we want everyone to hear. We are saying that it is true and it is good that members of the same gender can love each other and take responsibility in each other's lives. We are saying that homosexual feelings are healthy and natural for all human beings, whatever their sexual orientation. And we believe that public discussion of these ideas is essential, if gay children are to grow up healthy and proud, and *all* children are to grow up free from fear of their homosexual feelings, and from prejudice and hate.

20. Should gay people come out?
For centuries lesbians and gay men in our culture have been told that we must hide our homosexuality. We have been asked to live a lie. We have been forced to deny who we really are and whom we love. We have lived with enormous fear—for our jobs and homes, for the loss of those we care about, even for our lives.

Yet coming out of hiding or "coming out of the closet" is an ongoing issue in the life of virtually every gay person, since it not only involves how we present ourselves to the world, but how we perceive ourselves. For most of us, it is a lifelong process of integrating our homosexuality into the fabric of our lives, and of judging the extent to which we may operate as whole human beings in a repressive and hostile society. Some of us never go beyond a single step in the process; some take a very long while between steps; but for most of us the question is not whether we *should* come out. It is whether, and how far, we can afford to do so in any given situation.

The first step in the coming out process is to come out to ourselves: to acknowledge and accept our homosexual orientation as part of our total humanity, and say, "This is who I am." A next step may involve seeking out other gay people, and sharing with them an openness that seems impossible elsewhere.

Coming out to those who are not gay always involves the fear of personal rejection, but many of us have taken the risk of confiding in our close friends, believing that no real friendship exists when deception plays a part. Gradually more and more of us have risked coming out to our schoolmates or co-workers. Some of us have made public declarations and work openly for lesbian and gay rights. And more and more of us have come out to our families, where the fear of rejection often has been the greatest of all.

In some cases our fears have been realized: we have been rejected. In perhaps a majority of instances, we have established more honest and satisfying relationships with those around us. But whatever the immediate result, most of us who have engaged in the process of coming out have found that fear of rejection is worse than rejection itself. We have experienced a great sense of relief, and an increased sense of self-esteem. "Our findings," say researchers Martin Weinberg and Colin Williams of the Kinsey Institute, "show that being known about, rather than producing more stress for the homosexual in relation to the heterosexual world, can in certain ways make for a generally less stressful situation."

Despite the demonstrably positive effect that coming out has had on most of us who have emerged from the closet, no one can tell another gay person that they *should* come out. The reality of some people's lives demands that they keep their homosexuality a secret. And, in every case, coming out must be an individual decision.

But in many cases, this decision is affected not only by the potential effect on the person who makes it, but by the recognition that coming out of the closet has important implications for the community in which we live. Young gay people, as the result of seeing people like themselves they could admire or respect, may be spared the pain of self-hatred and self-doubt. And non-gay people, according to several national polls, are more likely to support gay rights if they are aware that they are personally acquainted with lesbians and gay men. There is no doubt that as more and more gay people *have* come out, we have come closer to the day when *all* gay people can afford to do so—a day when no one will challenge our right to a job and a place to live; our right to love whom we choose; our right to be ourselves; our right, if we choose to do so, to speak the truth.

WORKSHOP 2:
What We Know and How We Learned It

Purpose

• To understand how we have come to know what we know about ourselves and others' sexual orientation and gender identification.

Materials

• For large group exercises: newsprint (7-8 pages), masking tape, markers
• For small group exercises: none
• For individual exercises: none

Preparation

• Create seven stick figures on five pages of newsprint, putting one stick figure on three pages and two stick figures on two pages (see example below). Print the names above each stick figure.

• Create a chart on two pages of newsprint for the "How We Learned About . . ." exercise. See Sexual Orientation/Gender Identification Charts at the end of this workshop.

• Arrange chairs in a circle or semi-circle.

Workshop Plan

Opening/Chalice Lighting   (5 minutes)

Choose *one* of these openings. If you decide to bring readings, it is suggested that participants take turns with this responsibility each week.

• Lighting of chalice and reading.
  Reading: #502 by W. E. B. DuBois
  Hymn: #127 "Can I See Another's Woe?"

• Reading of leader's choice.
• Moment of meditation or prayer.

Check In   (5 minutes)

Ask participants to check in, saying in one sentence how they are doing and then sharing the reference about bisexual, gay, lesbian, and/or transgender people they noted from the previous week.

Word Brain Association   (55 minutes)

Hang the five pieces of newsprint in various places in the room. Split the group into five similar groups—one per newsprint page.

Have each group write and/or draw as many associations, stereotypes, and conceptions/misconceptions they have heard about their stick figure. Tell each group that these can be positive, negative, or neutral words, and it is more important to list as many words as possible than to avoid saying the "wrong thing." Stop after five minutes.

Allow for browsing and addition time. Give everyone 10 minutes to look at the other drawings and add to them. Ask the participants to make additions in such a way that it is clear they have been added to the group.

Go over what is written and drawn for each figure and discuss where this was heard and when this was learned as people are willing to share this information.

Process with the entire group what it felt like to do this exercise. Focus specifically on people's feelings and what specifically it would feel like to belong to one of these groups and hear all of these stereotypes and conceptions. You may also wish to spend a few minutes talking about how age has affected what people believe—particularly as the

Page 1	Page 2	Page 3	Page 4	Page 5
Gary Gayman	Lizzie Lesbian	Bobby & Betty Bisexual	Harry & Helen Heterosexual	Terry Transgender
1 stick figure	1 stick figure	2 stick figures	2 stick figures	1 stick figure

bisexual, gay, lesbian, and transgender civil rights movements have evolved.

How We Learned About . . . . (50 minutes)

Split the group into pairs and ask people to discuss the following questions. Allow each person two minutes to speak. For questions five and nine, participants may have more than one answer.

Sexual Orientation

1. When did you learn that there were gay men in the world? Were the connotations associated with this positive, negative, or neutral?

2. When did you learn that there were lesbians in the world? Were the connotations associated with this positive, negative, or neutral?

3. When did you learn that there were bisexual people in the world? Were the connotations associated with this positive, negative, or neutral?

4. When did you learn that there were heterosexual people in the world? Were the connotations associated with this positive, negative, or neutral?

5. When did you learn about your own sexual orientation? Was this a positive, negative, or neutral thing?

Gender Identification

6. When did you learn that there were boys/males in the world? Was this a positive, negative, or neutral thing?

7. When did you learn that there were girls/females in the world? Was this a positive, negative, or neutral thing?

8. When did you learn that there were transgender people in the world? Was this a positive, negative, or neutral thing?

9. When did you learn what gender you were? Was this a positive, negative, or neutral thing?

Return to the large group. Use the charts you've prepared to graph responses to the above questions.

For example, you might say, "How many of you learned about gay men between the ages of 0-5?" Record that answer and ask about the 6-10 age group and so on. When you have finished this for each age group, ask people, "If you raised your hand in the 0-5 age bracket, how many of you learned this in a positive way?" Record answer. "Negative way?" Record answer. "Neutral way?" Record answer. Continue this for each category. It will go more quickly than you think. Note: Participants may have more than one answer for questions 5 and 9.

After you have completed the information for each chart, ask participants what they notice about the information they have compiled. You may need to prompt with questions such as "Which sexual orientation did most of us know about first? Last? Why do think that is?" Notice trends and patterns.

You might also process with the group how it felt to do this exercise—what was easy, hard, thought-provoking?

Closing/Check Out (5 minutes)

End by asking people to share one thing they have learned, relearned, or unlearned tonight. Choose one or both of the following:

• Unison Reading: #689 by Paul Robeson

Sorrow will one day turn to joy. All that breaks the heart and oppresses the soul will one day give place to peace and understanding and everyone will be free.

• Hymn: #402 "From You I Receive"

Assignment/Follow-up

• Notice various oppressions during the week.
• Have each person talk to at least one other person with whom she or he feels comfortable and ask that person how and at what age she or he learned about gay men, lesbians, bisexuals, heterosexuals, or transgender people.

Sexual Orientation/Gender Identification Chart

	Age in Years								
	0-5	6-10	11-15	16-20	21-30	31-40	41-50	51+	Totals
Gay Men									
+,-,N									
Lesbians									
+,-,N									
Bisexuals									
+,-,N									
Heterosexuals									
+,-,N									
Your Own Sexual Orientation									
+,-,N									
Male									
+,-,N									
Female									
+,-,N									
Transgender									
+,-,N									
Own Gender Identification									
+,-,N									
(+ = positive, - = negative, N = neutral)									

Completed Sexual Orientation/Gender Identification Chart

	Age in Years								
	0-5	6-10	11-15	16-20	21-30	31-40	41-50	51+	Totals
Gay Men		2	5	5	2	1			15
+,-,N		0-2-0	0-4-1	0-4-1	1-1-0	0-1-0			1-12-2
Lesbians			4	6	3	1	1		15
+,-,N			0-3-1	1-3-2	1-1-1	0-1-0	0-0-1		2-9-4
Bisexuals		2	4	4	3	1	1		15
+,-,N		0-2-0	0-3-1	1-3-0	1-1-1	0-0-1	1-0-0		3-9-3
Heterosexuals	7	3	5						15
+,-,N	5-0-2	2-0-1	5-0-0						12-0-3
Your Own Sexual Orientation*	2	2	6	5	1			1	17
+,-,N	2-0-0	1-1-0	3-1-2	2-2-1	0-0-1			0-1-0	8-5-4
Male	15								15
+,-,N	11-0-4								11-0-4
Female	15								15
+,-,N	5-2-8								5-2-8
Transgender				2	5	5	2	1	15
+,-,N				0-2-0	0-4-1	0-5-0	0-1-1	0-1-0	0-13-2
Own Gender Identification*	15								15
+,-,N	8-2-5								8-2-5
(+ = positive, - = negative, N = neutral)									

* People may have more than one answer for this.

WORKSHOP 3:

The Common Elements of Oppression

Purpose

- To illustrate the commonalities between various oppressions.

Materials

- For large group exercises: newsprint (2 pages), marker
- For small group exercises: newsprint (1 page per group), masking tape, markers/crayons, Definitions of Oppression cards
- For individual exercises: "Oppression Observation" sheet (optional)

Preparation

- Create a chart on newsprint as shown below:

Oppression in Our Society

Social Group	Dominant Group	Target Group	Name of Oppression
Gender			
Race			
Ethnicity			
Ability			
Religion			
Affectional/ Sexual Orientation			
Class			
Age			
Species (Human/ Non-human)			

- Copy handouts for participants: "Definitions of Oppression" and "Oppression Observation" sheet (optional).

- Copy the "Definitions of Oppression" handout and cut out two oppression cards for each group.
- If you plan to do the "Oppression Observation" sheet, it is useful to familiarize yourself with "The Common Elements of Oppression" in *Homophobia as a Weapon of Sexism* by Suzanne Pharr. (See Program Resources)
- Arrange chairs in a circle or semi-circle.

Workshop Plan

Opening/Chalice Lighting   (5 minutes)

Choose *one* of these openings. If you decide to bring readings, it is suggested that participants take turns with this responsibility each week.

- Lighting of chalice and reading.
  Reading: #584 "A Network of Mutuality" (*Singing the Living Tradition*)
  Hymn: #170 "Singing for Our Lives" (*Singing the Living Tradition*)
- Reading of leader's choice.
- Moment of meditation or prayer.

Identified Norms   (20 minutes)

Tell participants that this workshop will focus on oppression and how it works. Ask the group to think about oppression as it exists in United States or Canadian society. Brainstorm a list of the various oppressions the group can identify.

Refer to the chart "Oppression in Our Society" and ask the group to study it for a minute. Tell the group to look at the top row and ask what they think "Dominant Group" and "Target Group" mean. Ask why they think these words are used here.

Look together at the chart and complete it as a whole group. Some of your answers may not match exactly the example on page 64, but trust your judgment.

Discuss the chart and allow for free-flowing conversation. Encourage people to discuss what provokes them into further thinking and reflection. Feel free to ask if there are other oppressions that participants feel need to be listed.

Oppression in Our Society

Social Group	Dominant Group	Target Group	Name of Oppression
Gender	Male	Female, Transgender	Sexism
Race	European-American (White)	All Others	Racism
Ethnicity	Anglo-Saxon	All Others	Ethno-centrism
Ability	Temporarily Able-Bodied	Disabled	Ableism
Religion	Christians	All Others	Anti-Semitism (example)
Affectional/ Sexual Orientation	Heterosexuals	Bisexuals, Gays, Lesbians	Heterosexism (& Homophobia)
Class	The Top 1%/10%	All Others	Classism
Age	Adults 30-50	All Others	Ageism
Species (Human/ Non-human)	Humans	All Other Living Things	Specie-ism

Oppression Pictures   (90 minutes)

Assess the group size and composition and choose three oppressions that are represented by people in the room. For example, you might choose sexism if you have a large number of women and/or transgender people in the room—or racism for a high number of people of color, or ageism if there are a fair number of older people. One of the oppressions, regardless of the group's make-up, should be heterosexism/homophobia. Divide the group into two or three smaller groups and assign an oppression to each.

Give each group a sheet of newsprint and some markers/crayons and ask each to draw a detailed picture illustrating how their assigned oppression works in our society. Allow 20-30 minutes.

You may wish to write some prompts on a sheet of newsprint that will help. These prompts would be particular ways oppression is experienced: immigration, schools, government, taxation, reproductive rights, health care, welfare, family, work, crime, misconceptions, and so on.

Give each group two oppression cards. Tell them that they are going to have to "teach" the whole group these words and their definitions after 15 minutes of planning time. They may do this in any way they would like, but encourage creativity. Offer suggestions such as drama, art, role plays, and human sculptures.

After 15 minutes have each group separately present their words, and afterwards ask every group to find examples, if they have them, of those words in their pictures.

Distribute the Definitions of Oppression handout and ask groups to identify the rest of the terms as portrayed in their pictures. *Allow groups to add to their pictures if needed.*

Have each group present its picture to the entire group, explaining it in no more than three minutes. Allow people from other groups to ask questions of the presenters.

After finishing this, ask the groups to rotate to the left to another picture. Give them five minutes to list privileges of the dominant, non-oppressed group. (For example, for the picture of heterosexism, list privileges given to heterosexual people and denied to bisexual, gay, lesbian, and/or transgender people. Share these with the total group.

Process the activity. What did people learn, or find interesting, challenging, or confusing in doing this activity?

Closing/Check Out   (5 minutes)

End by asking people to share one thing they have learned, relearned, or unlearned tonight. Choose one or both of the following:

• Unison Reading: #689 by Paul Robeson

   Sorrow will turn one day to joy. All that breaks the heart and oppresses the soul will one day give place to peace and understanding and everyone will be free.

• Hymn: #402 "From You I Receive"

Assignment/Follow-up

• Distribute the Oppression Observation sheet and the Suzanne Pharr reading (optional). You might wish to post one or more of these on the bulletin board.

Definitions of Oppression

These are from "The Common Elements of Oppression" by Suzanne Pharr.

DEFINED NORM

Definition: a standard of rightness which is backed up with institutional and economic power as well as institutional and individual violence. For example, in the United States there exists a defined norm which takes its form as the white, heterosexual male, of the middle or upper classes, temporarily able-bodied, and of a Christian (usually Protestant) background.

Example: Heterosexuality is a defined norm. Those who do not fit into this norm are denied civil rights such as fair employment and housing and the economic benefits of marriage. BGLT people suffer a high rate of hate crimes against them.

Example: Whiteness is a defined norm. Those who are not white face greater challenges than those who are. Most of the "standard" examples given of who people are in our society portray this "standard" as overwhelmingly white.

ECONOMIC POWER

Definition: the control of economic resources through laws and policies that reinforce the status quo.

Example: Recent prohibitions of new Native American-owned and -run gambling casinos after the first casinos have shown themselves to be quite profitable.

Example: Redlining: lines are drawn which divide neighborhoods by race and class with the result that insurance and mortgage rates are highest in neighborhoods in which people have the least economic resources.

INSTITUTIONAL POWER

Definition: majority status at the upper levels of the major institutions that comprise a society.

Example: In the US, white males (presumably heterosexual) hold the majority of top positions in federal and state governments, financial institutions, the legal system, military, etc. A quick look at the history of the presidency reveals who holds the greatest institutional power in this society.

Example: Most sports teams are owned by white males, even when the majority of the players are not white. Often entire cities are held hostage for new stadiums and arenas.

MYTH OF SCARCITY

Definition: the idea that resources are limited in such a way that those not in power are to blame for economic problems.

Example: The targeting of immigrants from Mexico as the cause of the decline of the middle class in California, despite the fact that the cheap labor performed by immigrants is essential to the economy of the state and that tax laws have increasingly favored the wealthy at the expense of the middle class.

Example: The threat of cutting social security with the promise of lowering taxes. By many people's standards, this is unethical. It also is based on a myth of scarcity. The wealthiest people receive the highest tax breaks, but some members of Congress prefer to blame the elderly and disabled for the high tax rates of middle income Americans.

VIOLENCE/THREAT OF VIOLENCE

Definition: the sanctioning of violence either through direct threat or through lack of protection.

Example: As Asian American communities started to profit in California in the nineteenth century, their farms and businesses were burned down, and they were physically assaulted with little recourse to justice.

Example: Recent statistics indicate that one in three women are targets of sexualized violence in their lifetime. Most women live with the understanding and fear that they may be targets of rape.

LACK OF PRIOR CLAIM

Definition: exclusion from being part of a defined norm in which those not originally present in the founding of institutions are considered to have no rightful claim to inclusion. ("You were never meant to do this.")

Example: The Constitution of the United States understood the term "all men are created equal" to mean white males. White women and all people of color were largely considered by the nation's founders to be less than fully human. Although most (not all) members of Congress would now agree that the case for genetic inferiority is not valid, most of them would recognize that the white male norm still runs the business of Congress and that white women and people of color are still significantly considered outsiders.

Example: "Marriage has always been about a man and a woman, not a man and a man." (Or even, "God created Adam and Eve, not Adam and Steve." It is interesting to note that no one ever questions the racism of that statement or the skin color of Adam and Eve.

THE OTHER

Definition: those who are not part of the defined norm.

Example: Aristotle believed that women were simply a weaker version of men, and Freud defined women in terms of lack (lacking the phallus). Although women are not a minority, this culture sees them as the Other in relation to a male norm. Cast from the norm, women in western society have often been viewed as mysterious and as something to be discovered.

Example: Parallels with the historical development of views toward people of color offer evidence that "the Other" is not simply a chance of relations between different groups of people, but rather a carefully and consciously constructed set of power relations based on discernible differences.

INVISIBILITY

Definition: a method of continual re-inscription of the Other in which the histories and achievements of certain groups of people go untold, unheard, and unseen.

Example: Most Americans, regardless of race or ethnicity, are taught history in such a way that they do not know what various communities of color and what white women were doing over the course of US history. The absence of visibility gives the impression that aside from a few exceptional people, they were not "doing" anything worthy of discussion.

Example: Many people believe they do not know anyone who is gay. Yet many BGLT people do not reveal their identities to family, friends, and co-workers out of fear of rejection or discrimination.

DISTORTION

Definition: the selective presentation and false representation of the lives and histories of particular groups of people.

Example: The continued dissemination of information regarding sexual abuse of children which tells us that gay men are out to seduce boys. Statistically speaking, the vast majority of sexualized crimes against children is committed by heterosexual men.

Example: After the Civil War, many racist portrayals of black people were created by white people who feared black equality. Among them was the new image of the black male rapist of white women, by which hundreds of lynchings were carried out. Ironically, white men had systematically raped black women in slavery, often as a means for reproduction of laborers.

STEREOTYPING

Definition: defining people through beliefs about a group of which they are a part; usually a product of ignorance about the diversity among individuals within any given group.

Example: Bisexual people are promiscuous. This stereotype erases the humanity and diversity of bisexual people and disregards the processes by which individuals of all sexual orientations go about choosing a way of life appropriate to their values.

Example: Jewish people as stingy. Many Jewish individuals, organizations, and communities are dedicated to work which helps the underprivileged, much as many Christian and other non-Jewish individuals, organizations, and communities are dedicated to this work. Both selfish and giving people can be found among every group. In many Jewish communities today, the obligation to "tikkun olam," to heal and transform the world, guides individual and community involvement.

BLAMING THE VICTIM

Definition: assigning blame to the targets of oppression for the oppression itself and for its manifestations.

Example: A rapist says that a woman "asked for it." Historically, women of color have been especially vulnerable to these accusations because part of racist devaluation has been to sexualize women of color in order to inflate the purity of white women.

Example: In situations of violence against people who are bisexual, gay, lesbian, and/or transgender, the charge is often made by attackers that the targets of violence were flaunting their sexuality. Consider that few, if any, heterosexual couples are attacked for holding hands in public (unless they are interracial).

INTERNALIZED OPPRESSION

Definition: the devaluing of one's own identity and culture according to societal norms.

Example: Rates of suicide are high among bisexual, gay, lesbian, and/or transgender youth in part because they have grown up in a culture that has taught them that their identity is not and will not be valued.

Example: Some women do not pursue full medical care because they feel they do not deserve good medical care.

HORIZONTAL HOSTILITY

Definition: acting out internalized oppression toward other members of the target group; safer than confronting oppressive forces.

Example: Gang violence.

Example: Discouraging people of one's cultural group from succeeding in the larger society with accusations of selling out.

ASSIMILATION

Definition: taking on the appearance and values of the dominant culture. It is important to recognize that assimilation occurs under varying conditions: sometimes it is forced, other times it is desired, and its success is usually mitigated by recognizable differences such as skin color.

Example: Native American people have experienced forced assimilation through the taking of their children to white schools to unlearn their culture. This is considered cultural genocide.

Example: In the nineteenth century many African American people desired to assimilate (while others did not), but were allowed only a limited assimilation due to the racism of the dominant culture.

ISOLATION

Definition: a necessary component of oppression that frames injustice in terms of individuals rather than recognizing commonalities between members of a group or between groups.

Example: A group coming out of isolation in the US are people with disabilities at community, state, and national levels. This movement gained momentum in the early 1980s and got the American Disabilities Act passed in 1990. Until then, people with disabilities were often pitied.

Example: BGLT youth have often been isolated because adult BGLT organizations fear being accused of "converting" youths. However, BGLT youth organizations are on the rise, often with the leadership of young people themselves.

TOKENISM

Definition: a limited number of people (pick one and only one) from non-dominant groups are chosen for prestigious positions in order to deflect criticism of oppression.

Example: Getting a person of color on an otherwise white board of directors with no intention of actually serving the needs of people of color.

Example: Appointing a woman to a high faculty position at a university with the intention of preventing the need to hire other women faculty.

INDIVIDUAL SOLUTIONS

Definition: seeking to create change at an individual level rather than at the level of social change.

Example: Welcoming individual BGLT people into congregational life without examining how heterosexism operates within one's denomination and society.

Example: Giving spare change to homeless people without organizing as a community to address poverty at local, national, and global levels.

Oppression Observation Sheet

Look for examples of these elements of oppression and record them on this sheet. Refer to "The Common Elements of Oppression" by Suzanne Pharr.

Element of Oppression	Heterosexism/ Homophobia	Other Oppression (Racism, Sexism, Ageism, Ableism, Classism, Ethnocentrism, Anti-Semitism)
Defined Norm		
Institutional Power		
Economic Power		
Myth of Scarcity		
Violence/Threat of Violence		
Lack of Prior Claim		
The Other		
Invisibility		
Distortion		
Stereotyping		
Blaming the Victim		
Internalized Oppression		
Horizontal Hostility		
Isolation		
Assimilation		
Tokenism		
Individual Solutions		

WORKSHOP 4:
Gender Socialization and Homophobia

Purpose

- To understand how homophobia and heterosexism maintain gender-role stereotyping and limit choices, regardless of sexual orientation and gender identification.

Materials

- For large group exercises: newsprint, markers, masking tape
- For small group exercises: none
- For individual exercises: drawing paper, markers/crayons

Preparation

- Create a chart on newsprint, as shown below.

	Boys	Girls
Age 7		
Age 15		
Present Age		

- Arrange chairs in a circle or semi-circle.

Workshop Plan

Opening/Chalice Lighting   (5 minutes)

Choose *one* of these openings. If you decide to bring readings, it is suggested that participants take turns with this responsibility each week.

- Lighting of chalice and reading.
  Reading: #569 "Stand by This Faith"
  Hymn: #121 "We'll Build a Land"
- Reading of leader's choice.
- Moment of meditation or prayer.

Childhood Memories   (80 minutes)

Distribute drawing paper. Ask participants to draw pictures of what they understood in their childhood about the following descriptions: good girl, bad girl, good boy, bad boy.

Reassure participants that this is not art class and stick figures are fine. Encourage the participants to add words associated with these drawings. Allow 20 minutes and encourage conversation as people are drawing.

Ask each participant to briefly talk about their drawings for the entire group. If you have a larger group, feel free to put people into two or three smaller groups.

When done, discuss what these pictures tell us about gender roles in our society, using the following questions as a guide.

- How did these pictures promote stereotypes of boys and girls?
- What, if any, connections can participants make from these pictures to homophobia and heterosexism?
- How does entrenched thinking about gender affect bisexual, gay, lesbian, and/or transgender people?
- What did participants feel and learn from doing this project?

Break the group into same-gender pairs and ask them to talk about other rules from their childhood. Ask them to remember themselves at age seven. What were they like? Who were their friends? Where did they live? What year was it and what was going on in the world around them at the time? Then repeat the process for age 15.

The upcoming discussion is about noticing what they were told—and by whom—about the "correct" ways boys and girls should act and what affect that has on them today. The discussion works on a couple of levels. One is the obvious message—we learn what is "right" about girls and boys at a very young age and it continues to affect who we are. On another level, the exercise connects us to a time when we knew less and were open to suggestion and teaching, and it subtly reinforces the idea that if that was possible then, it's also possible now.

Ask partners to remember and discuss the "rules" about friendships (both same and opposite gender friendship) that they knew at ages 7, 15, and now at their present age. Ask the following questions, one at a time, for them to discuss.

- Were there different rules for being friends with boys and girls at age seven? What were they? Who taught them to you?
- How did you feel about them?
- What were the rules about these friendships at 15? How and why did they change from age seven?
- How did you feel about this?
- What rules do you operate under now at your present age? How and why have these changed?
- How do you feel about this?
- If you could make the rules now, what rules would you make?

Return to the large group and discuss observations, learnings, and feelings that came up for participants. Ask people to listen for similarities and differences in experiences as the entire group talks. Record the "rules" on newsprint.

You may wish to ask if, at their present age, sexual/affectional orientation might affect the answers given. Would a straight person have a different set of rules than a gay or lesbian or bisexual person? There is no correct answer here. As a leader, you might encourage participants to speak from personal experience by asking a question like, "How do you know this?" or, "Why do you believe this?"

Ways to Avoid Being Called "Queer" (30 minutes)

In the large group, ask participants to remember what they had to do to avoid being called "queer," "fag," "gay," or "dyke." You may wish to prompt with a few examples:

- Boys must not hug each other.
- Girls must not be aggressive.
- Girls must sit with their knees together.
- Boys must be athletic.
- Never wear green on Thursdays (from the 1950s).

After 10-15 minutes, ask participants to look at the list and ask if and how things have changed today from their childhood.

Close with the following questions:

- Are there things people still do today to avoid being called "queer"?

- What connections do you notice doing this activity and gender stereotyping?
- What connections do you see between the stereotypes (from Workshop 2) of bisexual, gay, lesbian, and/or transgender people and gender stereotyping?
- How are homophobic slurs (fag, queer, dyke, etc.) used to reinforce gender stereotyping?
- Are there ways in which items from the list affect you and limit you in the way you are in your life? How?

Closing/Check Out (5 minutes)

End by asking people to share one thing they have learned, relearned, or unlearned today. Choose one or both of the following:

- Unison Reading: #689 by Paul Robeson

  Sorrow will turn one day to joy. All that breaks the heart and oppresses the soul will one day give place to peace and understanding and everyone will be free.

- Hymn: #402 "From You I Receive"

Assignment/Follow-up

Ask participants to note gender role expectations they hear from their peers at work or social events or on television during the upcoming week.

WORKSHOP 5:

Racism and Homophobia/Heterosexism

Purposes

- To reinforce the fact that there are bisexual, gay, lesbian, and/or transgender people of color.
- To understand the connections between racism and homophobia/heterosexism.

Materials

- For large group exercises: newsprint, markers
- For small group exercises: newsprint, markers (enough for whole group), masking tape
- For individual exercises: none

Preparation

- Prepare newsprint for brainstorming and listing exercises.
- Create six pages of newsprint and place on walls. Each page should look like the example below. Give each page a different title: Work Issues, Legal/Government Issues, Education Issues, Media Issues, Family Issues, and Other Issues.

Racism and Heterosexism/Homophobia	
Commonalities	Differences

- Arrange chairs in circle or semi-circle.

(Note to facilitator: It is important to acknowledge that people will have different levels of experience in dealing with issues of racism as they have had with homophobia and heterosexism. This workshop is meant to be a place of learning and not of judging. Each person's ideas, impressions, and insights are to be valued as a part of an ongoing process.)

Workshop Plan

Opening/Chalice Lighting (5 minutes)

Choose *one* of these openings. If you decide to bring readings, it is suggested that participants take turns with this responsibility each week.

- Lighting of chalice and reading.
  Reading: #550 "We Belong to the Earth"
  Hymn: #305 "Des Colores"
- Reading of leader's choice.
- Moment of meditation or prayer.

Famous People (10 minutes)

As a large group, name as many famous bisexual, gay, lesbian, and/or transgender people as you can and record on newsprint. Accept no concerns over whether or not someone on the list actually is or is not bisexual, gay, lesbian, and/or transgender.

After five minutes, look at the list and ask how many of these folks are also people of color. Circle the names of people who are.

Ask the group what they make of this. In many groups, there will be very few people of color on the list. If this is the case in your group, ask why they think this is so. If you do have a good percentage (such as 20 percent) of people of color, let the group know that this is unusual.

In either case, share with the group that more often than not only white people are ever portrayed as bisexual, gay, lesbian, and/or transgender people. Rarely are African Americans, Native Americans, Latino/a's, Asian Americans, Arab Americans, or Pacific Islanders portrayed as being bisexual, gay, lesbian, and/or transgender.

Allow for a few comments on this and proceed to the next exercise.

People of Color Who Are Bisexual, Gay, Lesbian, and/or Transgender (25 minutes)

Divide the groups into pairs. Each person gets five minutes to talk with his or her partner about any impressions or experiences they have had concerning bisexual, gay, lesbian, and/or transgender people of color. Be clear with people that each person should listen to the other for the whole five minutes without interjecting their own thoughts. Keep time for the groups, giving a one-minute warning and then an announcement to switch. (Facilitation tip: Make sure that everyone understands the format. It is fine if some participants cannot think of any impressions—they can talk about a lack of impressions and experiences as well, especially if they can reflect on why this is.)

Return to the large group. On a sheet of newsprint record what people report back from their small groups. Instruct people that they are only to report their own thoughts and not those of the other person. Again, people are encouraged to also report a lack of impressions or experiences. After everyone has had time to respond, ask people for any reflections they have. For example, what do the responses say about the place of the group and the individuals within it in terms of further learning?

Similarities and Differences (55 minutes)

Tape your six prepared sheets of newsprint to the wall. Try to allow enough room between the sheets so that each group can talk without distracting the others.

Divide participants into six groups. Give each group 10 minutes at their first newsprint page to list as many commonalities and differences as they can on the newsprint. Then ask groups to move to a new sheet and give them three minutes to add to it. Continue rotating until groups have completed a turn at all sheets.

If they get stuck, offer some examples, such as, "One commonality is that both people of color and bisexual, gay, lesbian, and/or transgender people face job discrimination." Or, "A difference is that people of color look to their families of origin for support, whereas bisexual, gay, lesbian, and/or transgender people often experience alienation from family members."

Gather everyone together. Visit each station and as an entire group discuss their responses. Allow for questions and brief comments. There will be more time for discussion. Allow approximately three minutes per station. Then ask the group what they have learned from this exercise. What surprised them? How can they further their learning?

Privilege (10 minutes)

Ask the group to look again at the newsprint pages. What are some common examples of the privileges white people and straight people have in our society? List these privileges on newsprint if you wish.

Passing (10 minutes)

Explain to the group that passing is a word used to describe people who appear to be part of the dominant cultural group. For example, many light-skinned people of color appear to be white and benefit from this. Many bisexual, gay, lesbian, and/or transgender people appear to be heterosexual. Usually this is maintained by not coming out. Because this is so predominant among bisexual, gay, lesbian, and/or transgender people, many people are not the vicitms of overt homophobia because they are assumed to be heterosexual.

Ask the group these questions for brief conversation:

- How does the ability to pass as heterosexual help bisexual, gay, lesbian and/or transgender people? How does it help light-skinned people of color?
- How does passing hurt bisexual, gay, lesbian, and/or transgender people? How does it hurt light-skinned people of color?
- How does the ability to pass affect the way these two oppressions are compared in our society? Would things be different if bisexual, gay, lesbian, and/or transgender people could not pass as heterosexual? How?

Closing/Check Out (5 minutes)

End by asking participants to share one thing they have learned, relearned, or unlearned tonight. Choose one or both of the following:

- Unison Reading: #689 by Paul Robeson

  Sorrow will one day turn to joy. All that breaks the heart and oppresses the soul will one day give place to peace and understanding and everyone will be free.

- Hymn: #402 "From You I Receive"

WORKSHOP 6:
AIDS

Purpose

- To understand how AIDS is linked to homophobia and heterosexism.

Materials

- For Option 1: VCR, TV, video
- For Option 2: none
- For Option 3: The book *When Plague Strikes* by John Cross Giblin, newsprint, markers

Preparation

- For Option 1: obtain video (available from your local video rental store or from the UUA Video Loan Library), preview movie, and arrange room for adequate viewing.
- For Option 2: Invite speakers from local, regional, or state AIDS groups (try for a balance of representatives, including a gay man with AIDS, a family member of a person with AIDS and caregivers who work with AIDS patients); arrange chairs in a circle.
- For Option 3 (an additional exercise to use with Options 1 or 2): Have a participant read *When Plague Strikes* by John Cross Giblin (New York: Harper Trophy, 1997) and prepare a report on what they learned from it. This is ideal if you show *Common Threads*, which is shorter than either of the other two movies.

Workshop Plan

Opening/Chalice Lighting   (5 minutes)

- Reading: #463 by Adrienne Rich
- Hymn: #295 "Sing Out Praises for the Journey"

Option 1—Video   (time varies)

Show the video *Common Threads* or *Longtime Companion* or *And the Band Played On*.

Use the following questions as the basis for discussion after the video:

- How did you feel after watching the video?
- What are your reactions to the stories you heard?
- What connection do you see between homophobia and AIDS?
- How do people you know talk about AIDS?
- How are people with AIDS treated in the community?

Option 2—Panel Discussion   (time varies)

Invite the panelists to share their experiences with AIDS. After they have finished telling their stories, allow for questions and answers. If necessary, ask questions about such topics as fears, discrimination, how AIDS is changing, blaming the victim, and what language like "innocent" victims implies.

After the discussion, invite the participants to talk about what they learned. Ask participants:

- How did you feel after listening to the speakers?
- What were your reactions to the stories you heard?
- What connection do you see between homophobia and AIDS?
- How do people you know talk about AIDS?
- How are people with AIDS treated in the community?

Option 3—*When Plague Strikes* by John Cross Giblin   (time varies)

Do this only as an addition to Options 1 or 2, or in combination with another shortened session from elsewhere in the curriculum. Ask the person(s) who read the book to share briefly what they learned about AIDS, disease, and human behavior.

Closing/Check Out   (5 minutes)

End by asking people to share one thing they have learned, relearned, or unlearned tonight.
Choose one or both of the following:

- Unison Reading: #689 by Paul Robeson

  Sorrow will one day turn to joy. All that breaks the heart and oppresses the soul will one day give place to peace and understanding and everyone will be free.

- Hymn: #402 "From You I Receive"

Assignment/Follow-up

Have participants look for examples of the Radical Right and their actions and beliefs in the upcoming week.

WORKSHOP 7:
The Radical Right

Purpose

- To gain greater understanding about the Radical Right and our options for conversation, response, and clarity.

Materials

- For large group exercises: newsprint, markers
- For small group exercises: newsprint, markers/crayons, case studies
- For individual exercises: index cards, copies of case study, readings

Preparation

- Copy "The Christian Right" and "Public Speaking Tips for People of Faith" handouts for each participant.
- Make four copies of the case studies for small group work.
- Have newsprint ready for the discussions and small group work.
- Arrange chairs in a circle or semi-circle.

Workshop Plan

Opening/Chalice Lighting   (5 minutes)

Choose *one* of these openings. If you decide to bring readings, it is suggested that participants take turns with this responsibility each week.

- Lighting of chalice and reading.
  Reading: #632 "Passover Remembered"
  Hymn: #162 "Gonna Lay Down My Sword and Shield"
- Reading of leader's choice.
- Moment of meditation or prayer.

Clarity and Rigidity   (20 minutes)

Ask participants to remember a time when they or someone else they knew had a very rigid way of being and thinking.

Break the group into pairs. Ask each person to share with his or her partner what she or he or the acquaintance did that demonstrated being rigid in thought.

After five minutes, ask participants to remember a time when they or someone else they knew was very clear in their thinking. Have each person describe to the partner what she or he or the other person did that demonstrated clarity of thought.

After each person has had a turn, ask each pair to find another pair and have that group work to articulate the difference between clear thinking and rigid thinking. Tell the groups they are going to be asked to tell the larger group their thoughts on the discussion they have.

Give them the two statements below as additional ideas to consider, and tell each group they have five minutes for discussion. You may wish to put these statements on newsprint. Tell the groups you will have one person from each group report on their conversation after five minutes and let each group know they need not arrive at consensus. You might wish to have the groups think of UU examples of rigid and clear thinking.

Rigid Thinking

Rigid thinking allows for only one possibility. It often applies to everyone in all situations. Often information is ignored or rejected when it contradicts the one possibility.

Clear Thinking

Clear thinking follows a process that allows for more than one possibility. Usually, it is a conscious choice that applies to a particular choice and individual(s). Other decisions may result when the choice and/or individual(s) are different.

After five minutes, allow each group to report briefly about their conversation. After the groups have reported, let them know that this exercise was to stimulate their thinking and not to create one answer for the group to define these two words. However, the conversation and thinking may be useful in the next exercise.

Evil   (35 minutes)

Ask the entire group to do some brainstorming for a moment. On newsprint, create a list of examples of evil as it exists in the world. Remind the group that this is brainstorming and all responses will be recorded.

Give each person an index card. Have each person write a personal definition of "evil." Ask participants to gather back in their groups of four. (Individual group size may vary depending on total number of people present.) Each group should now be given the task of defining what evil is for them. Tell the participants they may define evil in whatever way works best for them—words, images, pictures, and combinations of these. They will have 20 minutes to discuss, to listen, and to create their definition of evil and will then present these definitions to the larger group. Have newsprint, markers, and crayons available. Tell them that the only restriction is that they should not use black to represent evil in their drawings. Have a brief discussion about how the association of black or darkness with evil is viewed as racism by many. While some do not consider the use of black as evil to be racist, the producers of this curriculum have made a clear choice to be anti-racist in preparing it and urge participants to trust that the use of the color black in only this way is offensive to many. Tell the participants that they have 20 minutes to create their project and that these definitions will then be shared.

After 20 minutes, allow each group to briefly present its definitions.

Discuss what similarities and differences arose after all groups are done.

Process the activity by asking people what surprised them or intrigued them as they thought about evil.

Analysis   (25 minutes)

Distribute copies of the reading, "The Christian Right," by Suzanne Pharr. Divide the participants into four groups. Tell them to quickly look over the article but they should spend the majority of their time on a particular area that will be assigned to them. They will have 10 minutes to become an expert in their area and report the key points to the rest of the class.

Group 1: Introduction, Section 1
Group 2: Sections 2 and 3
Group 3: Section 4
Group 4: Sections 5 and 6

Give each group a sheet of newsprint and a marker and encourage them to be creative in their presentations. Tell them they will each have two minutes to present their learnings to the rest of the class.

After 10 minutes, have the groups present their information in order. Allow for conversation throughout and after the presentations.

Case Studies   (30 minutes)

Tell the participants their groups will now be given a case study to analyze. They will have 15 minutes as a group to read, analyze, and begin a response as a task force speaking on behalf of the congregation. Encourage each group to examine the suppositions that base the arguments given and to see how their own suppositions are different or similar. Each group will have two minutes to share their responses and/or thinking. Ease concern by telling groups they need not have a finished product after fifteen minutes and need only share their thinking and plan to that point.

Give each group a case study and each person a copy of the article, "Public Speaking Tips for People of Faith," by the Reverend Meg Riley. Tell them that the speaking tips are to help their thinking as they prepare a response. (If there is a relevant case being debated in your community at this time, feel free to substitute that for a case study.) Pick any four of the five or give every group the same case study.

At the end of 15 minutes, ask each group to present their progress. Remind the groups they need not have final answers at this point and may simply reflect on their conversation, particularly the suppositions that formed the bases for the arguments. Allow each group two minutes to present and allow for some discussion.

Conclude by asking each person to continue to think about these cases and their conversations during the week and to be aware of other cases in their community.

Closing/Check Out   (5 minutes)

End by asking people to share one thing they have learned, relearned, or unlearned tonight. Choose one or both of the following:

• Unison Reading: #689 by Paul Robeson

Sorrow will one day turn to joy. All that breaks the heart and oppresses the soul will one day give place to peace and understanding and everyone will be free.

- Hymn: #402 "From You I Receive"

Assignment/Follow-up

Ask people to think, over the upcoming week, about the importance of their religious/spiritual life.

The Christian Right: A Threat to Democracy

Suzanne Pharr

(Author's note: From January until July 1992 I was on loan to Oregon's Coalition for Human Dignity and the Lesbian Community Project to provide analysis and strategies in the effort to end the right wing Christian attack against the lesbian and gay community. Though I grew up among the Christian Right in the South and now work daily among them in Arkansas, my six months in Oregon gave me an opportunity to study them with a single focus. Shortly before I left Oregon, violence against the lesbian and gay community (and other progressive groups) was escalating, and people are beginning to understand what the threat of legislated discrimination can bring. Human rights are in peril: if the Oregon constitution is amended, it will be the first time in US history that a constitution has been amended to take away rights rather than to extend them. What a precedent that would set. The importance of this national test case will take me back to Oregon for work on the final days of the campaign in September and October. This essay was written for the Oregon Democracy Project Research provided by the Coalition for Human Dignity.)

In Oregon and throughout the US there is a battle going on to determine the political, social, and economic principles that shape our lives and our freedom. The conflict is in schools, in courts, in legislatures, in every institution of our society. It is the battle between the forces of repression and the forces of liberation, between the politics of exclusion and the politics of inclusion. It is the battle between the authoritarian ideology of the Christian Right and the liberation ideology of the Civil Rights Movement.

In contrast to the majority of Christians who believe in the separation of church and state, the Christian Right consists of organized right wing Christians who merge politics and theology to produce a system of social control. Positioned within a conservative movement made up of the secular, political Right and the neo-Nazi Far Right, the Christian Right provides the grassroots activists who create the groundwork for sweeping societal change. Ordinary citizens would likely have their most direct contact with the politics of the Right through encounters with these "foot soldiers" of the Christian Right who pound away at the fundamental principles of democracy.

A Brief Overview of the Christian Right

The Christian Right is reformist and its goal is the influence and infiltration of institutions to put in place Christian authority. It is fundamentalist in its literal interpretation of the Bible and its belief in absolutist "law and order" and morality dictated by God's elect. It is made up of Christian fundamentalists (church-based) and born-again Christians (from Televangelism conversion). Not all Christians belong to the Christian Right nor do all fundamentalists. There are approximately 50 million Christian fundamentalists in the US. Of that number, only 15 to 20 million are organized into the political and social agenda of the Christian Right. The remainder range from conservative to progressive, and all are simply exercising their basic right to practice the religious and spiritual beliefs of their choice.

The Christian Right organized in response to the Civil Rights movement, coming together under the racist agenda of the presidential campaign of George Wallace. They viewed the Civil Rights movement and eventually the legacy of this movement—the Women's Movement, the Lesbian and Gay Movement—as the cause of the breakdown of authority, stability, and law and order.

While both the Christian Right and the Civil Rights movements of the sixties were church-based, they were completely opposite in point of view. The Civil Rights movement put forth the message that true democracy calls for justice, liberation, and participation, and that call was heard by oppressed groups throughout the country, creating a basis for other movements, and giving hope to disenfranchised people for the future. The white Christian Rights movement put forth the message that inclusion and participation by diverse groups will destroy the old order of the forties and fifties when segregation was legally enforced, male authority was unchallenged by women as a class, and lesbians and gay men were invisible. It called for a return to the past. (These two divergent points of view—the politics of inclusion and the politics of exclusion—were supported by the respective theologies of the African American churches and that of the white fundamentalist churches. As Loretta Ross of the Center for Democratic Renewal has said, for white fundamentalist Christians the original sin is considered to be sex whereas for Jews and African Americans the original sin is thought to be slavery. Exploration of these two beliefs might help us to understand why the African American Civil Rights movement (with strong Jewish involvement) is a movement of liberation, and the Christian Right is a movement of repression.)

During the seventies and eighties, the Christian Right had considerable success in their attack against the gains of the Civil Rights movement. In particular, they gained strength through initiating a campaign against homosexuality led by Anita Bryant, the defeat of the ERA led by the Eagle Forum, and the attack against abortion rights led by Operation Rescue.

Their greatest success came from the coalition formed to elect Ronald Reagan, who in return legitimized them and gave them open access to influencing and infiltrating institutions. This reinforcement allowed them to speed up their campaign to eliminate affirmative action, gut welfare programs, broaden the death penalty, and fill the federal courts with judges of their theological/political position. (Reagan appointed 425 judges to federal district courts and US circuit courts of appeals.) A strong, highly organized movement for social control and Christian authoritarianism is fully entrenched.

Most remarkably, though, many people during these two decades dismissed the Christian Right as a temporary aberration on the US political scene. Perhaps they were minimized and trivialized because their public faces were those of buffoons: Jerry Falwell, Jimmy Swaggart, Jim and Tammy Faye Baker. Or perhaps it was because the movement originated out of the South and attracted some of the national anti-Southern sentiment. Many saw this growing "army of God" as working class and uneducated, and thereby incapable of designing a plan for dramatic, far-reaching social and political change. In retrospect, we must recognize that the New Right, with the Christian Right deployed as grassroots "foot soldiers," has controlled the public agenda for almost two decades and has affected virtually every US institution.

One cautionary note. While there is crossover in belief and activities of the Far Right and the secular and Christian New Right (i.e., David Duke and Pat Buchanan), it is important not to confuse the two by calling the Christian Right Nazis or their agenda the Holocaust. The Far Right is revolutionary and its goal is the takeover of institutions for white supremacist authority. Made up of neo-Nazis, racist skinheads, Christian patriots, Christian identity churches, the KKK, and Aryan Nations, it is racist, anti-Semitic, and focuses on white racial purity.

This belief that the original sin is sex points to an explanation of why the Christian Right becomes so strident and passionate about abortion and homosexuality, two areas of sexuality, freedom of choice and expression, which strike at the heart of male power and control. Also, if we understand the parallel fundamentalist Christians' reading of the Adam and Eve story, where Eve eats from the tree of knowledge (sin), we gain insight into the Christian Right's determination to suppress information through banning books, preventing sex education, and eliminating artistic expression, their disseminating mis/disinformation to the ignorant, and their battling against secular humanism (critical thinking) to enforce the teaching of creationism instead of evolution in the schools.

Some of the Major Players

In order to accomplish this widespread movement that has achieved everything from placing Christian Rightists on local school boards to placing them on the Supreme Court, there has to be a complex array of institutions and organizations to support the work. Here are a few of the most important cornerstones of the New Right movement:

Heritage Foundation. The most prestigious conservative think tank in the US, located in Washington, DC, and funded by the Coors family. It produces policy and strategies for the Right and acts as a watchdog of US government activity.

Rutherford Institution. The legal arm that develops legislative initiatives and legal challenges.

Christian Broadcasting Network. Led by Pat Robertson, CBN is one of the televangelism networks that control 1,000 fulltime radio stations and 200 television stations that function worldwide. These networks perform two important functions: they get out the message of Christian moral absolutism and authority, and they raise enormous sums of money through their viewers.

Operation Rescue. Grassroots anti-abortion activists who, ironically, employ tactics copied from the Civil Rights movement to deny constitutionally-protected rights.

Eagle Forum and Concerned Women of America. Grassroots anti-feminist networks that train women ("kitchen table activists") to generate thousands of letters and phone calls to public officials, to do street activism, and to apply pressure on institutions, particularly school boards. Eagle Forum has 80,000 members, and CWA is the largest conservative US women's organization, with a reported 565,000 members and a $5.4 million budget.

Oregon Citizen's Alliance. Born out of the 1986 Joe Lutz campaign for the US Senate, the OCA has worked as a "religious army" of supposedly 15,000 to shape the politics of Oregon to "divine authority" and to reinstate the "traditional family" among its citizens. Since 1987, the OCA has organized against gun control, euthanasia, separation of church and state, divestment from corporations doing business in South Africa, reproductive rights, homosexuality, state-aided pre-kindergarten programs, gay foster parents, parental leave, and for prayer in schools.

A Tested Agenda

The ultimate goal of the Christian Right is to dismantle the gains of the Civil Rights movement and to subject social and political life to Christian authoritarianism. To achieve this goal, they must attack not only African Americans and other people of color who gained from the Civil Rights movement but also the gains of the Women's Movement, the Lesbian and Gay Movement, and eventually, the People with Disabilities Movement.

They have found fertile ground in economic hard times marked by societal and political chaos. Generally, people feel assaulted, at risk, and in search of stability and meaning in their lives. Perhaps the greatest sense of loss is economic, providing an easy arena for scapegoating. The Christian Right offers an explanation of disorder by saying that it stems from social and economic disruption caused by people of color, women, lesbians, and gay men who have unfairly taken jobs from white men, destroyed the economy by welfare fraud, and demolished the traditional family by demanding autonomy and choice.

In response to this climate of fear, the New Right has built a national campaign centered on the idea of "No special rights." Their position is that the Constitution already covers everyone equally, and that, despite racism, sexism, and homophobia, to ask for anti-discrimination laws of laws providing equal protection and access is to ask for "special rights."

During 1991 and 1992 we have been able to see their agenda at work through three national testing sites. In each of these, strategies are tested for replication throughout the country.

The racist agenda was tested in Louisiana with the campaign of David Duke where Far Right and Christian Right politics were merged. Duke was defeated by the extraordinary effort of the African American community, which turned out 80 percent of its registered voters; otherwise, the 55 percent white vote would have elected Duke. In this case, the messenger (Duke) was defeated but the message was won by getting widespread publicity.

The sexist agenda was tested in Wichita, KS, with the highly orchestrated attack on abortion clinics by Operation Rescue which bussed in thousands of people for street activism. Thanks to a principled federal judge, they were thwarted. However, immediately thereafter, Operation Rescue held a press conference to say that their next targets would be two sites in North Carolina, one each in Massachusetts, Louisiana, and Arkansas. They had established a successful model.

The homophobic agenda is being tested in Oregon through city initiatives and a state initiative to declare homosexuality, sadism, masochism, and pedophilia to be "abnormal and perverse" behavior. Though initiatives are on the ballot in five other states, the Oregon initiative is the centerpiece because of its breadth and because it calls for a constitutional amendment. This initiative calls for two primary restrictions: for all policies and laws offering protection and access for homosexuals to be eliminated, and for all state and local governments (including schools) to eliminate funding that would "promote homosexuality." An almost identical ballot measure is being tested in Colorado as well.

Strategies of Confusion and Division

In each of these sites major strategies or tactics of the Christian Right can be observed. The "wedge approach" is a central strategy. The point of the wedge, or the point of entry, is on an emotionally charged issue such as abortion, homosexuality, or the failing economy. The Right then uses this issue to gain widespread support and to build a broad constituency base that can then be expanded to include the other issues on its agenda. For example, they provide information about abortion, affirmative action, parental leave, welfare, etc., to the membership and voting base built around the issue of homosexuality and then organize them to vote on these issues.

The second way the wedge is used is to divide communities against themselves and to break up the progressive base for social change. For instance, in Portland, the OCA is entering African American churches and writing letters to the African American newspaper to say that homosexuals are trying to take a share of the small piece of pie that African Americans earned the hard way.

A second critical strategy is to frame the issue as one of morality rather than civil rights. To do this, the Christian Right names certain behavior as immoral, attaches that behavior to a category of people, and then identifies that entire group as immoral and to be restrained and controlled. For example, David Duke, following a long line of racist politicians such as George Wallace, Reagan, and Bush, furthered the development of coded language to get the public to think spontaneously that when crime or drugs or welfare or affirmative action are mentioned, African Americans are the problem. Hence, when he and others name drugs, crime, and illegitimacy as immoral, then connect them to a single group of people—African Americans—the next step is to think that these people are not only connected to immorality but are immoral themselves.

Similarly, the tactic is to say that abortion is immoral, feminists support the right to choice, therefore feminists are immoral. Another is to say that lesbianism is immoral and the equation goes like this: feminists = manhaters = lesbians. Therefore, feminists are immoral.

For this attachment of morality/immorality to a class of people, the Right must produce not only generalized and stereotyped information but also false and twisted information. An example of such information is their basic premise that the Constitution provides rights and protections for everyone equally. They present this distorted information to a population that is essentially uninformed. While being taught to think with pride about the framing of the Constitution, we have not been taught that women and African Americans were not accorded full human status by the men who created a document to protect the rights of property and slave owning males.

The Christian Right's campaign against homosexuality and for "traditional family values" illustrates clearly the use of mis/disinformation to support the idea of morality as the central issue instead of civil rights. Lesbians and gays are particularly vulnerable because even though in existence for centuries, there has been group visibility only since the beginning of the lesbian and gay movement with Stonewall in 1969. This brief period of visibility creates vulnerability for two primary reasons. Lack of visibility means that there is widespread ignorance on the part of the general public concerning this area of sexuality and culture. Thus, when the Right puts out the information that lesbians and gay men are child molesters, the public accepts it as truth, despite the data that demonstrates that 95 percent of those sexually abusing children are heterosexual men. Once again, immoral behavior gets attached to a group and the issue of gay and lesbian rights is presented in such a way that the voters think that they enter the polling booth to pull the lever on whether it is right or wrong to be homosexual (which is simply a sexual identity, like heterosexuality), not whether it is right or wrong to deny basic human rights.

The second way the lesbian and gay community is vulnerable is because the policies and laws providing rights and protection are so new and therefore more easily attacked. Through providing misinformation, Christian rightists can get voters to overturn these laws, thereby setting precedent in the attack against all the gains of the Civil Rights movement and beginning the domino effect.

Naming the Real Issue

What is facing us in this "holy war" is not a battleground for morality but a direct assault on democracy. While the Right keeps public debate focused on the issue of right and wrong behavior, good and bad people, their political agenda goes unheeded and is on a course to limit participation in the democratic process by those they consider less capable of their narrow definition of morality: people of color, women, lesbians and gay men, Jews.

This fundamental threat to democracy is a clear and present danger: a small number of people through the merger of church and state will soon determine and limit the freedom of those who differ from them in religion, politics, or culture. Democracy must always protect the minority voice, must always guarantee the participation of everyone. In the efforts of the Right we see the politics of exclusion, the politics of authoritarianism and domination.

The central question is one of self-determination and choice. Do we as a people get to have determination of our own lives and communities through a governing system that provides access, opportunity, and protections equally to all citizens, no matter who we are? Or do we have a governing system of rigid societal control determined by a theologically-based political group?

Do we all get to sit down at the decision-making table of this society? Or do only the few? And who decides?

Crisis and Opportunity

An insistence upon democracy as named by the Civil Rights movement—requiring justice, liberation, and participation—is the greatest threat to the Christian authoritarian agenda. It is the work of those of us who believe in freedom to develop a local and national movement of liberation that claims our communities in the name of all the many diverse peoples who occupy them. It is incumbent upon us at this critical juncture of history to establish the values that are inclusive of everyone and to reject the values of exclusion and repression.

Nothing is more central to democracy than an informed populace able to make critical judgments. We must remember, as Eric Fromm said in the forties when reflecting upon the Second World War, "The human automaton is fertile ground for the seeds of fascism." For instance, one of the great battlegrounds is schools. The Christian Right has entered school boards throughout the country to oppose sex education, school-based clinics, dispensing condoms, secular humanism (critical thinking and values clarification), teaching evolution, and to promote prayer in the schools, to insist upon teaching creationism, and banning "objectionable" books. This work is at the heart of the greatest threat to democracy, for this is the highly orchestrated effort to gain control of the minds of our children to limit their access to information and their ability to do critical thinking.

Finally, to create this great movement for liberation, we must figure out how to include everyone in full opportunity and participation. We have no model for this work for a true democracy. To live the politics of inclusion means that we must first get over ourselves, that is, put an end to our own barriers to inclusion. It is bigotry that *unites* the right wing because they see people of color, women, lesbians, and gay men as the enemy to their power and control. And it is our bigotry— the racism, sexism, and homophobia within our organizations—that *divides* us on the progressive Left and prevents us from developing a fully inclusive movement.

Our most critical work is to eliminate these divisions and to recognize the connection we have as targeted groups and the common ground we share in our dream of justice and liberation for all of us.

Our work is more difficult than that of the Christian Right. Their vision is modeled on the past, the time of the television Cleavers, when the power to exclude gave a few white people security. Our vision, on the other hand, has no model because we look to our present diversity and to the future which requires building a democratic society that includes everyone. We have to protect the democracy that we have in the present while building the new inclusive society.

We have the excitement and challenge of developing new ground. While the massive homophobic attack of the OCA against the people of Oregon and Colorado has created an alarming crisis, it has also created an opportunity. The Christian Right has chosen these two states as testing sites for exclusion; so may we make them testing sites for inclusion. In the face of this clear and present danger, we have the opportunity to bring people together to overcome old divisions and to build in our communities and our nation a true inclusive, participatory democracy. It is a test of the thoughtfulness, goodwill, courage, and dignity of our people.

Public Speaking Tips for People of Faith

Reverend Meg Riley

DON'T respond defensively to homophobic scriptural citations by engaging in a "boxing match" style of dialogue about them. *"God made Adam and Eve, not Adam and Steve!"* "But that's ridiculous! The creation story is just a myth to explain human creation—surely you don't believe it literally happened that way! Why, all scientific evidence shows that the original person was a woman in Africa."

DO use humor and keep a light touch. *"God made Adam and Eve, not Adam and Steve!"* "Yeh, well, and look at the trouble they got themselves into!" "Are you saying heterosexuals are responsible for the fall of humankind?" OR "'Just Say No' didn't even work in the Garden—and that time it was God talking directly!"

DON'T fight with an idiot. Someone looking in from the outside won't know which one of you is the idiot. *"Gay people deserve to be killed."* "And you call yourself a Christian? That's the most hateful thing I've ever heard someone say!"

DO appeal to moderate observers. *"Gay people deserve to be killed."* "Did you hear what he just said? I know that the majority of Americans are as repulsed by these mean-spirited words as I am. Every poll shows that we Americans believe in fair, non-violent treatment of all people, even when we disagree with them."

DON'T let someone else set the agenda/frame the parameters of the discussion. *"Our founding fathers intended this to be a Christian nation!"* "That's absurd. This is not a Christian nation, and never has been."

DO speak positively. *"Our founding fathers intended this to be a Christian nation!"* "The wise people who founded this country bequeathed us a wonderful Constitution and a Bill of Rights that affirms the rights of all people. These, not any religion, provide the covenant that is our basis for living together in peace in the United States."

DON'T demonize or insult the proponents of the initiative. "Only a bigot or a homophobe would support this Initiative, and the people who thought it up are fascists!"

DO differentiate the leaders from the followers in these initiatives; use language of compassion and reconciliation. "I am concerned that Americans, who are shown in every poll to oppose discrimination against any group of people, are being misled about exactly what this ballot measure means."

DON'T allow homophobes to monopolize religious language. *"God is opposed to homosexuals; I read it in the Bible and that's good enough for me."* "Regardless of what you read in the Bible, this is not a Christian country and the Bible should not govern our laws."

DO claim the moral high ground; cite verse you like, use your own religious language. *"God is opposed to homosexuals; I read it in the Bible and that's good enough for me."* "Neither Jesus nor the ten commandments mention homosexuality at all, but they do condemn bearing false witness against our neighbors. Many of the statistics cited in the materials for this ballot measure are provably false. As a person of faith, concerned for the spiritual well being of my community, I cannot allow this false witness to go unchallenged. My faith demands that I tell the truth, and the truth shall set me free."

DON'T use the word "religious" to describe the leaders of the initiatives. "Those who want special righteousness," "radical right" are more accurate, and are generally received much more negatively.

DO speak openly about your own faith as it informs your commitment to this issue. "Jesus' injunction to love your neighbor as yourself demands that I speak up on this issue. Gays are my neighbors." "I believe it's up to God to judge us. My own faith warns me to beware of wolves in sheeps' clothing."

DON'T get sidetracked into discussions of whether people "choose" to be homosexual, or whether gay people are 1 percent of the population or 10 percent. *"Homosexuals could choose to be heterosexual if they wanted."* "That's ridiculous! You're either born gay or you're not!" *"Homosexuals are only 1 percent of the population. The Kinsey study was skewed because it studied perverts and prisoners."* "That study that says they are only 1 percent is skewed because who would tell an anonymous person at the door they were gay?"

DO stay focused on your primary talking points. "No matter how many or how few members there are of a group such as a religion or a race, and no matter whether they are born that way or choose it, such as a Catholic who converts to Judaism versus someone who is born and remains Catholic, our constitution supports their civil rights equally."

DON'T globalize the issues or use rhetoric. "This is just the first step toward death camps! First they came for the Jews, and I did not speak up because I was not a Jew. . ." You may believe it, but the average person does not.

DO speak specifically about how the initiative will affect your local community. "What exactly will this ballot measure mean to my gay son who was fired from his job simply because he's gay? It will mean that he has no legal recourse, as any other citizen would."

DON'T try to terrorize people into voting on our side.

DO lift up a vision of unity. "I wish that, instead of using all of my energy in fighting this ballot initiative, I could be working together with all of the citizens of our community to confront the economic and ecological crises we face. I know that, together, we could solve these problems! What I regret most about these initiatives is the way they tear up the community."

Case Studies

1. After School Group

In the local high school, a group of students wishes to start an after school group to dialogue about gay-straight issues. This new gay-straight alliance group has gained public attention. Many conservatives have taken issue with the group and letters to the editor opposing the existence of the group have appeared in the newspaper.

Some of the more heated arguments have included statements about how groups like this will encourage children to experiment with homosexuality, that school is not a suitable place to discuss this topic, that homosexuality is immoral and we need to keep it out of the school, and that children will be harmed by the presence of open homosexuals in the school. A few people have suggested there are other places for homosexuals to meet and that the students do not need a space in the schools. The after school Bible study group has said it will be offended if the group is allowed to exist on school grounds.

Tension is very high in the community. You have been asked to speak as a liberal voice of faith at an upcoming school board meeting. What will you say and how will you say it?

2. Sex Ed Curriculum

The school board is adopting new health curricula including new sex education materials. There are two leading contenders. One sex ed curriculum will be a bare bones minimal curriculum which will talk about the physical nature of sex and how it happens. There is very little emphasis on decision making and emotional content, though it does recommend abstinence and it is exclusively heterosexual. The second curriculum engages students in both the biological and emotional aspects of sexuality. The program encourages value development, conversation, and obtaining as much information as possible. Topics include gay and lesbian issues, safer sex, and values discussions on abortion, responsibility, and sexual harrassment.

The debate gained public attention. Many conservatives have expressed concern that they do not find the second curriculum appropriate for their children. Sex education should be taught in the home. Topics like abortion, safer sex, and homosexuality should not be taught or encouraged in schools. Many feel they are more equipped than the schools to talk to their children about

sexuality. Several have said that those who support the second curriculum must be either homosexuals or baby-killers. Words like "immorality" and "evil" are a part of the conversation. Many feel the new curriculum will put strange new ideas into the heads of youth.

There will be a public hearing on the matter and your congregation has been approached to speak out on the curriculum. As a task force, you have been given the authority by the board to respond. What will you say?

3. Public Funding of the Arts

An art show that depicts nudity and references to homosexual behavior is on exhibit at a nearby art gallery. The show becomes highly controversial when several folks learn public funds were used to bring it to the gallery. Many in the community are upset that this happened and want to close the exhibit and prohibit the use of public funds for anything like it in the future.

Some have said that public monies should not be used to fund pornography and express tolerance of homosexuality.

Many feel this is an unfit display for their community and that it gives their town a bad name and its children the wrong message about art and sexuality. There is a move to pass legislation that will prohibit funds to be used for such art exhibits.

There will be a public hearing on the matter and your congregation has been approached to speak out on the use of funds for the arts. As a task force, you have been given the authority by the board to respond. What will you do?

4. Special Rights

Some concerned citizens feel a need to keep gays and lesbians from obtaining special rights and have introduced a law to your community that excludes gays and lesbians from other civil rights legislation.

The arguments say that gays and lesbians already have equal rights and that this law would keep them from having an unfair advantage. Also, as gays and lesbians have become more visible in the community, it is important that the community take a stand so as to not be encouraging of homosexuals or homosexuality. Some have expressed concern that if special rights are given to homosexuals, their community will become a gay haven and the city will be taken over by them.

Many say simply about the non-discrimination clauses, "We don't need that here."

There will be a public hearing on the matter and your congregation has been approached to speak out on the legislation. As a task force, you have been given the authority by the board to respond. What will you say?

5. Marriage

There is great concern in your community about allowing same-gender couples to marry. Many are opposed to the idea and wish to enact legislation that will "stop this abomination."

The arguments against same-gender marriage have been expressed in different ways. Marriage is and always has been between a man and a woman. God made Adam and Eve, not Adam and Steve. Homosexuality is immoral and should not be encouraged. With AIDS being so prevalent among gays, the health insurance costs will bankrupt most companies required to give health benefits. The next thing you know, some have said, they'll want to adopt children.

There will be a public hearing on the matter and your congregation has been approached to speak out on the legislation. As a task force, you have been given the authority by the board to respond. What will you say?

WORKSHOP 8:
Religion and Homosexuality

Purpose

- To explore our religious beliefs for doing this work, or
- To explore how Judeo-Christian thinking has shaped our beliefs around sexual orientation.

Materials

- For Option 1:
  For large group exercises: none
  For small group exercises: chart paper and crayons or markers for groups of four
  For individual exercises: UUA Principles and Purposes
- For Option 2:
  For large group exercises: none
  For small group exercises: none
  For individual exercises: handouts

Preparation

- Copy handouts: "What Does the Bible Say About Homosexuality?," "Biblical Perspectives on Homosexuality," "Inclusive Liturgy and Preaching," "UUA Principles and Purposes" (for Option 1 only), "Sentence Completion Exercise" (for Option 1 only).
- Arrange chairs in a circle or semi-circle.

Workshop Plan

(Note: You have two options here, depending on the needs of your group. Option 1 explores Unitarian Universalism and thinking around sexual orientation and gender identification. People respond to a series of four questions. Option 2 explores individuals' perceptions about Hebrew and Christian Scriptures from the Bible around homosexuality. Both are valuable, and you may choose to do both.)

Opening/Chalice Lighting   (5 minutes)

Choose *one* of these openings. If you decide to bring readings, it is suggested that participants take turns with this responsibility each week.

- Lighting of chalice and reading.
  Reading: #598 "Without Hate" or #638 "Love"
  Hymn: #392 "Hineh Mah Tov"
- Reading of leader's choice.
- Moment of meditation or prayer.

Option 1: Unitarian Universalism, Sexual Orientation, and Gender Identification

Ask participants to form groups of four (though other size groups will work as well). Tell participants that they are going to be asked four questions. Each person in the group will respond to each question and then there will be time for the group to continue the conversation. Remind participants of the Participation Guidelines and encourage all people to participate fully.

Question 1   (20 minutes)

"How does your spirit get fed (or nurtured or uplifted)?"

Give each person two minutes to speak and then another 10 minutes for group conversation. Keep track of time and tell groups when the two-minute segments are complete.

At the end of this time tell participants the next question shifts from the personal to the congregational. Distribute markers/crayons and chart paper or poster board. Tell the participants that they will first talk again for two minutes and then as a small group discuss and draw the answer(s) to the question.

Question 2   (40 minutes)

Ask the second question: "What would a Welcoming Congregation look like here?" Encourage specific examples as well as generalities. Tell participants they will have 30 minutes in all to create their picture.

After the time is complete, ask participants as a whole group to briefly discuss if there are any connections they can make for themselves between the first two questions. Take about three to five minutes for this. Then ask each group to share their drawing with the larger group. Give each group two minutes to present.

After completing this piece, you may ask or decide to place these pictures on a bulletin board for the whole congregation to see.

Question 3 (20 minutes)

Ask the participants to now explore the third question in this series in their small group. Remind participants that each person will have two minutes to speak before entering into a group conversation. The third question is: "What keeps you in the struggle for justice?"

You may need to expand this question with information about how the work of justice-making is continual and many people choose not to do this kind of work. This question takes people from the congregational to the visionary/community concerns. Allow 20 minutes in all for this question.

Take a few minutes as a whole group to share your responses before moving to the last question.

Question 4 (30 minutes)

Distribute a copy of the Unitarian Universalist Association Principles and Purposes. Tell participants these will be used to help answer the last question: "How do our Principles and Purposes (and the faith of Unitarian Universalism) speak to you about engaging in the work of becoming a Welcoming Congregation and dismantling homophobia and heterosexism?"

Again, give each group member two minutes to answer. Encourage each person to speak personally and specifically to answer this question. Tell the participants they will have 20 minutes in all for this question.

After the time is complete, allow for 10 minutes of conversation about their response to the last question and their thoughts on all of the questions. What new things did they think about? How is this work religious work? Distribute the follow-up assignments and proceed to the closing.

Option 2: The Bible and Homosexuality

Sentence Completion (20 minutes)

Give each participant a Sentence Completion Exercise and a pencil. Ask them to complete each sentence. Tell them not to write their names on the sheets, and that you will collect and redistribute the sheets so that the sentences will be read aloud anonymously.

When all participants have finished, collect the sheets and redistribute them.

Ask each participant to read the first sentence only. Go on to the second sentence, and continue until all the sentences have been read. Ask participants not to comment until all have been shared.

If the group is large (20 or more), not all of the sentences need to be read. To save time, invite a sampling by asking participants to volunteer to read the ones they have.

Discussion (20 minutes)

Ask if anyone would like to share a reaction to the activity. Review the Participation Guidelines to encourage respectful listening and sharing.

Reading and Reacting to the Readings (70 minutes)

Give each participant the readings, "What Does the Bible Say About Homosexuality?," "Biblical Perspectives on Homosexuality," and "Inclusive Liturgy and Preaching" and allow for 15 to 20 minutes of reading time. Have participants form pairs or trios. Ask them to respond to the following questions. (Write questions on newsprint for their referral.)

- What was your overall reaction to the readings?
- What new information did you learn?
- What was most troubling to you?
- What do you need more information about?
- How do these readings affect your spiritual perspective on homosexuality?

Ask the group to rejoin in a circle. Invite participants to share some of their discussion from the small groups. (Use the same questions as a guide to frame this discussion.)

If discussion in the whole group is difficult, return to small groups. Often, people feel more comfortable talking with a partner or two.

Closing/Check Out (5 minutes)

End by asking people to share one thing they have learned, relearned, or unlearned tonight. Choose one or both of the following:

- Unison Reading: #689 by Paul Robeson

  Sorrow will one day turn to joy. All that breaks the heart and oppresses the soul will one day give place to peace and understanding and everyone will be free.

- Hymn: #402 "From You I Receive"

Assignment/Follow-up

- Distribute readings "What Does the Bible Say About Homosexuality?," "Biblical Perspectives on Homosexuality," and "Inclusive Liturgy and Preaching" if you used Option 1.
- Tell people about the panel scheduled for the next session and ask them to think of questions they have for the panelists.

Unitarian Universalist Association Principles and Purposes

We, the member congregations of the Unitarian Universalist Association, covenant to affirm and promote:

- The inherent worth and dignity of every person
- Justice, equity, and compassion in human relations
- Acceptance of one another and encouragement to spiritual growth in our congregations
- A free and responsible search for truth and meaning
- The right of conscience and the use of the democratic process within our congregations and in society at large
- The goal of world community with peace, liberty, and justice for all
- Respect for the interdependent web of all existence of which we are a part.

Sentence Completion Exercise

Biblical passages used to condemn homosexuality are . . .

The biblical passage I am most concerned about is . . .

What I need to know about the Bible and homosexuality is . . .

People who use the Bible to condemn homosexuality are . . .

A good way to sum up my perspective on homosexuality and the Bible is to say . . .

What Does the Bible Say About Homosexuality?

Reverend Dr. F. Jay Deacon

Do the Hebrew and Christian scriptures tell us homosexuality is immoral or unnatural?

It all depends on how you understand the Bible. It depends on whether your faith is a living, dynamic one, or whether it's just a lot of rules and formulas. There have always been those who, despite their sincerity, misunderstand faith as a set of legalistic moralisms. Remember, such folks demanded the death of Jesus, on the grounds that he took the legalisms of their common religious tradition too lightly.

And in recent times there have appeared those who want to read the Bible literally and legalistically, like a technical manual. Read literally, certain sections of the Bible support slavery, the property status of women, racial segregation, and genocide on religious grounds. And sure enough, several American Church denominations were split not long ago when Christians used the Bible to support slavery and racial segregation. Some Christians have earned a reputation for being on the least human side of every issue!

Jesus was quite different. To him, the living God was always greater than even the words of the Bible, which his opponents used to attack him.

Fact is, those who now go around condemning gay people base their arguments on about six "proof texts" of Scripture, while missing the main point of Scripture as a whole. And they've even misunderstood their "proof texts"!

The Bible and Gay People
It is unfortunate that a society which considers itself tolerant of all religious beliefs should attempt to base its civil legislation on the Bible or on any other arbitrarily selected holy book of scriptures. But because this is so, it's important to realize exactly what the Bible does and does not say about sexual and emotional relations between individuals of the same sex.

It is sometimes said that the Bible will justify nearly anything. When isolated verses are pulled out of context, anything can happen. But when considered in the literary and historical contexts, these passages do not mean what many people think they mean. Have a look.

Leviticus 18:22 and 20:13
No section of the Bible has made more trouble for gay people than these frequently mentioned verses in Leviticus. They were probably composed during a late period of Israel's history while under Persian domination. These texts call for the death penalty for sexual acts between men. But then, the same book of Leviticus prohibits eating rabbit, oysters, clams, shrimp, pork (Leviticus 21). And much, much more. Why should two verses in Leviticus be considered still valid when so much else in the same book is not?

Genesis 19:4-11 and Judges 19:22
The Sodom story (Genesis 19:4-11) is one of a mob's violation of the ancient value of hospitality toward two angelic visitors to their city, in the form of an attempted homosexual rape. The Gibeah story (Judges 19:22) is strikingly similar, but the rape is heterosexual. In Ezekiel 16:49, Isaiah 1:9-17 and 3:9-15, and Jeremiah 23:14, the sins of Sodom are described as arrogance, adultery, lies, insincere religious practices, political corruption, oppression of the poor, and neglect of the fatherless and widows. Homosexuality is not mentioned. When Jesus refers in Luke 10:10-13 to Sodom's sin, he's speaking about inhospitality. So much inhospitality has been practiced against homosexuals!

Romans 1:26-32
Saint Paul believed homosexual acts to be unnatural. In fact, he viewed all sexuality with fear and disapproval, urging those who can to abstain. But today's psychological, sociological and scientific knowledge indicates that it is unnatural for a gay man or lesbian to defy his or her own "nature" and personality structure by attempting heterosexual relationships and sexual activity. And the language about "giving up" heterosexual relations does not describe a homosexual person, who did not deliberately choose to be homosexual just to defy God!

One could also argue that much of Paul's writing on social issues has little bearing on modern society. No one today would argue for the restoration of slavery in the United States, based on Paul, although Paul very clearly condones slavery. Paul also commands women to be silent and not to teach men, yet these views have not deterred Anita Bryant at all!

I Corinthians 6:9-10 and I Timothy 1:5-10
Problems of mistranslation arise in these epistles, one by Saint Paul and the other by an unknown author. The word "homosexuals" is not justified by the Greek text, which reads "malakoi" and

"arsenokoitai." Scholars do not know what these words mean (they have something to do with prostitution) so some translations have arbitrarily inserted the word "homosexual." Earlier editions of the Revised Standard Version of the Bible read "homosexual" here, but the later (1977 and on) editions of the same fine translation have dropped the word.

Of course, many zealously self-righteous folks would rather go on reading certain select passages of Scripture literally and even inaccurately, to use as ammunition against people they hate or fear. Such literalism is always selective, though! No one—repeat, *no one*—actually takes the *whole* Bible literally. If they did, they would:

- Not allow women to speak in church or ever teach men, demanding, instead that women wear veils (1 Corinthians 14:34-35, 11:1-16).
- Demand the death penalty for lending money with interest (Ezekiel 18:5-18, Deuteronomy 23:19-20). Should bankers be ordained? Should they be protected by civil rights statutes? Should they live?

Those who use the Bible like ammunition, singling out homosexual people for special abuse, miss the main point of the Bible as a whole. Here are some of the themes they miss.

The Gospels

That Jesus, who had a great deal to say about the impossibility of the rich attaining salvation, had nothing to say about homosexuality.

That Jesus is hardly a "role model" for heterosexual family life. Jesus' lifestyle represented a dramatic break with the way almost all people, especially religious people, were expected to live. Instead of marrying he associated intimately with 12 men. One loved him so much he was called "The Beloved Disciple," or "The disciple whom Jesus loved." One of the last times Jesus was seen alive by the twelve, this disciple was lying with his head on Jesus. He wrote a deep, emotional book about Jesus, called "John." Jesus seems to define an alternative style of family in Mark 3:19-35.

That the Bible is essentially a history of Love—divine love, reaching out to ever broadening circles of humanity as one category of prejudice and exclusion after another is overcome by Love, the cohesive force that draws all God's creation together into one whole. Jesus preached and practiced an inclusive, universal Gospel that set aside cheap moralisms in favor of Love.

About Jonathan and David

Here's Scripture the opponents of homosexual people won't quote. It's the moving story of love between Jonathan and David (I Samuel 16-20, 1:19-27). Jonathan's father, King Saul, is clearly disturbed by the relationship: "You son of a perverse, rebellious woman, do I not know that you have chosen David the son of Jesse to your own shame?" But Israel has celebrated David as its greatest hero. In this passage, we read: "Your love to me was wonderful, passing the love of women." (Incidentally, the story of Ruth and Naomi, in the book of Ruth, portrays woman's love passing, for a woman, the love of men.)

For many of these reasons, many progressive theologians, Catholic, Protestant, and Jewish, now believe the real message of the Bible is not in conflict with gay and lesbian lifestyle.

Those who attack the rights, dignity and decency of gay people say they do so in the name of love. *We* don't believe it. Love always wants to *know* those it loves. The opponents of gay and lesbian people refuse to learn the truth about them and about sexual orientation.

They insist, contrary to evidence, that sexual orientation is chosen and can be changed. Yet it is known that sexual orientation is determined, usually, within the very earliest years of life, by factors no one understands. And the bold claims of "evangelical ex-gay" movements about "faith-cures" to heterosexuality have been proven cruel hoaxes.

They insist that gay people are famous for raping and corrupting people, especially the young—even though the vast majority of such incidents are attributable to heterosexuals, even within the family!

But then, they aren't interested in the truth about gay and lesbian people. They never were. And 1 Corinthians 6:10 declares that "revilers"—those who lie and falsely defame others—cannot see the kingdom of God. What they call "love" is perfect hatred!

Now here's tragedy. Some of God's children, who happen to be gay, have discovered themselves to be gifted by God with the holiest gift of all—the ability to give and receive love, an affinity and will to union toward another person—but still fear and doubt the holy gift, holding it at arm's length, with reserve.

It is tragic that anyone should elevate an imperfect and primitive set of moralisms above the holy gift of human loving. We hope you don't make that mistake.

Inclusive Liturgy and Preaching

Chris Glaser

Naming is of primitive religious importance. God called creation into being by naming light and darkness, earth and seas, living creatures in water, sky, and earth. Then God pronounced each aspect of creation "good." Adam was charged with naming the creatures, indicating both human participation in creatorship and human stewardship of God's creation. God was to be left unnamed, or divine names used advisedly and sparingly, but creatures were named one by one. God's existence, value, and responsibility were not dependent on naming, but the creation's existence, valuing, and responsibility stemmed from naming. Throughout scripture, naming and re-naming also became a commissioning for God's service.

Recent human rights movements have reminded us of the importance of naming. The majority of blacks rejected "Negro" as well as more intentionally derogatory terms, women struggle against diminutive terms (such as "girl") and non-inclusive words (such as "man" as a generic for men and women), and physically challenged people still debate the labels "handicapped" and "disabled," to give a few examples. All point to the need to be mentioned and included in the words and deeds of everyone from politicians to preachers. Naming recognizes their existence, values their humanity, and reminds us all of our responsibility to them as part of God's creation of which they and we alike are called to be good stewards. And the choice of new names to designate themselves indicates a new understanding of their place and mission in life.

Gays and lesbians experience the same need to have their existence acknowledged, their humanity valued, societal responsibility exercised on their behalf, and their commissioning to God's service affirmed. Surviving shifts in popular mood that have sometimes accepted and sometimes rejected it, "the love which dare not speak its name" has endured name-calling and treatment that denied its existence or its humanity.

Whether one calls it sin or variation, a product of The Fall or another aspect of God's creation, homosexuality is part of the church's experience. Even those who want to "hate the sin, but love the sinner" must recognize the existence of homosexual persons, value their humanity, and discover what the church's stewardship should be regarding them. This begins with the naming process. Ironically, it is often those opposed to homosexual behavior who most often name homosexual persons as loved and valued by God. Those who view homosexuality as one more aspect of God's creation often fail to do that much.

As other minorities, gays and lesbians generally reject derogatory terms applied to them, though sometimes a label originally used derogatorily is taken and used proudly as a counter-cultural statement. The term "homosexual" is unsatisfactory because it narrowly and clinically defines an aspect of personality, rather than indicating a broader naming of life experience. Compare the inadequate use of "heterosexual" to name the life experience of those who have a loving, opposite-gender relationship.

The term "gay" dates from the 14th century. It is used to name homosexual males and often generically to include homosexual females (though the merits of this latter use is debated). "Lesbian" is a far more ancient term, recently broadly reclaimed by homosexual females (though many prefer or feel comfortable with the term "gay"). Generally both terms are applied to homosexual persons who have at least begun a process of acceptance of their sexual orientation. In addition, they imply a life experience inclusive of sexuality, society rejection, and mistreatment, as well as community-building and celebration with others who share both the sexuality and the survival of oppression.

Though linguistically not unusual, the apparent "borrowing" of a "perfectly good word" to name another phenomenon is often cited as a "reasonable" objection to the use of the word "gay" to describe homosexual males and (sometimes) females. But behind this seemingly reasonable objection lurks a heterosexist if not homophobic attitude. Generally speaking, no one objects to manufacturers identifying their products with other "perfectly good words," so that, when one hears words like "crest" or "tide" or "mustang," one thinks first of the product and then (if at all) of the original phenomenon so named. That no one objects to these new uses of words, but many object to the new use of the word "gay," suggests that their objection comes from some other source than reason: such as heterosexism or homophobia. Compare how whites reacted to Negroes choosing to call themselves "black" in the 1960s: "Why, their skin isn't black!" Despite mainstream society's objections, the right of a minority to name itself is generally appreciated, and currently the majority of homosexual women and men prefer the words lesbian and gay, sometimes capitalized, sometimes not.

"Homophobia" is linguistically awkward because it literally means "fear of same," but has come to mean an irrational fear of gays and lesbians and same-gender relationships of intimacy (not necessarily erotic) which often leads to hatred and disdain. "Homophobia" is no less clumsy than "homosexual," which literally means "of the same sex." "Heterosexism" refers to provincial and prejudicial attitudes of society (including unliberated homosexual persons) toward gays and lesbians and same-gender relationships. "Homophobia" connotes illness from which one is healed or recovered; "heterosexism" connotes attitudes for which one must take account and responsibility.

Lesbians and gays do not expect, need, nor want to be named as a category frequently to feel welcomed in church and society. But, when naturally listing categories of persons deprived of full communion within church and society, liturgists and preachers should keep in mind that listing "blacks, women, etc." is not sufficient in alerting lesbians and gays that their concerns are recognized and they themselves welcomed. Unintentionally, too, the church may be encouraging only the participation of traditional families if various activities are designed around "the family." Advertising "family worship services" does not make gays or lesbians feel welcome, even though they themselves may have developed nontraditional family units. Clearly, this may be problematic for nongay singles and single parents as well. Emphasizing "the family of faith" as Jesus did might encourage participation of gay and lesbian singles and couples, as well as nongay singles and family units.

Note the use of "nongay" in the previous paragraph. The heterosexual majority also has a right to name itself, and within that majority, the words "heterosexual" and "straight" are not popular self-namings. I use "nongay" simply as a nonjudgmental term descriptive of those who do not share the gay and lesbian experience.

Overcoming homophobia and heterosexism in the church requires naming gays and lesbians with all its incumbent meaning, valuing, and responsibility. "Simply say the word and I shall be healed" could be applied collectively to the church's need for healing between the community of believers and its gay and lesbian members, as well as healing between the church and the broader gay and lesbian community.

Although much emphasis is placed on the content, style, and delivery of the sermon, the rest of the liturgy is an important place to be inclusive of gays and lesbians and exclusive of homophobia and heterosexism. The sermon may be the reflections of the preacher alone, but the liturgy carries the weight of the institution. The common liturgy at best tries to avoid any references to which the congregation cannot assent. The liturgy may be developed and/or approved by the whole pastoral staff and possibly the church's worship committee. And it is in print for all to see. This gives it significant weight and authority.

If gays and lesbians are welcomed with others in the call to worship, or mentioned in new words to an old hymn, a concern of theirs prayed for in a litany, the sin of homophobia (or heterosexism) confessed in the prayer of confession, or aspects of their faithful experience expressed in an affirmation of faith, the effect is powerful. It makes lesbians and gays feel that this is their church, too, and awakens nongays to the presence and concerns of gays, lesbians, their families, spouses, children, parents, and friends in the worshipping community. . . .

Needs keenly experienced in the gay and lesbian community may indeed be common to the whole community. Societal oppression and discrimination, stress in relationships unsanctioned by church and society, loneliness, lack of self-esteem, even homophobia itself may be manifest among lesbians and gays. Yet touching on them in litanies and confessions will reach out not only to lesbians and gays, but also nongays who experience the same.

Gifts of gays and lesbians may not be unlike those of others of the congregation: sensitivity, creativity, commitment to a relationship, acceptance of sexuality, professional, educational, and financial contributions—all need to be affirmed and celebrated within the context of worship, and, in doing so, the same gifts are affirmed and celebrated in the entire congregation. An irony exists in that gays are often accused of not forming committed relationships or of forming transient ones by the very church which refuses to affirm such relationships in the context of common worship where nongay relationships of loving fidelity are routinely affirmed. This needs to be remedied by the church that wishes to be inclusive of gays and lesbians.

It must also be recognized that the needs and gifts of lesbian women may differ from the needs and gifts of gay men, and vice versa. Lesbian women may experience less power in the church than their gay male counterparts because of male/female power issues; gay men may experience discomfort in the church with the power thrust on them as males and the incumbent challenge to compete when they'd rather cooperate. Most lesbian women and gay men are in the middle of this seesaw of the balance of power, but all are tugged by the gravity of societal expectations.

Biblical Perspectives on Homosexuality

Walter Wink

There is no biblical sex ethic. The Bible knows only a love ethic, which is constantly being brought to bear on whatever sexual mores are dominant in a given country, culture, or period.

No more divisive issue faces the churches of this country today than the question of ordaining homosexuals. Like the issue of slavery a century ago, it has the potential for splitting entire denominations. And like the issue of slavery, the argument revolves around the interpretation of Scripture. What does the Bible say about homosexuality, and how are we to apply it to this tormented question?

We may begin by excluding all references to Sodom in the Old and New Testaments, since the sin of the Sodomites was homosexual rape, carried out by heterosexuals intent on humiliating strangers by treating them "like women," thus demasculinizing them. (This is also the case in a similar account in Judges 19-21.) Their brutal gang-rape has nothing to do with the problem of whether genuine love expressed between consenting persons of the same sex is legitimate or not. Likewise Deuteronomy 23:17-18 must be pruned from the list, since it most likely refers to a heterosexual "stud" involved in Canaanite fertility rites that have infiltrated Jewish worship; the King James version inaccurately labeled him a "sodomite."

Several other texts are ambiguous. It is not clear whether I Corinthians 6:9 and I Timothy 1:10 refer to the "passive" and "active" partners in homosexual relationships, or to homosexual and heterosexual male prostitutes. In short, it is unclear whether the issue is homosexuality alone, or promiscuity and "sex-for-hire."

Unequivocal Condemnations

With these texts eliminated, we are left with three references, all of which unequivocally condemn homosexuality. Leviticus 18:22 states the principle: "You [masculine] shall not lie with a male as with a woman; it is an abomination." The second (Lev. 20:13) adds the penalty: "If a man lies with a male as with a woman, both of them have committed an abomination; they shall be put to death, their blood is upon them."

Such an act was regarded as an "abomination" for several reasons. The Hebrew prescientific understanding was that male semen contained the whole of nascent life. With no knowledge of eggs and ovulation, it was assumed that the woman provided only the incubating space. Hence the spilling of semen for any nonprocreative purpose—in coitus interruptus (Gen. 38:1-11), male homosexual acts or male masturbation—was considered tantamount to abortion or murder. (Female homosexual acts and masturbation were consequently not so seriously regarded.) One can appreciate how a tribe struggling to populate a country in which its people were outnumbered would value procreation highly, but such values are rendered questionable in a world facing total annihilation through overpopulation.

In addition, when a man acted like a woman sexually, male dignity was compromised. It was a degradation, not only in regard to himself, but for every other male. The patriarchalism of Hebrew culture shows its hand in the very formulation of the commandment, since no similar scripture was formulated to forbid homosexual acts between females. On top of that is the more universal repugnance heterosexuals tend to feel for acts and orientations foreign to them. (Left-handedness has evoked something of the same response in many cultures.)

Whatever the rationale for their formulation, however, the texts leave no room for maneuvering. Persons committing homosexual acts are to be executed. The meaning is clear; anyone who wishes to base his or her beliefs on the witness of the Old Testament must be completely consistent and demand the death penalty for everyone who performs homosexual acts. This was in fact the case until fairly recent times—hence the name "faggots," which homosexuals earned while burning at the stake. Even though no tribunal is likely to execute homosexuals ever again, a shocking number of homosexual people are murdered by "straights" every year in this country.

The third text is Romans 1:26-27, which like Leviticus 18 and 20, unequivocally denounces homosexual behavior:

> For this reason God gave them up to dishonorable passions. Their women exchanged natural relations for unnatural, and the men likewise gave up natural relations with women and were consumed with passion for one another, men committing shameless acts with men and receiving in their own persons the due penalty for their error.

No doubt Paul was unaware of the distinction between sexual orientation, over which one has apparently very little choice, and sexual behavior. He apparently assumes that those whom he condemns are heterosexual, and are acting contrary to nature, "leaving," "giving up," or "exchanging" their usual sexual orientation.

Likewise the relationships Paul describes are heavy with lust; they are not relationships of genuine same-sex love. Paul assumes that venereal disease is the divine punishment for homosexual behavior; we know it as a risk involved in promiscuity of every stripe, but would hesitate to label it a divine punishment, since not everyone who is promiscuous contracts it. And Paul believes that homosexuality is contrary to nature, whereas we have learned that it is manifested by a wide variety of species, especially (but not solely) under the pressure of overpopulation. It would appear then to be a quite natural mechanism for preserving species.

Other Practices

Nevertheless, the Bible quite clearly takes a negative view of homosexuality, in those few instances where it is mentioned at all. And the repugnance felt toward homosexuality was not just that it was deemed unnatural but also that it was considered un-Jewish, representing yet one more incursion of pagan civilization into Jewish life. But this conclusion does not solace the hermeneutical problem of our attitude toward homosexuality today. For there are other sexual attitudes, practices, and restrictions, which are normative in Scripture but which we no longer accept as normative:

1. Nudity, the characteristic of paradise, was regarded in Judaism as reprehensible, even within the family (Lec. 18:6-19; Ezek, 22:10; II Sam. 6:20; 10:5; Isa. 20:2-4; 47:3). For a son to look upon his Father's nudity was equivalent to a crime (Gen. 9:20-27). To a great extent this taboo probably even inhibited the practice of husbands and wives (this is still true of a surprising number of people reared in the Judeo-Christian taboo system). We may not be prepared for nude beaches, but are we prepared to regard nudity in the locker room or at the old swimming hole or in the home as an accursed sin?
2. Old Testament law strictly forbids sexual intercourse during the seven days of the menstrual period (Lev. 18:19; 15:18-24 contradicts this). Today many people on occasion have intercourse during menstruation and think nothing of it. Are they sinners?
3. The Bible nowhere explicitly prohibits sexual relations between unmarried consenting adults—a discovery that caused John Calvin no little astonishment. The Song of Songs eulogizes a love affair between two unmarried persons, though even some scholars have conspired to cover up the fact with heavy layers of allegorical interpretations. For millennia the church has forbidden sex outside of marriage. Today many teenagers, single adults, the widowed, and the divorced are reverting to "biblical" practice, while others continue to believe that sexual intercourse belongs only within marriage. Which view is right?
4. The Bible virtually lacks terms for the sexual organs, being content with such euphemisms as "foot" or "thigh" for the genitals, and using other euphemisms to describe coitus, such as "he knew her." Today we regard such language as "puritanical" and contrary to a proper regard for the goodness of creation.
5. Semen and menstrual blood rendered all who touched them unclean (Lev. 15:16-24). Intercourse rendered one unclean until sundown; menstruation rendered the woman unclean for seven days. Some people may still feel that uncleanness attaches to semen and menstrual blood, but most people who consider themselves "enlightened" regard these fluids as completely natural and only at times "messy" but not "unclean."
6. Social regulations regarding adultery, incest, rape, and prostitution are, in the Old Testament, determined largely by considerations of the males' property rights over women. Prostitution was considered quite natural and necessary as a safeguard of the virginity of the unmarried and the property rights of husbands (Gen. 38:12-19; Josh. 2:1-7). A man was not guilty of sin in visiting a prostitute, though the prostitute herself was regarded as a sinner. Even Paul must appeal to reason in attacking prostitution (I Cor. 6:12-20); he cannot lump it in the category of adultery (vs. 9). Today we are moving, with great social turbulence and at a high but necessary cost, toward a more equitable set of social arrangements in which women are no longer regarded as the chattel of men; love, fidelity, and mutual respect replace property rights and concern to reduce competition between

related males for the same woman. We have, as yet, made very little progress in changing the double standard in regard to prostitution. As the moral ground shifts, will moral positions remain the same?

7. The punishment for adultery was death by stoning for both the man and the woman (Deut. 22:22), but here adultery is defined by the marital status of the woman. A married man who has intercourse with an unmarried woman is not an adulterer—again, the double standard. And a bride who is found not to be a virgin is to be stoned to death (Deut. 22:13-21), but male virginity at marriage is never even mentioned. Today some Christians argue that the development of contraceptives makes even the social prohibition against extramarital intercourse passé—which is to say, they are prepared to extend to women the privileges which the Old Testament freely accords to men. Others, who believe that sexual intercourse requires a monogamous context for true love to flourish, would nonetheless be aghast at the idea of stoning those who disagree.

8. Polygamy was regularly practiced in the Old Testament. It goes unmentioned in the New—unless, as many scholars now believe, I Timothy 3:2,12 and Titus 1:6 mean, as the Greek plainly reads, that bishops and deacons should have only one wife, referring not to divorce and remarriage (surely a widowed and remarried bishop was not disallowed) but to polygamy. If so, polygamy was still being practiced sporadically within Judaism for centuries following the New Testament period. Christian missionaries to Africa in past centuries were ruthless in demanding that tribal chieftains divorce all but one wife, with tragic consequences for the ones rejected. Now many wonder whether some other arrangement might have been more humane, even if it included tolerance of polygamy in at least the first generation of believers.

9. A form of polygamy was the levirate marriage. When a married man in Israel died childless, his brother was supposed to marry the widow and sire children for his deceased brother. Jesus mentions this custom without criticism (Matt. 22:23-33). Today not even devout Jews observe this unambiguous commandment (Deut. 25:5-10).

10. In the New Testament, Paul taught that it was best not to marry (I Cor. 7). While he quali-fies this as his own advice and not a commandment of the Lord, it is clearly advice that most Christians choose to ignore. And here and elsewhere, in explicitly authoritative teaching, Scripture teaches patriarchal, male-dominant marital relationships as the norm. Do we wish to perpetuate that teaching?

11. Jews were supposed to practice endogamy—that is, marriage within the 12 tribes of Israel. Until recently a similar rule prevailed in the American South, in laws against interracial marriage (miscegenation). We have witnessed, within our own lifetimes, the legal battle to nullify state laws against miscegenation and the gradual change in social attitudes toward toleration and even acceptance of interracial couples in public. Sexual mores can alter quite radically even in a single lifetime.

12. The Old Testament regarded celibacy as abnormal (Jeremiah's divinely commanded celibacy is a sign of doom for the families of Israel [Jer. 16:1-4]), and I Timothy 4:1-3 calls compulsory celibacy a heresy. Yet the Catholic Church has made it normative for priests and nuns.

13. In many other ways we have developed different norms from those explicitly laid down by the Bible: "When men fight with one another and the wife of the one draws near to rescue her husband from the hand of him who is beating him, and puts out her hand and seizes him by the private parts [i.e., testicles], then you shall cut off her hand" (Deut. 25:11f). We, on the contrary, might very well applaud her. And just as we no longer countenance slavery, which both Old and New Testaments regarded as normal, so we also no longer countenance the use of female slaves, concubines, and captives as sexual toys or breeding machines by their male owners, which Leviticus 19:20 f., II Samuel 5:13, and Numbers 31:17-20 permitted—and as many American slave owners did slightly over 100 years ago.

The Problem of Authority

These cases are relevant to our attitude toward the authority of Scripture. Clearly we regard certain things, especially in the Old Testament, as no longer binding. Other things we regarded as binding, including legislation in the Old Testament that is not mentioned at all in the New. What is the principle of selection here? Most of us would regard as taboo intercourse with animals, incest, rape, adultery, prostitution, polygamy, levirate marriage, and concubinage—even though the Old Testament permits the last four and the New Testament is silent regarding most of them.

How do we make judgments that these should be taboo, however? There exist no simply biblical grounds, for as I have tried to show, in other respects many of us would clearly reject biblical attitudes and practices regarding nudity, intercourse during menstruation, prudery about speaking of the sexual organs and act, the "uncleanness" of semen and menstrual blood, endogamy, levirate marriage, and social regulations based on the assumption that women are sexual properties subject to men. Obviously many of our choices in these matters are arbitrary. Mormon polygamy was outlawed in this country, despite the constitutional protection of freedom of religion, because it violated the sensibilities of the dominant Christian culture, even though no explicit biblical prohibition against polygamy exists. (Jesus' teaching about divorce is no exception, since he quotes Genesis 2:24 as his authority, and this text was never understood in Israel as excluding polygamy. A man could become "one flesh" with more than one woman, through the act of intercourse.)

The problem of authority is not mitigated by the doctrine that the cultic requirements of the Old Testament were abrogated by the New, and that only the moral commandments of the Old Testament remain in force. For most of these sexual mores fall among the moral commandments. If Christ is the end of the law (Rom. 10:4), if we have been discharged from the law to serve, not under the old written code but in the new life of the Spirit (Rom. 7:6), then all of these Old Testament sexual mores come under the authority of the Spirit. We cannot then take even what Paul says as a new law. Even fundamentalists reserve the right to pick and choose which laws they will observe, though they seldom admit doing just that. For the same Paul who condemns homosexual acts as sinful is the Paul who tells women like Anita Bryant to remain silent in the church (I Cor. 14:34). If Anita Bryant were consistently biblical, she would demand that gays be stoned to death—though she would never be able to say so in church!

Judge for Yourselves

The crux of the matter, it seems to me, is simply that the Bible has no sexual ethic. There is no biblical sex ethic. The Bible knows only a love ethic, which is constantly being brought to bear on whatever sexual mores are dominant in any given country, or culture, or period.

Approached from the point of view of love, rather than of law, the issue is at once transformed. Now the question is not "What is permitted?" but rather "What does it mean to love my homosexual neighbor?" Approached from the point of view of faith rather than of words, the question ceased to be "What constitutes a breach of divine law in the sexual realm?" and becomes instead "What constitutes obedience to the God revealed in the cosmic lover, Jesus Christ?" Approached from the point of view of the Spirit rather than of the letter, the question ceases to be "What does Scripture command?" and becomes "What is the Word that the Spirit speaks to the churches now, in the light of Scripture, tradition, theology, psychology, genetics, anthropology, and biology?"

In a little-remembered statement, Jesus said, "Why do you not judge for yourselves what is right?" (Luke 12:57). Such sovereign freedom strikes terror in the hearts of many Christians; they would rather be under law and be told what is right. Yet Paul himself echoes Jesus' sentiment immediately preceding one of his possible references to homosexuality: "Do you not know that we are to judge angels? How much more, matters pertaining to this life!" (I Cor. 6:3). The last thing Paul would want is for people to respond to his ethical advice as a new law engraved on tablets of stone. He is himself trying to "judge for himself what is right." If now new evidence is in on the phenomenon of homosexuality, are we not obligated—no, free—to reevaluate the whole issue in the light of all available data and decide, under God, for ourselves? Is this not the radical freedom for obedience which the gospel establishes?

It may, of course, be objected that this analysis has drawn our noses so close to texts that the general tenor of the whole is lost. The Bible clearly considers homosexuality a sin, and whether it is stated three times or 3,000 is beside the point. Just as some of us grew up "knowing" that homosexuality was the unutterable sin, though no one ever spoke of it, so the whole Bible "knows" it to be wrong.

I freely grant all that. The issue is precisely whether that biblical judgment is correct. The whole tenor of the Bible sanctions slavery as well, and nowhere attacks it as unjust. Are we prepared to argue that slavery today is biblically justified? The overwhelming burden of the biblical message is that women are inferior to men. Are we willing to perpetuate that status? Jesus himself explicitly forbids divorce for any case (Matthew has added "except adultery" to an unqualified statement). Are we willing to forbid divorce, and certainly remarriage, for everyone whose marriage has become intolerable?

A Profound Prejudice

The fact is that there is, behind the legal tenor of Scripture, an even deeper tenor, articulated by Israel out of the experience of the Exodus and brought to sublime embodiment in Jesus' identification with harlots, tax collectors, the diseased and maimed and outcast and poor. It is that God sides with the powerless, God liberates the oppressed, God suffers with the suffering and groans toward the reconciliation of all things. In the light of that supernal compassion, whatever our position on homosexuals, the gospel's imperative to love, care for, and be identified with their sufferings is unmistakably clear.

Many of us have a powerful personal revulsion against homosexual people—a revulsion that goes far beyond reason to what almost seems to us an instinctual level. Homosexuality seems "unnatural"—and it would be for most of us. I myself have had to struggle against feelings of superiority and prejudice in regard to homosexual people. Yet for some persons it appears to be the only natural form their sexuality takes. This feeling of revulsion or alienness, or simply of indifference, is no basis, however, for ethical decisions regarding our attitudes toward homosexuality. It seems to me that we simply need to acknowledge that for the majority of us who are heterosexual by nature, this deep feeling amounts to nothing more than prejudice when applied to others. It has no sure biblical warrant, no ethical justification. It is just the way we feel about those who are different. And if we can acknowledge that profound prejudice, perhaps we can begin to allow others their preferences as well.

I want to close by quoting a paragraph from a 1977 address by C. Kilmer Myers, Bishop of California, before the Episcopal House of Bishops:

> The model for humanness is Jesus. I know many homosexuals who are radically human. To desert them would be a desertion, I believe, of our Master, Jesus Christ. And that I will not do no matter what the cost. I could not possibly return to my diocese and face them, these homosexual persons, many of whom look upon me as their father in God, their brother in Christ, their friend, were I to say to them, "You stand outside the hedge of the New Israel, you are rejected by God. Your love and care and tenderness, yes, your faltering, your reaching out, your tears, your search for love, your violent deaths mean nothing! You are damned! You have no place in the household of God. You are so despicable that there is no room for you—in the priesthood or anywhere else." There are voices in this country now raised proclaiming this total ostracism in the name of Jesus of Nazareth. What will be the nature of the response to this in the House of Bishops?

Now that this issue has become one that none of us can dodge, what will be the nature of our response?

WORKSHOP 9:

Experiences of Bisexual, Gay, Lesbian, and/or Transgender People

Purpose

- To learn about the experiences of bisexual, gay, lesbian, and/or transgender people through face-to-face contact with bisexual, gay, lesbian, and/or transgender people willing to talk openly about their lives and answer questions.

Materials

- For large group exercises: a sheet of newsprint, masking tape
- For small group exercises: none
- For individual exercises: index cards, pens

Preparation

- Arrange chairs in a circle, including extra chairs for the speakers.
- Display the Participation Guidelines from Workshop 1.
- Before the session, talk with the speakers about your purposes and the typical workshop format. Ask them what you need to do to make them comfortable and prepare the group for their visit. Tell them that your group meets for two hours, but you want to save the last 30 minutes for processing the speakers' presentations, so their commitment is for 90 minutes. Meet with them before the workshop and spend time getting to know them so they feel that they have allies in the group. This is helpful to experienced speakers and a necessity for inexperienced ones. If your group has already formed some questions, tell the speakers what they are so they can think about answers. Give the speakers some basic information about your group.

Workshop Plan

Opening/Chalice Lighting   (5 minutes)

Reading: #576 "A Litany of Restoration"
Hymn: #128 "For All That Is Our Life"

Panel   (85 minutes)

Introduce the speakers by name and suggest that the group go around the circle and give their names as well. Remind participants that the speakers are making themselves vulnerable for the benefit of the group, and that following the presentation the group will have an opportunity to reflect on the experience.

If your group is quiet and not likely to ask questions, have them write questions ahead of time and turn them in anonymously. Give the speakers the cards before they begin so they can prepare. Or, have note cards available, and if participants are too shy to ask questions, have them ask them anonymously during the panel by handing cards to you.

Turn the agenda over to the speakers in whatever way you have negotiated ahead of time. If the speakers do not have a favorite format, suggest that one of the speakers review these discussion guidelines:

- Respect the confidentiality of personal information shared.
- Speak from personal experience.
- Remember that the speakers do not represent the views of all bisexual, gay, lesbian, and/or transgender people—just their own.
- There is no such thing as a "stupid" question.
- Speakers have the right to pass on any question that they feel is too personal or inappropriate.
- Be respectful and courteous when disagreeing.

Each speaker should offer a brief (3-10 minute) autobiographical introduction and ask people who may have specific questions for her or him to jot them down and ask them after the last speaker has introduced her- or himself. After the last speaker's introduction, ask for questions from the group, either directed to a particular speaker or to the panel as a whole. Speakers answer the questions and engage in discussion until time runs out.

You should keep track of the time and let everyone know when there are about 10 minutes left so everyone will have a chance to make any final comments.

Thank the speakers, and ask them if they would like written or oral feedback from the group, or any kind of follow-up. Have someone accompany them out of the room.

Discussion   (25 minutes)

Ask for the group's reactions to the panel. You may want to structure the discussion by asking the following processing questions:

- What surprised you?
- What made you feel uncomfortable?
- What was something new you heard?
- What interested you?
- What questions were left unanswered?
- What emotions and feelings came up for you? In response to what?

Closing/Check Out   (5 minutes)

End by asking people to share one thing they have learned, relearned, or unlearned tonight. Choose one or both of the following:

Unison Reading: #689 by Paul Robeson

> Sorrow will one day turn to joy. All that breaks the heart and oppresses the soul will one day give place to peace and understanding and everyone will be free.

Hymn: #402 "From You I Receive"

Assignment/Follow-up

Ask people to think about what life must have been like for bisexual, gay, lesbian, and transgender communities in the early part of the 1900s. How have things changed?

WORKSHOP 10:
History

Purpose

- To understand some of the history of the bisexual, gay, lesbian, and transgender civil rights movement.

Materials

- For large group exercises: video, VCR, television
- For small group exercises: none
- For individual exercises: none

Preparation

- Obtain and preview the video.
- Set up room for viewing the video.
- Copy the "History of Unitarian Universalist Involvement in Support of Bisexual, Gay, Lesbian, and Transgender Issues" as a handout for participants (optional).

Workshop Plan

Opening/Chalice Lighting   (5 minutes)

Choose *one* of these openings. If you decide to bring readings, it is suggested that participants take turns with this responsibility each week.

- Lighting of chalice and reading.
  Reading: #447 by Albert Schweitzer
  Hymn: #348 "Guide My Feet"
- Reading of leader's choice.
- Moment of meditation or prayer.

Video and Discussion   (time varies)

Video Option 1:
Before Stonewall   (90 minutes)

This video chronicles the lives of bisexual, gay, lesbian, and/or transgender people in the twentieth century prior to the Stonewall Riots in 1969. It is available in many progressive video stores.

Introduce this video by saying that before 1969, most bisexual, gay, lesbian, and/or transgender people were closeted. Only since then have things begun to change. This video will show how life was and how it changed for people who were bisexual, gay, lesbian, and/or transgender prior to 1969.

Video Option 2:
The Life and Times of Harvey Milk   (90 minutes)

This Academy Award-winning documentary chronicles the life of San Francisco Supervisor Harvey Milk. This video may be harder to find than the others.

Introduce *The Life and Times of Harvey Milk* by saying that the video is an uplifting documentary about the first openly gay man elected to political office in California. The film follows Milk from his days as a Castro Street businessman, to his triumphant election to the San Francisco Board of Supervisors in 1977. One year later, Milk and San Francisco Mayor George Moscone were shot and killed by Dan White, another San Francisco supervisor. Milk's assassination has become a symbol for the continuing struggle for gay rights across the country.

Video Option 3:
The Celluloid Closet   (90 minutes)

This Academy Award-nominated video chronicles how bisexual, gay, lesbian, and/or transgender people have been portrayed since the beginning of the film industry. It is available in many progressive video stores.

Introduce this video by saying one way to learn about the history of bisexual, gay, lesbian, and/or transgender people is to explore how the film industry has portrayed them in the movies. This film is a good reflection of how slowly attitudes have changed over nearly 100 years. Encourage people to think about what it must have been like for a bisexual, gay, lesbian, and/or transgender person to see these movies when they originally came out.

Video Option 4:
Pink Triangles   (40 minutes)

This video chronicles the story of gays and lesbians in the Holocaust. It is available through the Unitarian Universalist Association Video Loan Library, (716) 229-5325. Order well in advance.

Introduce *Pink Triangles* by saying that it describes gay and lesbian oppression in a historical context, focusing especially on the origin of the symbol of the pink triangle used by the Nazis to identify homosexuals. The documentary contains excellent examples of institutional and cultural heterosexism, as well as personal interviews from a wide variety of perspectives.

Discussion

Invite discussion of the films. You may wish to use the following questions—as time and needs allow—to guide you.

- What emotional reactions did the film generate in you? What segments caused them?
- What did you learn?
- What made you uncomfortable? Why?
- What questions did the video leave you with?
- How have silence, invisibility, and ignorance been a part of homophobia and heterosexism?
- How have things changed in our society? How have they not changed?

Local/Congregational History   (20 minutes, optional)

If you have time, you may wish to examine the history of your local congregation, the Unitarian Universalist Association, and/or your community concerning bisexual, gay, lesbian, and/or transgender rights. You may wish to have someone do some research in each of these areas to report back later as well—especially if the history is sketchy. Also, note times when apparently nothing happened. This is a statement as well. You might use this time as an opportunity to create an oral history of your community and/or congregation by talking with a person or people with a long personal history in that setting.

Closing/Check Out   (5 minutes)

End by asking people to share one thing they have learned, relearned, or unlearned tonight.
Choose one or both of the following:

- Unison Reading: #689 by Paul Robeson

  Sorrow will one day turn to joy. All that breaks the heart and oppresses the soul will one day give place to peace and understanding and everyone will be free.

- Hymn: #402 "From You I Receive"

Assignment/Follow-up (optional)

- Ask each person to talk to a long-time member of the congregation or community who can reflect on changes she or he has seen.
- Distribute copies of the "History of Unitarian Universalist Involvement in Support of Bisexual, Gay, Lesbian, and Transgender Issues."

History of Unitarian Universalist Involvement in Support of Bisexual, Gay, Lesbian, and Transgender Issues

1967   Unitarian Universalist Committee on Goals publishes results of its survey on beliefs and attitudes within the denomination: 7.7% of Unitarian Universalists believe that homosexuality should be discouraged by law; 80.2% that it should be discouraged by education, not law; 12% that it should not be discouraged by law or education; .1% that it should be encouraged.

1969   LaForet, Colorado—the Reverend James L. Stoll publicly declares himself to be homosexual at a Liberal Religious Youth Conference.

1970   General Assembly General Resolution to end discrimination against homosexuals and bisexuals, especially with regard to ending legal regulations against private consensual behavior among adults, discrimination in employment, granting of visas, security clearances, and citizenship. Also calls on congregations to develop sex education programs that promote healthy attitudes toward all forms of sexuality.

1971   The Reverend Richard Nash and Elgin Blair co-found Unitarian Universalist Gay Caucus, to lobby for the creation of an Office of Gay Affairs.

1971   Publication of *About Your Sexuality,* a curriculum for youth that attempts to foster more positive attitudes toward homosexuality and bisexuality.

1972   Publication of *The Invisible Minority,* an adult curriculum about homosexuality.

1973   *Invisible Minority* wins an award from the National Council on Family Relations.

1973   General Assembly General Resolution to create a denominational Office of Gay Affairs, staffed by gay people, to be a resource to the Unitarian Universalist Association (UUA).

1974   General Assembly votes funding for the UUA Office of Gay Affairs.

1975   Arlie Scott hired as director of Gay Affairs.

1977   General Assembly General Resolution urging Unitarian Universalists to fight negative propaganda against gays.

1977   The Reverend Robert Wheatley becomes new director of Office of Gay Concerns; starts BUUGL (Boston Unitarian Universalist Gays and Lesbians), which meets on Sunday evenings at Arlington Street Church for worship and socializing.

1979   GALA (Gay and Lesbian Affirmed), is founded by the Reverend Robert Wheatley and co-sponsored by the Office of Gay Concerns and Ferry Beach Park Association. The week-long conference, including workshops, worship, fun, and fellowship, continues to be held every year.

1980   General Assembly Business Resolution urging Unitarian Universalists, the UUA, and the Unitarian Universalist Ministers Association to assist in the settlement of openly-gay ministers.

1984   General Assembly Business Resolution affirming the practice of Unitarian Universalist clergy performing services of union between same-sex couples, and requesting that the Department of Ministerial and Congregational Services develop and distribute supporting materials.

1986   General Assembly General Resolution encouraging Unitarian Universalists to work to end AIDS discrimination through education and advocacy.

1986   The Reverend Jay Deacon becomes director of Office of Lesbian and Gay Concerns; UUA Board of Trustees appoints AIDS Advisory Panel, which recommends the formation of the AIDS Action Working Group.

1986   UUA adds to personnel manual non-discrimination clause for employees who are HIV-positive.

1987   General Assembly General Resolution encouraging Unitarian Universalists to work to overturn legislation restricting the rights of gays, lesbians, and bisexuals, including boycotting products and services of organizations that have a policy of discrimination.

1987   The Reverend Mark Mosher DeWolfe, Unitarian Universalist minister in Ontario, Canada, dies of AIDS.

1989   General Assembly Business Resolution adopting Welcoming Congregation Program to combat homophobia in Unitarian Universalist congregations and to educate individual Unitarian Universalists.

1989   General Assembly General Resolution: opposing discriminatory practices toward people with AIDS/HIV, and urging fuller effort towards education and treatment, including institution of clean needle program.

1989   General Assembly Resolution of Immediate Witness condemning the Helms Amendment to restrict the travel rights of HIV-infected people into the US.

1989   The Reverend Scott Alexander becomes director of Office of Lesbian and Gay Concerns.

1990   Publication of *The Welcoming Congregation Handbook*, edited by Scott Alexander and Steve L'Heureux. Handbook to be used as resource material for implementing The Welcoming Congregation Program.

1991   The Reverend Meg Riley becomes director of Office of Lesbian and Gay Concerns.

1992   Welcoming Congregation trainers conference held in Boston to train district leaders in conducting homophobia workshops.

1992   General Assembly Resolution of Immediate Witness opposing legalization of discrimination against gays, lesbians, and bisexuals. A response to hate campaigns in Oregon and Colorado.

1992   UUA Board of Trustees passes resolution expressing disapproval of Boy Scouts of America policy of discrimination against gay and atheist scouts and leaders (revised and adopted 1997).

1993   General Assembly stages public protest against North Carolina's "crime against nature" laws. As required by GA 1987 resolution, UUA Board, staff, members, and GA delegates participate in candlelight vigil and witnessing.

1993   UUA Board of Trustees vote unanimously to make director of Office of Lesbian and Gay Concerns a full-time position; Office title changes to "Office of Lesbian, Bisexual and Gay Concerns" to reflect commitment to the bisexual community.

1993   General Assembly Resolution of Immediate Witness protesting the ban of openly lesbian, gay, and bisexual persons in the military.

1993   UUA endorses the March on Washington for Lesbian, Gay, and Bisexual Equal Rights and Liberation. UUA Board adjourns its quarterly Boston meeting to reconvene in the nation's capital to attend the March. Opening service at All Souls Unitarian Church. Closing worship at Sojourner Truth Congregation. Thousands of Unitarian Universalists attend the March.

1994   General Assembly Resolution of Immediate Witness sponsored by the Youth Caucus urging that public school sexuality education be comprehensive, unbiased, up-to-date, and inclusive of all sexual orientations.

1996   Keith Kron becomes director of Office of Lesbian, Bisexual, and Gay Concerns.

1996   UUA Board of Trustees passes resolution in support of same-sex marriage.

1996   Office title changes to Office of Bisexual, Gay, Lesbian, and Transgender Concerns (OBGLTC) to reflect commitment to the transgender community.

1996   General Assembly Resolution of Immediate Witness in support of the right to marry for same-sex couples.

1997   General Assembly Action of Immediate Witness in support of non-discriminatory corporate and other business policies is passed. This resolution:
- urges support for corporations with customer and employment policies that respect bisexual, gay, lesbian, and/or transgender individuals
- urges the UUA and Unitarian Universalists to encourage corporate managers to institute policies that acknowledge a respect for the diversity of the human community.

1997   General Assembly stages sodomy law protest in the form of an educational panel in Phoenix, AZ.

1997   OBGLTC sponsors training on transgender issues for Ministerial Fellowship Committee, at their request.

1997   OBGLTC provides training on transgender issues for the UUA's Religious Education department.

1999   Publication of second edition of *The Welcoming Congregation Handbook*.

WORKSHOP 11:
Bisexuality and Biphobia

Purpose

- To gain greater understanding of bisexuality.

Materials

- For large group exercises: newsprint, markers, the book *Am I Blue?: Coming Out of the Silence* edited by Marion Dane Bauer
- For small group exercises: none
- For individual exercises: none

Preparation

- Obtain copy of *Am I Blue?* from bookstore or library. Read the story "Am I Blue?" by Bruce Coville several times and decide whether to retell it aloud, shorten it, or read it in its entirety.
- Print out the Kinsey and Klein Scales on newsprint and post.
- Arrange chairs in a circle or semi-circle.

Workshop Plan

Opening/Chalice Lighting   (5 minutes)

Choose *one* of these openings. If you decide to bring readings, it is suggested that participants take turns with this responsibility each week.

- Lighting of chalice and reading.
  Reading: #420 by Annie Dillard
  Hymn: #298 "Wake Now My Senses"
- Reading of leader's choice.
- Moment of meditation or prayer.

Pairs   (40 minutes)

Ask people to find a partner with whom they have not yet done much interacting. Tell them you are going to provide a series of questions for them to discuss. They will have about two minutes to answer each question.

After each question, ask the entire group to reflect on their conversations. After one person/group reflects, ask the entire group how many people had a similar answer and ask for a show of hands. Ask if there were other, different answers. You may wish to list these on newsprint. Remind them that each person should have time to speak.

- Most people have reported that they learned about heterosexual people first, gay and lesbian people next, and bisexual people third. Why do you think people learn about bisexuality last?
- The West—US and Canada, in particular white Westerners—is characterized as being much more dualisitic in its thinking than Eastern thought. We are much more into yes/no, right/wrong, man/woman, black/white, either/or thinking. Do you agree with this? How would this affect how bisexuality is viewed here?
- A man in a relationship with another man tells you he is bisexual. What's your reaction?
- Would it make any difference if he told you he was bisexual before telling you his partner was male?
- A woman in a relationship with another woman tells you she is bisexual. What's your reaction?
- Would it make any difference if she told you she was bisexual before telling you her partner was female?
- Is your reaction any different if the bisexual person is in a relationship with a person of another gender?
- Is your reaction any different if the bisexual person is not in a relationship with anyone?
- Is your reaction any different if the bisexual person is in relationships with both a person of another gender and a person of the same gender at the same time?

Process the questions as a whole group. Listen for language as people process. Where did they stumble? Did people fall into calling the relationships gay or straight relationships? Did you? Where were the strongest reactions?

Am I Blue?   (25 minutes)

Tell the group you are going to read or tell them a story from a book called *Am I Blue?* The story is about a teenage boy trying to figure out his sexual orientation. You are advised that telling the story or shortening it with a summary is better than reading all of it, but it is a great story regardless. Ask participants to listen for what the story has to say about sexual orientation and bisexuality.

After telling the story, ask participants about their reactions to the story, what they liked and disliked about it, and what the story has to say about sexual orientation and bisexuality.

Ask participants to form groups of four. Using the story's metaphor of blue for sexual orientation, what would determine how blue a person is? (If participants need a prompt, reframe the question as, "Is sexual orientation just about who you are attracted to sexually?")

After five minutes, ask the groups to report on their conversations briefly.

Kinsey and Klein Scales   (25 minutes)

After the reports, ask the group if they have heard of the Kinsey scale. Explain that Alfred Kinsey's reasearch into sexuality led to the creation of the Kinsey Scale, which defines sexuality as a continuum as opposed to a category. Display the Kinsey Scale and tell participants Kinsey believed that few people fell at either end, that most were between one and five. Ask if there are any questions about the scale. Remind participants that for some people, behavior and identity may differ. For example, someone who is bisexual may have only different gender partners or someone who is predominantly homosexual may be married and behave bisexually or predominantly heterosexually.

Tell the participants that psychologist Fritz Klein has put further thought and depth into sexual orientation. He has developed scales similar to Kinsey's scale but measuring nine different areas.

Explain that Fritz Klein also asks each of these questions against a time frame.

1. How would you answer these questions for your past—beyond a year ago?
2. How would you answer these questions for the present—in the last twelve months?
3. How would your answers be if you could answer ideally for yourself?

Invite comments and learnings from these scales. Do the nine scales make your understanding of attraction and sexual orientation any different? Allow for brief conversation, but point out that these scales are used to help people become more comfortable with the complexity of their lives and are not a judgment or definitively saying that everyone is bisexual.

Case Studies   (20 minutes)

Ask each participant to find a partner. Tell each pair that you are going to make a statement to them. Each partner will have an opportunity to respond to the statement. Encourage participants to answer as honestly and directly as possible. Tell participants they will each have a minute to respond.

1. "Sure, he says he is bisexual, but I think he just has not made up his mind yet."
2. "She just told me she has two partners—one male, the other female. I don't know whether to be offended or jealous. I guess all bisexual people are like that."
3. "I think ultimately everyone is bisexual."

After the questions and responses are done, process the questions with the group. What assumptions were implied by the questions? What was hard to answer? What questions do you still have about bisexuality?

Closing/Checkout   (5 minutes)

End by asking people to share one thing they have learned, relearned, or unlearned tonight. Choose one or both of the following:

• Unison Reading: #689 by Paul Robeson

Sorrow will one day turn to joy. All that breaks the heart and oppresses the soul will one day give place to peace and understanding and everyone will be free.

• Hymn: #402 "From You I Receive"

Assignment/Follow-up

Ask participants to notice examples of dualistic thinking as they see them in the world during the week.

Kinsey Scale

0	1	2	3	4	5	6
Exclusively Heterosexual	Predominantly	Somewhat	Bisexual	Somewhat	Predominantly	Exclusively Homosexual

Klein Scales

The nine scales are as follows:

1. Sexual Attraction (Who are you attracted to?)

0	1	2	3	4	5	6
Exclusively Heterosexual	Predominantly	Somewhat	Bisexual	Somewhat	Predominantly	Exclusively Homosexual

2. Sexual Behavior (Who do you engage in sex with?)

0	1	2	3	4	5	6
Exclusively Heterosexual	Predominantly	Somewhat	Bisexual	Somewhat	Predominantly	Exclusively Homosexual

3. Sexual Fantasies (Who do you fantasize about?)

0	1	2	3	4	5	6
Exclusively Heterosexual	Predominantly	Somewhat	Bisexual	Somewhat	Predominantly	Exclusively Homosexual

4. Emotional Preference (Do you love and like members of one or both genders?)

0	1	2	3	4	5	6
Exclusively Heterosexual	Predominantly	Somewhat	Bisexual	Somewhat	Predominantly	Exclusively Homosexual

5. Social Preference (Who do you socialize with, which may be different from whom you emotionally prefer?)

0	1	2	3	4	5	6
Exclusively Heterosexual	Predominantly	Somewhat	Bisexual	Somewhat	Predominantly	Exclusively Homosexual

6. Self-Identification (How do you identify? This may not match the other scales.)

0	1	2	3	4	5	6
Exclusively Heterosexual	Predominantly	Somewhat	Bisexual	Somewhat	Predominantly	Exclusively Homosexual

7. Lifestyle (Where do you tend to spend time with whom?)

0	1	2	3	4	5	6
Exclusively Heterosexual	Predominantly	Somewhat	Bisexual	Somewhat	Predominantly	Exclusively Homosexual

8. Community Affiliation

0	1	2	3	4	5	6
Exclusively Heterosexual	Predominantly	Somewhat	Bisexual	Somewhat	Predominantly	Exclusively Homosexual

9. Political Identity

0	1	2	3	4	5	6
Exclusively Heterosexual	Predominantly	Somewhat	Bisexual	Somewhat	Predominantly	Exclusively Homosexual

WORKSHOP 12:
Transgender Identity: What It Means

Purpose

- To gain a better understanding of transgender people.

Materials

- For large group exercises: newsprint, markers
- For small group exercises: "Twenty Questions About Transgender Identity" cards
- For individual exercises: "Transgender 101" handout, paper, pen/pencil

Preparation

- Create chart on newsprint as shown in the Words and Meanings activity.
- Copy "Transgender 101" handout for participants.
- Duplicate one copy of "Twenty Questions About Transgender Identity" and create cards by cutting out each question and answer so that no two questions are on the same page.
- Arrange chairs in a circle or semi-circle.

Workshop Plan

Opening/Chalice Lighting   (5 minutes)

Choose *one* of these openings. If you decide to bring readings, it is suggested that participants take turns with this responsibility each week.

- Lighting of chalice and reading.
  Reading: #595 "Free From Suffering"
  Hymn: #407 "We're Gonna Sit At the Welcome Table"
- Reading of leader's choice.
- Moment of meditation or prayer.

Words and Meanings   (40 minutes)

Ask participants to find a partner. Tell them you are going to say a word. Ask them to share with their partner when they first learned this word and how they learned what it means. If this is the first time they have heard the word, encourage them to share that as well. Some of these words will be new for many people. Each person will have one minute for each word. Do not provide any definition or clarification of any of these words:

transvestite
male-to-female transsexual
female-to-male transsexual
intersexuals
hermaphrodites
third gender
two spirit
drag queen
drab king

After you have completed this list, re-gather as a large group. Tell participants you are going to complete a chart just as they did in Workshop 2 (see page 61). Ask participants to share when they learned about each of these terms and whether it was a positive, negative, or neutral experience. Proceed through the chart. Upon completing the chart, discuss briefly what they know and do not know and when they learned it. Also, compare this to their learnings about sexual orientation from Workshop 2.

Transgender 101   (20 minutes)

Distribute the "Transgender 101" handout. Review the definitions and ask for comments and questions.

Spend some time discussing the difference between gender identification and sexual orientation. You may wish to ask people why the phrasing "bisexual, gay, lesbian, and/or transgender" is used as opposed to "bisexual, gay, lesbian, and transgender."

Twenty Questions   (40 minutes)

Distribute a sheet of paper and pencil or pen to each person. Tell them you are going to read a series of questions about transgender people and issues facing them. Tell them they will have a brief period of time to try to write answers to these questions.

Read each of the "Twenty Questions About Transgender Identity" (questions only) and give the participants half a minute to a minute to write the answer to the question. Encourage guessing.

After you have completed the questions, distribute the question slips (including answers) to the participants. For example, if there are 10 people in the group, give each person two question slips.

Then in the order they were read, have each person read the question out loud and ask the rest of the group for answers. If someone's answer matches the given answer, have the reader acknowlege this or have them read the answer to the question as written. Allow for brief comments and questions. Proceed through all the questions.

At the end of the questions, ask the participants to share two things they learned from this session with the person next to them.

Further Questions　　　　　　(10 minutes)

Ask participants to re-gather as an entire group and ask them what they have learned. Then ask what questions they still have and record these questions on newsprint. Encourage individuals to take a specific question to research and report back to the larger group at a later time. Remind participants that there is a lot of information we do not know and that the learning is ongoing.

Closing/Check Out　　　　　　(5 minutes)

Choose one or both of the following:

* Unison Reading: #689 by Paul Robeson

  Sorrow will one day turn to joy. All that breaks the heart and oppresses the soul will one day give place to peace and understanding and everyone will be free.

* Hymn: #402 "From You I Receive"

Assignment/Follow-up

Spread out an assortment of gay- and transgender-supportive buttons and/or pink triangle stickers on a table. Include buttons that express support for gay, lesbian, and bisexual rights or pride—pink triangles, interlocking male or female signs, "Don't Presume I'm Heterosexual," "Gay and Proud," "Support Gay and Lesbian Rights," "Gay Is Beautiful," etc. Provide enough buttons for each participant to choose one.

Ask each participant to take a button and wear it for at least one day. Ask participants to note their thoughts and feelings about wearing the button as well as the reactions of others. Participants may want to write down these reactions to share with the group at the next workshop. If some participants choose not to take a button, or take one but will not wear it, ask them to think about how they made these decisions, and their thoughts and feelings about the activity.

Twenty Questions About Transgender Identity

1. What does "transgender" mean?

The word "transgender" is an umbrella term used to include people who are transsexual, cross-dresser/transvestite, intersexual (formerly known as hermaphrodite), and people who see themselves as neither or both male and female gender, such as two spirit or third gender people.

2. What is the difference between gender identification and sexual/affectional orientation?

Gender identification is about how you understand your gender—man, woman, or third gender, for example. Sexual/affectional orientation is about who you are attracted to—asexual, bisexual, gay, heterosexual, lesbian. Everyone has both a gender identification and a sexual orientation. This explains the "and/or" usage in "bisexual, gay, lesbian, and/or transgender" listings. A person who identifies as transgender may be of any sexual/affectional orientation—asexual, bisexual, gay, heterosexual, lesbian. A person who is gay may or may not identify as transgender. Both are related directly to sexism in our culture.

3. Define genderism.

Genderism is the name for the oppression that suggests that there are only two genders in our world and that there are only certain ways to be each of these genders in our culture.

4. What issues do both the transgender and bisexual communities experience?

Both groups are the last groups seen and recognized in their respective arenas (transgender for gender identification, and bisexual for sexual orientation). Both suffer from the dualism of Western (predominantly white) culture. Both are more misunderstood in our culture than gays or lesbians.

5. **What is the difference between transvestite and transsexual?**

A transvestite finds satisfaction and pleasure in dressing and appearing as the gender opposite that which she or he was born, as both in clothing and overall appearance. The term is used considerably more for biological males. Cross dressers, Drag Queens and Drab Kings would fit here. This identity may not be readily apparent, because for some, it may mean only undergarments. For others it means hair, facial features, clothes, and make-up. A transsexual is a person who was born in one gender body but understands their gender to be the opposite of the one she or he was born as. A biologically born woman who understands her- or himself to be a man is a female-to-male (FTM) transsexual. A biologically born man who understands him- or herself to be a woman is a male-to-female (MTF) transsexual.

6. **List the different stages of "transition" that some transsexual people go through.**

1. Pre-operational—Sexual reassignment surgery is planned for the future. This eventually will include hormone therapy which prepares the body for surgery and helps the body more fully achieve the desired gender appearance. 2. Operational—The surgery has begun. This can be done in sections. For example, female to male transexuals may have the top part of their body undergo the surgery before the lower half. 3. Post-operational—Surgery complete. Hormone therapy continues. The term is often not used by the transsexual at this point. 4. Non-operational—This may or may not be a transitional stage. For various reasons, individuals decide to not pursue surgery or further surgery. Some are waiting for further medical advances.

7. **What is sexual reassignment surgery (SRS)?**

This is the surgery where individuals choose to alter their genitalia and chest area to match the internal gender identity they hold for themselves.

8. **Why do some transsexual folks choose not to have sexual reassignment surgery?**

Economics is one reason. Sexual reassignment surgery is expensive and generally not covered by insurance. Other medical conditions such as cancer often preclude the surgery. To live their lives, some people just do not feel a need or desire for the surgery. Some are waiting for medical technology and information to improve.

9. **What are the Benjamin Standards?**

These are the explicit standards of care that determine who is allowed to be applicants for hormonal therapy and sexual reassignment surgery—as determined by the Harry Benjamin International Gender Dysphoria Association, Inc. These tend to be very limiting in terms of who and how a person can be an applicant for sexual reassignment surgery. Nowhere in the document does it mention transgender people having any power or access to making these decisions.

11. **Define intersexual.**

A person born with mixed sexual physiology, with a physical manifestation of genital/genetic/endochrinological differentiation that is different from the cultural norm. Intersexuals often are "assigned" a boy/girl gender, and surgery is done after birth to "correct" their "problem." The problem may well be our society's tightly held view that there are only two genders.

10. **What is involved in changing a person's gender identification?**

This is a three-part answer: 1. the coming-out process, 2. the surgery and hormone treatment, and 3. the legal documentation that needs to be changed. The surgery may be the easiest piece. Coming out to people one knows often takes quite a toll on the individual and the process is continual. The legal aspects of changing one's gender identification are daunting and potentially expensive. This includes driver's license, social security, birth certificate, credit cards, medical records, and all other legal documentation where gender and/or name is listed.

12. **What does DRAB mean? What does DRAG mean?**

<u>D</u>ressed <u>A</u>s a <u>B</u>oy. Women who appeared as men in clothing and appearance in performances were often called DrAB Kings. It is used very rarely today. <u>D</u>ressed <u>A</u>s a <u>G</u>irl. Men who appeared as women in performances were and still are often referred to as DrAG Queens.

13. What is "third gender"?

A person whose understanding of her/hir/his gender identification transcends society's polarized gender system. Examples include male-to-third gender (biologically born male understands self to be neither or both genders) and female-to-third gender (biologically born female understands self to be neither or both genders). Transgender is usually the preferred term here as opposed to transsexual because transsexual refers to the male-female dichotomy.

14. Do you think the transgender movement is in the same place as the bisexual, gay, and lesbian movement?

No. The civil rights movement for transgender people is really just starting and is probably some 25 years behind the struggle for bisexual, gay, and lesbian civil rights. There is a fair amount of disagreement over terms, ideas, and strategies for moving forward. There are many different communities within the transgender community. Very few places have laws protecting the rights of transgender people or judges who are willing to interpret the law so that the rights of transgender people are protected.

15. Do transgender people from around the world face the same problems?

No. In some cultures, life is much better for transgender people. In particular, many Native American tribes view what we call transgender people as revered and special people. The Dagara people of West Africa have no word for transgender (or bisexual, gay, or lesbian) but they do hold all of these folks in special roles as gatekeepers of their society with special connections to the spirits. On the other hand, in many countries people who identify as transgender are far more closeted than they are here.

16. What percent of people in our culture identify as transgender?

No one knows for sure—which says something about the nature of the oppression and its scope. Some transgender people feel the numbers may rival the number of bisexual, gay, and lesbian people in our society. But until the oppression ends, we will never know for sure.

17. What are some common everyday problems transgender people face?

If a person is transgender, s/he may avoid going to any restroom in public places out of fear of being ostracized or attacked. There is virtually no legal protection in housing, job discrimination, and other areas for transgender people. A fear of physical safety is real and common for transgender people. A general fear of being outed is also an everyday concern of most transgender people. Thus, simple tasks like buying clothes and writing checks that require identification can be quite difficult. Adequate medical care is a perennial concern—not only in finding a doctor willing to treat a person who is transgender, but finding one with useful knowledge that will help the transgender patient.

18. How can transgender people fit into our culture?

They already do. Most transgender people in our culture are not seen. We all pay a price for that. A culture that promotes silence and dishonesty hurts itself in many ways. Eventually, society may move to a place where it trusts that transgender people know more about how they lead their lives and how transgender folks can fit and enrich our society. It may well be that transgender people, not fitting into traditional notions of gender, know more about gender because they must think about it more.

19. What can I do to help?

1. Educating one's self about transgender issues—especially in your geographic locale—is an excellent first step. What are the rights transgender people have in your community? What are the support systems? 2. Speak out against discrimination when you notice it. Challenge assumptions and educate others about transgender issues. 3. Be attentive to everyday language—from pronoun usage to gender options given. See if you can catch yourself using language that may exclude. 4. Be attentive to a polarized gender world as you encounter it—bathrooms, government forms, etc. 5. Ask transgender people and groups what they need from you as one person or one congregation. Follow their lead.

20. Are there historical connections between transphobia and racism?

Absolutely. When the Europeans came to colonize the North American continent, their experience with Native cultures where men were clearly living in female roles was one reason that they believed Native cultures were inferior and primitive compared to their own. Perhaps it is the Europeans who were primitive.

Draft
Transgender 101

Transgender

Our culture tends to limit its understanding of gender to man and woman. OBGLTC believes there are more than two genders and uses the word *transgender* as an umbrella term to describe the following people: crossdressers/transvestites, third gender people, transsexuals, intersexuals, and any self-identified transgender people.

Gender Identification

Transgender is a gender identification—*not* a sexual orientation. It expresses how you identify your gender rather than to whom you are sexually, affectionally, or romantically attracted. A transgender person can be of any sexual orientation.

Gender v. Sex

People are assigned a biological sex but define their own gender.

> Sex: Male, Female, Intersexual
> Gender: Man, Woman, Transgender

Language

OBGLTC believes that "transgender" is a noun equivalent to "man" and "woman", and as such should not be spelled or pronounced with an "-ed" suffix. Just as we would not say a person is "manned" or "womanned," we should not say a person is "transgendered".

When adding transgender to the list of bisexual, gay, and lesbian people, it is important to include transgender at the end, preceded by "and/or" because people can be bisexual, gay or lesbian, *and* transgender, but are not always both.

Whom the Umbrella Covers (We solicited these definitions from the communities they describe.)

Crossdressers (also known as *Transvestites*)
People who dress in the clothing, partially or completely, of the societal norm for the "opposite" gender. Most crossdressers are heterosexual men who crossdress for pleasure. Bisexual and gay men who crossdress usually do so for entertainment purposes, making fun of what it means to be a man.

DrAG Queens*—Dressed As a Girl
DrAB Kings*—Dressed As a Boy

* DrAG Queen and DrAB King are historical terms. Currently, "DrAG" refers to either.

Third Gender
A person whose understanding of her/hir/his gender identification transcends society's polarized gender system. OBGLTC believes that the dichotomized system of gender is limiting and encourages everyone to think outside and beyond this schema. *People who are third gender often prefer "transgender" to "third gender".*

> Male-to-Third Gender (born in body of male, believe self to be another gender)
> Female-to-Third Gender (born in body of female, believe self to be another gender)

Transsexual
A person born in the body associated with one gender who believes internally that s/he is of another gender.

> Male-to-Female (born in body of male, believe self to be female)
> Female-to-Male (born in body of female, believe self to be male)

Being transsexual may or may not involve sexual reassignment surgery (SRS). Some transsexuals use hormones to create the bodies they believe they were born to have. There seem to be some potential health risks for some hormone treatments. More research is needed to allow for better health care for transgender people. The Benjamin Standards are requirements set by a committee of the American Psychological Association in order for transsexuals legally to change their external identities and bodies.

> Pre-operative (considering or planning SRS)
> Post-operative (has had SRS)
> Non-operational (for personal and/or medical reasons—e.g., breast cancer—has chosen not to have SRS)

Intersexual (historically called hermaphrodite)

A person born with mixed sexual physiology, with a physical manifestation of genital/genetic/endocrinological differentiation that is different from the cultural norm. Intersexuals often are "assigned" a boy/girl gender, and surgery is done soon after birth to "correct" their "problem." The problem may well be our society's tightly held view that there are only two genders.

WORKSHOP 13:
How Homophobia Hurts Us All

Purpose

- To gain a greater understanding that homophobia, biphobia, transphobia, and heterosexism hurt everyone, regardless of sexual orientation or gender identification.

Materials

- For large group exercises: newsprint
- For small group exercises: large paper/poster board for murals, crayons/markers
- For individual exercises: none

Preparation

- Create the following chart on newsprint.

How Homophobia and Heterosexism Hurt All of Us	
oppression	homophobia, biphobia, transphobia, heterosexism
people hurt	bisexual, gay, heterosexual, lesbian, and/or transgender people
ways hurt	individual, congregation, community

- Arrange chairs in a circle or semi-circle.

Workshop Plan

Opening/Chalice Lighting   (5 minutes)

Choose *one* of these openings. If you decide to bring readings, it is suggested that participants take turns with this responsibility each week.

- Lighting of chalice and reading.
  Reading: #561 by Margaret Mead
  Hymn: #51 "Lady of the Seasons' Laughter"
- Reading of leader's choice.
- Moment of meditation or prayer.

Mural   (45 minutes)

Divide participants into four groups. Explain that each group will work together to create a mural that demonstrates how everyone is hurt by homophobia. Tell the participants they will have 45 minutes to create their mural on newsprint or posterboard. Refer them to the newsprint and ask them to think about the factors listed on the newsprint as they create their murals. Discuss the newsprint page briefly, pointing out that it lists the different oppressions for this mural, the different people hurt, and some ways people can be hurt (as individuals, in their congregation, in the wider community). Remind them that all types of drawings and word webs are acceptable. Ask for questions and begin.

Button Activity   (20 minutes)

(See Workshop 12 Assignment/Follow-up.) Ask participants to share in two sentences what button they chose to wear during the week, and when and where they wore it. If you used pink triangle stickers instead, simply ask when and where they wore it.

Then ask participants to briefly tell about their experience of wearing it. How did it feel to wear it? Did they behave differently when they wore it? Did others behave differently toward them when they wore it? What did they learn from this experience?

This may be difficult for some participants, so you may need to remind people that it is okay to pass and judgments about people's individual experiences are not useful. For some, this experience may bring up feelings of embarrassment and shame. Be very attentive to group process here.

If you have a large group you may wish to shorten another piece of the workshop to allow for more time for this conversation.

Sharing Murals   (25 minutes)

Ask each group to take five minutes to share their murals with the class. Allow for questions, if time, as each group presents.

Discussion (20 minutes)

Ask each participant to find a partner who was not in their mural group. Tell each pair they will have 10 minutes to discuss these three questions (you may wish to print them on newsprint):

1. What have you learned about homophobia today?
2. How does/has homophobia hurt you personally?
3. How does homophobia hurt all of us?

After 10 minutes, invite participants into the whole group and ask them to continue the discussion and reflect on their individual conversations. Listen for themes that you may wish to put on newsprint.

Closing/Check Out

End by asking people to share one thing they have learned, relearned, or unlearned tonight.
    Choose one or both of the following:

• Unison Reading: #689 by Paul Robeson

    Sorrow will one day turn to joy. All that breaks the heart and oppresses the soul will one day give place to peace and understanding and everyone will be free.

• Hymn: #402 "From You I Receive"

Assignment/Follow-up

Ask participants to begin to think about what they as individuals and as members of the congregation and larger community can do after completing the workshop series.

WORKSHOP 14:
What Now?

Purpose

- To reflect on what we have experienced and learned.
- To strategize on what we will do next.

Materials

- For large group exercises: newsprint, markers
- For small group exercises: newsprint, markers
- For individual exercises: Attitude and Action Continuum handouts

Preparation

- Copy the "Action Continuum" and "Attitude Continuum" handouts for each participant.
- Have three newsprint pages ready, with one titled "Individual," one titled "Congregational," and one titled "Community."
- Arrange chairs in a circle or semi-circle.

Workshop Plan

Opening/Chalice Lighting   (5 minutes)

Choose *one* of these openings. If you decide to bring readings, it is suggested that participants take turns with this responsibility each week.

- Lighting of chalice and reading.
  Reading: #443 "We Arrive Out of Many Singular Rooms"
  Hymn: #396 "I Know This Rose Will Open"
- Reading of leader's choice.
- Moment of meditation or prayer.

Partner Sharing   (15 minutes)

Ask participants to work with a partner to answer the following questions. Distribute sheets of newsprint, and have each pair write their answers on it to share with the rest of the group.

- What have you learned as a result of participating in these workshops?

- What questions do you still have about homosexuality, bisexuality, transgender identity, homophobia, and heterosexism?

Ask each pair to talk through their answers with the group. Then look over all the lists to identify common themes.

Attitude Continuum   (20 minutes)

Distribute the "Attitude Continuum" handout to participants. Describe the attitude that each step on the continuum represents. Give as many examples as you can think of for each attitude.

Ask participants to mark on the continuum where they were at the beginning of the workshop series. Ask them to identify where they are now. Encourage the group to mark for different groups if necessary. For example, a person might be at a different place on the continuum when answering about transgender people compared to lesbians. Participants may wish to place four marks on the continuum: (B) bisexuals, (G) gay men, (L) lesbians, (T) transgender people.

Ask participants to share their responses with the group, and how they decided to place themselves where they did.

Ask participants to share where on the continuum they would like to be in the future.

Explain that everyone should identify their own place on the continuum without feeling that there are right or wrong places to be. Of course, the workshop series aims to move people toward appreciation of bisexual, gay, lesbian, and/or transgender people and toward taking action against their oppression, but everyone begins in a different place. Everyone will learn and progress at his/hir/her own pace. Moving from actively participating in homophobic actions to ignoring them is as important a change for some people as moving from silent disapproval of homophobic actions to speaking out against them.

Action Continuum   (20 minutes)

Distribute the "Action Continuum" handout. Describe the continuum as a tool to help us think about how our attitudes about homosexuality can be translated into actions. It describes several categories of action, ranging from those that are homophobic to those that are anti-homophobic.

Ask participants to work in pairs to identify where they were on this continuum at the beginning of the workshop series, where they are now, and where they would like to be. Again, participants may wish to do this separately for bisexual people, gay men, lesbians, and/or transgender people.

What Next? (40 minutes)

Ask participants to work in pairs again to identify what the next steps could be in continuing to learn about bisexual, gay, lesbian, and/or transgender people, or to act on their commitment to address their oppression. Tell participants they will have 15 minutes to discuss what these steps could be for them as individuals, for their work in the congregation, and work in the wider community. After 15 minutes, ask participants to re-gather as a large group and report on their conversations.

On three separate sheets of newsprint (one for individual, one for congregational, and one for community) list, without comment, people's responses for each.

When done, ask the group to reflect on these lists and notice common themes. You may wish to spend the last ten minutes before closing agreeing on how to take these steps further and form smaller groups to begin to work on these steps.

Closing/Checkout (20 minutes)

You may wish to have a moment of silence. In a circle, ask participants to take a few minutes to think about the most important things they have learned during the workshop series. You may wish to play some meditational music. Then ask each participant to complete the following sentences and share them with the group:

- The most important thing I learned is . . .
- My next step is . . .

Answer each question separately, going around the circle.

Conclude the series by acknowledging all the hard work and attention participants have contributed. Stress that the workshops have not been easy, and that breaking silence is an important beginning. Note that this series is a beginning, not an end. Unlearning prejudice about any group is a life-long process of discovery and rethinking. Choose one or both of the following to close:

- Unison Reading: #689 by Paul Robeson

  Sorrow will one day turn to joy. All that breaks the heart and oppresses the soul will one day give place to peace and understanding and everyone will be free.

- Hymn: #402 "From You I Receive"

Assignment/Follow-up

Ask participants to keep working and learning and being open to the conversation.

Attitude Continuum

Repulsion—Pity—Tolerance—Acceptance—Support—Appreciation

Repulsion: Bisexual, gay, lesbian, and/or transgender people are sinful, sick, and immoral, and their behavior must not be tolerated in any way.

Pity: Bisexual, gay, lesbian, and/or transgender people are sad because they aren't normal. Why can't they just live as they are? They need our help.

Tolerance: Bisexual, gay, lesbian, and/or transgender people exist and always have. We must tolerate them even if we object to their lifestyle.

Acceptance: Bisexual, gay, lesbian, and/or transgender people are fine as long as they mind their own business, keep to themselves, and don't flaunt their lifestyle or ask for "special privileges" (civil rights, open acknowledgment).

Support: Bisexual, gay, lesbian, and/or transgender people deserve the same rights and respect as everyone else. I still may be uncomfortable, but I believe discrimination against bisexual, gay, lesbian, and/or transgender people is wrong.

Appreciation: Bisexual, gay, lesbian, and/or transgender people are valued members of the community and a valid part of the diversity of our community. My life is enriched because there are openly bisexual, gay, lesbian, and/or transgender people in my community.

Action Continuum

Oppressing—Denying/Ignoring—Recognizing/Not Acting—Recognizing/Acting—Educating Self—Educating Others—Supporting/Encouraging—Initiating/Preventing

Oppressing: Telling gay jokes; avoiding people who are (or might be) bisexual, gay, lesbian, and/or transgender; discouraging the open acceptance of bisexual, gay, lesbian, and/or transgender people; working to prevent the passage of gay-rights laws; participating in harassment of or violence against bisexual, gay, lesbian, and/or transgender people.

Denying/Ignoring: Allowing bisexual, gay, lesbian, and transgender oppression to continue. (This category includes behavior that is not actively anti-gay, but supports anti-gay actions with silent consent by denying or ignoring that such oppression is a problem.)

Recognizing/Not Acting: Recognizing oppression and its harmful effects, but taking no action to stop homophobic behavior, because of fear, lack of information, or confusion about what to do; feeling discomfort with the incongruence between your inner beliefs and your lack of action on these beliefs.

Recognizing/Acting: Recognizing oppression and taking action to stop it. (Though your response may go no further than objecting to homophobic behavior, this is an important step in the transition from silent disapproval of homophobic actions to choosing to speak out against them.)

Educating Self: Taking action to learn more about bisexual, gay, lesbian, and/or transgender people, homophobia, and heterosexism. This includes reading books, attending workshops, participating in discussion groups, joining organizations, and attending bisexual, gay, lesbian, and transgender cultural events. (This category is a prerequisite to the last three, which involve interacting with others about homophobia. To engage others comfortably and confidently, we need to learn more ourselves.)

Educating Others: Rather than only objecting to homophobic behavior, engaging people in dialogue to increase their awareness of bisexual, gay, lesbian, and transgender oppression.

Supporting/Encouraging: Supporting and encouraging others who are speaking out against homophobia, or who are working to be more inclusive of bisexual, gay, lesbian, and/or transgender people.

Initiating/Preventing: Working to change individual and institutional actions that exclude or denigrate people because of their sexual orientation and/or gender identification—for example, planning educational programs; including sexual orientation in institutional non-discrimination statements; explicitly inviting bisexual, gay, lesbian, and/or transgender people to become open and appreciated members of a community.

OTHER PROGRAM IDEAS

This section presents several less strenuous program possibilities that congregations might want to try in place of or in addition to the workshop series. These activities may help reach people who might not sign up for workshops, but would be willing to participate in an activity that demands less time and effort. Although these activities do not require a great deal of advanced planning and preparation, they nonetheless can be very meaningful, enjoyable, and transforming.

Film Series

A wide variety of excellent movies—available on videocassette—address bisexual, gay, lesbian, and transgender themes. Your congregation could offer a series of such films (for example, on the first Friday of every month for four months) with refreshments and a discussion after the viewing. You might preview each film to be shown and prepare discussion questions, or allow discussions to be spontaneous. A complete video bibliography is available from the Office of Bisexual, Gay, Lesbian, and Transgender Concerns (OBGLTC) at the Unitarian Universalist Association and on its Web site at http://www.uua.org/obgltc.

Specific discussion questions for the following films are also available:

Before Stonewall
Desert Hearts
Lianna
The Life and Times of Harvey Milk
A Question of Love
Torch Song Trilogy

Here are some questions which may apply to all the films suggested:

- Did you gain any insights from this film that will help you to better understand or relate to bisexual, gay, lesbian, and/or transgender persons? What are those insights, and how might they affect your attitudes and behavior?
- What in this film did you find particularly helpful, intriguing, or exciting?

- Did anything disturb you about this film? Did you find yourself challenged, perplexed, horrified, angered, scared, uncomfortable, sad? Did you find yourself arguing with the makers of this film?
- Which stereotypes about bisexual, gay, lesbian, and/or transgender people and culture does this film address? Does it challenge or confirm these stereotypes? Does this film help or hurt the cause of sexual and gender minorities?
- How were the bisexual, gay, lesbian, and/or transgender characters portrayed in this film? Were they likable, healthy, humane, decent? How would you feel about having them as your family or friends? Did anything make you uncomfortable about any characters?
- Would you recommend this film to others, particularly in regard to gaining a better understanding of bisexual, gay, lesbian, and transgender issues? If so, why? If not, why not?

Outside Speaker or Panel

Contact a local bisexual, gay, lesbian, and/or transgender organization (or leaders/spokespersons in your area) and ask them to speak at a forum, service, or other program sponsored by your congregation. They could address a variety of themes, including what it's like to be bisexual, gay, lesbian, and/or transgender, similarities and differences between gay and non-gay persons and relationships; the struggle of the bisexual, gay, lesbian, and transgender community; sexual minorities and the law; and AIDS in our community (by no means an exclusively bisexual/gay/lesbian issue).

Discussion Workshop

Form a group of heterosexual, homosexual, bisexual, and/or transgender members of the congregation or community (fairly well balanced between bisexual, gay, lesbian, straight, and transgender) to plan a two-hour workshop. Each could briefly speak on ways to increase our understanding and acceptance of one another. Some may share personal stories about moving toward self-acceptance, and acceptance of those who differ from them. You could also do one in regards to gender.

The planning group should meet several times to share what they have prepared for the workshop and to deal with the issues and emotions that arise in the group. Several groups that have tried such a program report that the process of preparing the workshop together was as rewarding as the actual discussion. By including both gay and straight participants, this program becomes safe and welcoming for all members of the congregation.

Workshop on Family Issues

Everybody has a family of some sort—birth families, families we create with our spouse or lover, and chosen or extended families of friends and other loved ones. Form a diverse group of people including bisexual, gay, heterosexual, lesbian, and/or transgender persons if possible to plan a workshop on family issues. The group might include a therapist, psychologist, or social worker who could address issues of human intimacy, commitment, and conflict. People could share the stories of their families to increase understanding and acceptance of the different kinds of families we build and cherish.

4 x 4 x 4

This deceptively simple idea comes from the Reverend Pete Tolleson of Swannanea, NC. Form groups of four straight persons together with four gay persons who agree to meet four times (4 x 4 x 4). There is no specific agenda for each meeting, other than to get to know, understand, and appreciate one another. Such meetings might be combined with dinner to make them more fun and less threatening to those who are nervous about meeting people different from themselves; food can be a great social lubricant. Where 4 x 4 x 4 programs have been held, people have reported their delight in participating, and have been surprised by how much they have learned.

Some congregations have enough bisexual, gay, lesbian, and/or transgender members to form such groups. In other communities, a congregation may have to contact local bisexual, gay, lesbian, and transgender groups to see if they can find people interested in participating.

An AIDS Program

The bisexual, gay, lesbian, and transgender community has been deeply affected by the AIDS epidemic. A program dealing with AIDS can help pull people together in a common effort at understanding. Your congregation could offer a wide variety of educational or outreach programs, including a medical update from a physician familiar with the disease, a speaker or panel of persons living with AIDS/HIV, a speaker or panel discussing the opportunities for getting involved in battling the disease in your community, a videotape program to foster greater understanding and compassion (for example, *Common Threads*, available through the Video Loan Library, (716) 229-5325), or a dinner for persons with AIDS in your community. The possibilities are limited only by your imagination and energy.

A Potluck Dinner and Dance for Everyone

Your congregation could sponsor a potluck dinner and dance and explicitly invite people of all sexual orientations. This event would provide a social occasion for people of all sexual orientations and gender identifications to interact and would be a safe place for men to dance with men, women with women, and women with men. An invitation could be extended to local bisexual, gay, lesbian, and transgender community organizations, who might help publicize, organize, and sponsor the event.

A Worship Service

A group of people from your congregation (possibly with input and participation from individuals from your local bisexual, gay, lesbian, and transgender community) could create a worship service focused on the theme of affirming bisexual, gay, lesbian, and/or transgender persons. Individuals could share what they have learned from their participation in the Welcoming Congregation Program, as well as personal stories and testimonies. You might want to ask your minister(s) to have a role in the service, offering his or her support to the goals of the Welcoming Congregation Program. It is important that the service itself be inclusive—with people of differing sexual orientations (including heterosexual) and/or gender identities participating in the service.

CHRISTIAN PERSPECTIVES

The materials in this section were compiled by a group of Unitarian Universalist Christians. The healing, communion, and union services that follow are not written specifically for bisexual, gay, lesbian, and/or transgender parishioners—there is no special service for such. These inclusive prayers and services focus on people relating to one another and to a community.

Unitarian Universalist Christians
Reverend Terry Burke

The roughly 20 percent of Unitarian Universalists who call themselves Christian are an extremely diverse group. Even as a past president of the UU Christian Fellowship, I cannot speak *for* Unitarian Universalist Christians or their congregations. However, I can attempt to speak *to* them.

My congregation's bond of fellowship is a version of the Ames Covenant: "In the love of truth and the spirit of Jesus, we unite for the worship of God and the service of humanity." That "spirit of Jesus" means many things to different people, but to me it speaks of the Kingdom or Reign of God that Jesus preached, a reign where sin, oppression, sickness, and death are overcome by God's saving, healing wholeness, a reign embodied in the resurrection.

I was baptized at King's Chapel on All Saints' Day in 1981. Part of my own profession of faith was, "In Christ there is neither male nor female, rich nor poor, black nor white, straight nor gay, young nor old, all are one." I believe that we are all people of God, all part of the body of Christ. We need to live that belief by working for greater connection and equality in the here and now.

Each church is a place where people try to learn how to remember God's love and do the justice of God's reign. We cannot love our neighbor in the abstract, only as a particular individual. We cannot seek greater connection with a hypothetical neighbor, but we can connect with a Samaritan, a Russian, or a Salvadoran. We *can* welcome the middle-aged black man, the working-class lesbian, and the disabled elder who come through our door.

As an all-too human institution, the Church has many sins that need healing, including sins of racism, sexism, classism, and heterosexism. The Church must especially confess that its teachings have been used as weighted truncheons in the oppression of same-sex relationships. In any consideration of biblical passages, we need to recognize new scholarship done in recent years that puts Scripture in a different light. Jesus Christ was not a "family man" of conventional social morality, nor do any of his recorded sayings refer to same-sex relationships.

The Church's attitude toward sexuality was formed by its imminent view of the End Time, and by the brutal and violent forms of sexuality in late Greco-Roman antiquity. However, I believe that sexuality in our time can be an important part of Christian spirituality. Through our sexuality we can be co-creators with God: co-creators of love, children, and of healing joy.

May our congregations and the Church confess its brokenness. May we reach out in welcoming neighborliness to our bisexual, gay, lesbian, and/or transgender brothers and sisters. In the Spirit of Jesus, may we learn how to be Christian ministers of reconciliation: to one another, to our communities of faith, and to all the people of God.

God's Love
Reverend Wendy Fitting

I was raised Unitarian Universalist, so my early experiences of Christianity were not so hurtful as have been those for too many of my lesbian and gay sisters and brothers. Learning about Christianity in church school was an experience of invitation for me and for a number of years I have enjoyed a deepening relationship with the teachings of Jesus. To me, the heart of this message is the great commandment, "Love one another as I have loved you." In a fundamentally Christian culture, one that rejects me for having the audacity and integrity to love according to my nature, I find an alternative meaning and an affirmation in the scriptural message that as I am, I am loved.

Lesbian feminist Sally Gearhart writes, "I think to love myself in a society that does not want me to do so is miraculous." The heart of the gospel is the proclamation of the good news of God's love for the faithful, regardless of their social position. In fact, the best news of the gospel is the proclamation of the power of God's love to draw into community those who have been cast out, to release the bonds of those held captive in prisons of stone, silence, fear, or hatred. To reclaim the meaning of the great commandment is to refuse to give Jesus over to those who would use him as an agent of hatred.

I reject that "Christianity" that engenders and promotes shame and self-hatred. I embrace a Christianity that affirms my worth and teaches me to live gently and intelligently as a participant in creation. What the cultures deny us, the gospel affirms: You are loved and accepted, not because of what you have learned or accomplished, but in all the imperfect completeness of your humanity. In this faith, love comes alive among us all. For enrichment, for comfort, and for celebration, I reclaim God's love for me. Finding renewed courage in deepening faith, I offer that love in the world.

How Can You Be a Lesbian and a Christian?

Occasionally, I am asked how, as a lesbian, I am able to consider myself a Christian. This question often reflects the perspective that Christianity and homosexuality are incompatible states of being, and is generally accompanied by one of two conflicting viewpoints. The first sees bisexual, gay, lesbian, and/or transgender people as intrinsically abhorrent to a Christian sensibility. According to this view, inclusion of such persons harms Christianity. The second view holds Christianity and homosexuality as incompatible because of the way the Church has harmed bisexual, gay, lesbian, and/or transgender people. My view is that these positions are not mutually exclusive.

Like many bisexual, gay, lesbian, and/or transgender Unitarian Universalists, I was raised in an orthodox religious community that invalidated my creation as a homosexual person and condemned my attempts to grow and to relate honestly within my religious community. As a result, my first coming out—to myself—was full of the fear, shame, and loss often felt by victims of social/religious heterosexism. In pain, rage, and confusion, I became an exile, as willing to reject as I had been rejected. Unknowingly, I had also relinquished the power of the vitally inclusive affirmation so central to the ministry and message of Jesus. The process of coming to name myself both lesbian *and* Christian is a process of reclaiming that affirmation and that power.

Jesus stood in opposition to the Spiritless theologies of his time; he gathered to him and honored the full humanity and integrity of those whom the hypocritical social order had marginalized. His vision of community was radically inclusive. Yet among the greatest "victories" and sins of traditional Christian theology is the effectiveness with which bisexual, gay, lesbian, and/or transgender people have been convinced that there is no place for us in the Christian community. That is a lie. There is a place for us. Regardless of sexual orientation, gender identification, age, ability, or color, we are "all one in Christ Jesus" (Galatians 3:28). Without the full and valued participation of bisexual, gay, lesbian, and/or transgender people, the Christian community is incomplete.

Unitarian Universalism has offered me reinterpretations and new understandings of religious concepts, symbols, and meanings. From my struggles with my church of origin have emerged the convictions that the dictates of conscience supersede those of dogma, that reason occupies a place alongside revelation, and that genuine inclusion is the hallmark of a truly religious community. Through involvement in Unitarian Universalist communities, the pain of earlier rejection healed, and I experienced a reawakening of my spiritual heritage. I heard, in the biblical message, an invitation to become an active co-creator of the justice I had envisioned, rather than simply reacting to its absence.

While much in the Christian tradition affirms the religious heritage by which we are called to empower justice and healing, it also contains dangerous perversions that result in continued exclusion. We must not abdicate our voices to theologies of oppression and hate.

As a *Unitarian Universalist* Christian, I acknowledge my commitment to the liberating witness of the religion *of* Jesus, rather than the heterosexist doctrines of the religion *about* Jesus. Along with many other Unitarian Universalist Christians of every sexual orientation, I continue to reject heterosexist and other exclusionary theologies as antithetical to the central message of

Christianity. As reflected in the life and teachings of Jesus, that message affirms and celebrates the fullness of my creation and offers me the comfort and challenge of God's love in communities that care about us all.

A Theological Statement
Reverend Harry H. Hoehler

Christian community, as Henri Nouwen says, "embraces *all* people, whatever their individual differences may be, and allows them to live together as brothers and sisters of Christ and sons and daughters of God."

To "live together as brothers and sisters of Christ"! What does this imply for the most intimate of our human relationships? For those of us who take discipleship to Christ with utmost seriousness, it entails more than loving one's neighbor as oneself, in the sense of willing the good or the welfare of one's neighbor. Rather, it means a willingness to lose oneself in the other to find oneself. It means a willingness to lay down one's life for the other in love. It means a willingness to become, as best as one is able, a channel of God's self-giving love for the sake of the other.

What is the nature of this love? The apostle Paul describes its qualities in his peerless hymn in 1 Corinthians 13. He speaks of a love that "is patient and kind, not jealous or boastful, not arrogant or rude, does not strive for its own advantage, is neither irritable nor resentful, does not rejoice in wrong but rejoices in the truth," a love that "bears all things, believes all things, hopes all things," a love that "never ends."

Granted, Paul is writing of the love that unites people in the bonds of Christian community. But don't these words also serve as criteria for defining the love that frames our most profound person-to-person relationships? A love freely bestowed, a love that says "yes" to the other, a love that does not subordinate the other, a love equally shared and born of the promise of never-ending faithfulness. A love, to follow Paul's thought, that has its ultimate source and empowerment in "the love that God has for us and pours into our hearts through the Holy Spirit who has been given to us" (Romans 5:5).

Surely such love, whenever or wherever found, is worthy of human praise. Surely such love makes valid same-gender as well as heterosexual unions.

What Does the Bible Say?
Marianne McCarthy Power

Some clergy and scholars have long held that scriptural translations and interpretations uphold moral and legal injunctions against same-sex relationships. However, recent biblical scholarship calls these traditional views into question.

In the area of translation, George R. Edwards notes, in his article "Moral Decisions in Bible Translation" that "translators of the RSV [Revised Standard Edition of the Bible] took a decisive step forward by removing the word 'sodomite' from the five passages where it had been used in the American Standard Version and the King James Version. . . . By deleting 'sodomites' in these texts, translators question the widespread illusion that 'homosexual' means 'sodomite' and that 'sodomite' means 'homosexual.' While the translators cannot effectively overturn this familiar assumption merely by eliminating 'sodomite' from the Old Testament, a definite forward step has been taken, and the occasion for more intelligent moral understanding has been created."

In the Hebrew Bible, in Genesis 19:4-11, the story of Sodom and Gomorrah has largely been interpreted as an example of God's condemnation of homosexuality. The word "sodomy" is itself derived from this passage. However, some biblical scholars have asserted that this passage, with its violent overtones, is about the exploitation of visitors and gang rape, rather than a general condemnation of homosexuality and homosexual behavior. The real sin of Sodom, it has been argued, was a lack of hospitality toward strangers. Writing in *Engage/Social Action*, Joseph Weber has noted, "It is questionable whether the sin in this story is 'sodomy' at all. The word 'know' in Hebrew in verse 5 [of this passage] appears 943 times in the Old Testament. Only 10 times does it refer to sexual intercourse, and in each of these cases it means heterosexual intercourse. . . . There is no evidence that Sodom's sin was homosexuality. In every other passage of the Bible referring to Sodom, the sins condemned are vain sacrifices, pride, and inhospitality. Even if the men of Sodom intended homosexual acts against the angels, the passage could only serve as a condemnation of homosexual rape."

These texts refer to same-sex relationships as "an abomination." It is important to understand the context in which the term occurs. L. Robert Arthur, in *Homosexuality and the Conservative Christian*, writes, "There are those who try to see in the word 'abomination' a reference to homosexual activity. However, a brief word study will show us quite otherwise. This Hebrew word, 'to`ebah' is found frequently in the Old Testament. If one were to read it in the context of every place it occurs, one would find it is always connected to or synonymous with idolatry."

Letha Scanzoni and Virginia Mollenkott, authors of *Is the Homosexual My Neighbor? Another Christian View,* have also noted that these verses represent part of Israel's Holiness Code, which prohibited other behaviors associated with pagan nations and cults viewed as idolatrous. Thus, it is plausible that the "abomination" referred to in this context is not homosexual behavior, but idolatry.

The prohibition in this passage is also currently understood as emerging from a pre-scientific understanding of male semen as containing "the whole of nascent life," as Walter Wink writes in *The Christian Century;* "hence the spilling of semen for any non-procreative purpose" undermined the Israelites' attempts to populate their outnumbered tribe. In addition, the impact of gender roles is evident. Arthur writes, "The Hebrews believed that men were created in the image of God, and that the earthly likeness of God must be treated with the same awe and respect as one would treat God. However, since they believed women were created in the image of men, they were one step removed from God, and not deserving of the same respect. . . . If a man were to treat another man in the same manner as he was free to treat women, that would be degrading the image of God to a mere possession, as women were. This would be a direct affront to God—God's image, the man. So to 'lie with a man as with a woman' was a blasphemous action degrading God to a mere possession."

Many scholars understand these passages as a condemnation of a variety of practices of pagan cult worship, including ritual male heterosexual and homosexual prostitution, rather than a condemnation of homosexuality or homosexual behavior in general. According to Hebrew Law, Wink writes, "the unique claim of one God over his [sic] people is denied" by such activity, because in the cults "such an act is infused with a sacral/mystical quality that is supposed to relate the persons involved to some form of Divine power." It appears likely that these texts refer to the removal of aspects of Canaanite fertility cults that had infiltrated Jewish worship.

The New Testament has also been re-examined. One studied passage is Romans 1:26-27, part of a larger component that encompasses Romans 1:18-3:20. Some interpreters feel that these two verses must be taken in the context of the entire chapter of Romans. In this context, according to Scanzoni and Mollenkott, Paul "shows how sin has alienated *all* people from God," both Jews and Gentiles. "The point of Romans, then, is not to set apart some category of persons as the worst kind of sinners possible." The relationship between homosexual behavior and idolatry evident in the Old Testament is also evident at several points in the writings of Paul (see below). The condemnation in these passages is of "a desire to avoid acknowledgment of God. . . . The emphasis is "entirely on sexual activity in a context of lust and idolatry" as understood within the social context of the era, rather than of homosexuality or homosexual behavior.

Other New Testament passages under scrutiny are 1 Corinthians 6:9 and 1 Timothy 1:10. According to Weber, the "question being dealt with [in these passages] is not homosexuality *per se,* but the kinds of action that exclude people from the kingdom of God. . . . What these acts have in common is that they either deny the sovereignty of God or do harm to one's neighbor. They are not evil in their very being, apart from their consequences. They are unrighteous because of what they do, namely, deny God as creator or harm fellow human beings. . . . Neither of these texts can serve to support condemnation of homosexuality in all its degrees and manifestations."

Interpretations of these two passages have also proven problematic due to the translations of the terms *arsenokoites* and *malakoi.*

Malakoi, translated as "effeminate" or "catamite" by many English versions of the Bible, "rarely connotes any sexual meaning. . . . It basically means 'soft.' But when applied to people, it usually means 'gutless.' Someone who will not stand up for what is right [is viewed as] certainly not fit for the Kingdom of God (e.g., Luke 7:62). This understanding of 'malakoi' certainly fits much better with Pauline theology than any homosexual meaning. Paul was continually urging his converts to stand for the truth, no matter what the cost. (Phillipians 1:19-30)." *Arsenokoites,* which has been translated as meaning same-sex relations between males, has also been linked to the term *godesh,* found in the Deuteronomic texts, in the context of cult prostitution. Thus, the reference is more properly to idolatry, not homosexuality.

As this brief survey indicates, translation and interpretation are integrally related. Other crucial areas of consideration are the social, political, and theological contexts from which the Scriptures emerged.

In light of these and other studies of the Scriptures, it appears that the Hebrew Bible and New Testament condemn certain specific kinds of same-sex practices rather than generally condemning homosexuality or homosexual relationships. Obvious heterosexual parallels are the commandments against lust ("thou shalt not covet thy neighbor's wife") and adultery—condemnations of certain kinds of heterosexual activity and not heterosexuality in general.

Thus, many theologians currently challenge the traditional use of these and other biblical texts to support a general condemnation and exclusion of bisexual, gay, lesbian, and/or transgender persons from the full acceptance and love of the Christian Church. As Weber writes, "Christian ethics, if it is based upon the fullness of God's word, cannot condemn homosexuality in all of its forms and expressions in an absolute manner, but must examine the use made by a person of his or her sexuality in relationship to the sovereignty of God and the good of fellow human beings."

According to Edwards, those ethics call us to return to the true mission of the Christian Church: "To proclaim the gospel of freedom and love in Jesus which is not compromised by requirements based on race, nationality, class, gender, or sexual orientation."

Prayers and Readings

A Prayer
Reverend Terry Burke

O loving God,
we give thanks for gathering today in this community,
in this faithful body.
We give thanks for gathering in the Spirit of Jesus.
We remember Jesus,
who lived and embodied God's love and forgiveness,
and who issued a call to the healing and transforming Kingdom of God's Reign.
As individuals and as a community,
may we embody that love of God,
that Spirit of Jesus.
May we embody God's creative Spirit as we create through our work,
as we create the lives of children,
as we create justice,
and as we create healing love.
May we create with our hands and our bodies.
May our hands be God's hands;
may our bodies be part of Christ's body.
Through our bodies may we know God's peace,
God's passion,
and God's joy.
With our bodies may we bless,
may we give thanks,
and may we praise God.
Through our divinely created sexuality may we know
that physical closeness and graceful intimate
touch which gives us a glimpse of God our Lover,
a God who spoke through the prophet Isaiah the words,
"When you pass through the waters, I will be with you;
and through rivers, they shall not overwhelm you;
when you walk through fire, you shall not be burned,
and the fire shall not consume you . . . because
you are precious and honored and I love you."
May our knowledge of the love of God
help us to be willing to risk loving our brothers and sisters.
As people of a loving God,
part of the varied body of Christ,
may we know that we are one people—
whether lesbian, straight, or gay;
elderly, middle-aged, or young;
Asian, African-American, or white;
man, woman, or child.
May we know that we are all connected and all part of God's healing reign,
a reign that ultimately triumphs over sin, sickness, injustice, and death.
Help us by our shared love to be part of the birthing of that divine reign.
In the spirit of Jesus we pray.
Amen.

Homosexual
Frederick Buechner

One of the many ways that we are attracted to each other is sexually. We want to touch and be touched. We want to give and receive pleasure with our bodies. We want to know each other in our full nakedness, which is to say in our full humanness, and in the moment of passion to become one with each other. Whether it is our own gender or the other that we are chiefly attracted to seems a secondary matter. There is a female element in every male just as there is a male element in every female, and most people if they're honest will acknowledge having been at one time or another attracted to both.

To say that morally, spiritually, and humanly, homosexuality is always bad seems as absurd as to say that in the same terms heterosexuality is always good, or the other way round. It is not the object of our sexuality that determines its value but the inner nature of our sexuality. If (a) it is as raw as the coupling of animals, at its worst it demeans us and at its best still leaves our deepest hunger for each other unsatisfied. If (b) it involves some measure of kindness, understanding, and affection as well as desire, it can become an expression of human love in its fullness and can thus help to complete us as humans. Whatever our sexual preference happens to be, both of these possibilities are always there. It's not whom you go to bed with or what you do when you get there that matters so much. It's what besides sex you are asking to receive, and what besides sex you are offering to give.

Here and there the Bible condemns homosexuality in the sense of (a), just as under the headings of adultery and fornication it also condemns heterosexuality in the sense of (a). On the subject of homosexuality in the sense of (b), it is as silent as it is on the subject of sexuality generally in the sense of (b). The great commandment is that we are to love one another—responsibly, faithfully, joyfully—and presumably the biblical view is implied in that.

Beyond that, "Love is strong as death," sings Solomon in his song. "Many waters cannot quench love, neither can floods drown it" (Song of Solomon 8:6-7). Whoever you are and whomever you desire, the passion of those lines is something you are quick to recognize.

Sex
Frederick Buechner

Contrary to Mrs. Grundy, sex is not sin. Contrary to Hugh Hefner, it's not salvation either. Like nitroglycerin, it can be used either to blow up bridges or heal hearts.

At its roots, the hunger for food is the hunger for survival. At its roots, the hunger to know a person sexually is the hunger to know and be known by that person humanly. Food without nourishment doesn't fit the bill for long, and neither does sex without humanness.

Adultery, promiscuity either heterosexual or homosexual, masturbation less as an expedient than as an escape—one appealing view is that anything goes as long as nobody gets hurt. The trouble is that human beings are so hopelessly psychosomatic in composition that whatever happens to the *soma* happens also to the *psyche*, and vice versa.

The lonely orgasms of Portnoy, the discreet adulteries of suburbia, the proud promiscuities of the commune, the self-conscious seductions of the boys in the band—who is to say who gets hurt and who doesn't get hurt, and how? Maybe the injuries are all internal. Maybe it will be years before the X-rays show up anything. Maybe the only person who gets hurt is you.

In practice, Jesus was notoriously soft on sexual misbehavior. Some of his best friends were chippies. He saved the woman taken in adultery from stoning. He didn't tell the woman at the well that she ought to marry the man she was living with. Possibly he found their fresh-faced sensualities closer to loving God and man than the thin-lipped pieties of the Pharisees. Certainly he shared the Old Testament view that the body in all its manifestations was basically good because a good God made it.

But he also had some hard words to say about lust (Matthew 5:27-28) and told the adulterous woman to go and sin no more. When the force of a person's sexuality is centrifugal, pushing farther and farther away as *psyches* the very ones being embraced as *somas*, this sexuality is of the Devil. When it is centripetal, it is of God.

Excerpts from *Embracing the Exile*
John Fortunato

This long reading may be presented by two or more people, if desired.

Reader: When I moved to Washington, having had to grieve the loss of a four-year lover all by myself in the wilds of southern Maryland, I was resolved never to be in the closet again. So when I took a job, I planned to be out. And I was. I started slowly, coming out to only a few people. But by the time I left that job, everyone knew. And few cared. It was a pleasant surprise. I thought I was safe.

Wayne's and my relationship deepened, blossomed. We knew we had found something special. We were awed by it. We recognized it as a gift—from God. It was a healing time.

Our church community at the Episcopal church of St. Stephen and the Incarnation in Washington, DC, a kind of crazy, renegade, progressive parish at that time, embraced our love for each other. They wanted to literally *celebrate* it with us. A service, a union, a covenant, a marriage. Nobody knew what to call it. But it was to be a time of lifting something special up, blessing it, and publicly affirming it. That's when the trouble started.

Reader: With tremendous naivete, we greeted the larger Christian community. Our sisters and brothers of the faith—and many outside of it—listened but didn't respond quite the way we expected. The planned service got a lot of press, something we neither expected nor desired. We thought this was just going to be a service for our community.

The publicity opened up a hornet's nest of hate. Hate mail and obscene phone calls, condemnation by a conclave of bishops and tirades from a few theologians. I was called everything from a corrupter of children to an abomination; psychotic, a deviant, an aberration—and worse! The local bishops declared *ex cathedra* that the planned service would bring ridicule and disgrace on the Episcopal church and forbade it to take place, threatening this and that if it did. I lost my job. My family abandoned me. And it soon became clear that there was a substantial silent minority of our parish community that hadn't liked the idea of who I was, who *we* were, or what we were doing, at all. They left.

All in all, short of physical violence, all of my worst fears during all of those years in a closet came true. It was awful.

The service did take place—somewhere else. And I suppose it was wonderful, as services being held under siege go. I was too much in shock by then to really be there. The joy had been pretty well laced with bitter herbs.

Reader: The publicity and notoriety went on for some time; television appearances, radio, newspaper features, speaking engagements. I had become what is called in the gay community *a professional faggot*. But through all the hype, I felt myself withdrawing. I wanted out. It was all crazy.

I remember one night in particular. I got up in the middle of the night, leaving Wayne in bed. I went and sat in the dark in the living room, smoked too many cigarettes, and rocked in the recliner, and I meditated, I guess you'd say. I pondered the whole mess in my heart of hearts.

It all welled up. All the doubt, the pain, the outrage, the hostility and hate, the rejection. All of my brokenness. I sat and rocked and cried and raged. And I waited. Waited for something. Some insight. Some revelation. Something to help me get out of the mess I was in. I think I rocked a long time.

Slowly it all began to drift away—all of the insanity, all of the pain—I kind of went numb. And then I had a vision. I know, that's crazy. "Woogie," as a friend of mine would say. It was all my imagination, right? Well, maybe it was, but I had a vision. I imagined something.

I imagined I was sitting there and God was sitting there, too, on the couch right in front of me. It was very peaceful and dark. But I could see him. He was bright. We were talking.

I was saying, "You know, sometimes I think they're right, that being gay and loving a man is wrong." God smiled and said quietly, "How can love be wrong? It all comes from me."

Reader: But I was a wreck, you'll remember. It was going to take more than that. "Sometimes, I just want to bury that part of me," I said, "just pretend it isn't real." "But I made you whole," God replied. "You are one as I am one. I made you in my image." I knew he was trying to soothe me, but I had just been through four months of good Christian folk trying to cram down my throat that I was an abomination, so all this acceptance was just getting me very frustrated. So I tried again. "*Your* church out there says that you don't love me. They

say that I'm lost, damned to hell." "You're my son," God said in a way both gentle and yet so firm that there could be no doubt of his genuineness. "Nothing can separate you from my love. I redeemed you before the beginning of time. In my Father's house, there's a mansion waiting just for you." I started to fill up. "What do I do with all this?" I asked, weeping now and clenching my teeth—at my wit's end trying to have it all make sense. "What do I do with *them*?" And in the same calm voice, God said, "I've given you gifts. Share them. I've given you light. Brighten the world. I empower you with my love. Love them."

Reader: That did it. After all I had been through, I had had it with sweet words. Who was he trying to kid? I pounded my fist in exasperation and cried, "*Love* them? What are you trying to do to me? Can't you see? They call my light darkness! They call my love perverted! They call my gifts corruptions! What the hell are you asking me to do?"

My words echoed in the silence. My breath stopped. It felt vaguely like eleven years before when I had lain on a football field at Milton Academy and cursed the God who sat before me. Only now it was different. Now he was *here*. Now I believed. God, was I scared.

There was silence. God didn't move a muscle, though his gaze was much more intense. And with a voice filled with compassion, a voice that enveloped me with its love, God spoke.

"Love them anyway," he said. "Love them anyway."

Reader: "Love them anyway?" I moaned. "But how?"

"You begin by just being who you are," God said, "a loving, caring, whole person created in my image, whose special light of love happens to shine on men, as I intended for you."

"Is that all?" I asked fearfully.

God shook his head. "No, you must also speak your pain and affirm the wholeness I've made you to be when they assail it. You must protest when you are treated as less than a child of mine."

"Is there more?" I asked.

"Yes," God said gently, "and this is the hardest part of all. You must go out and teach them. Help them to know of their dependence on me for all that they really are, and of their helplessness without me. Teach them that their ways are not my ways, and that the world of their imagining is not the world I have made. Help them to see that all creation is one as I am one, and that all I create I redeem. And assure them by word and work and example that my love is boundless, and that I am with them always."

Reader: "You know they won't listen to me," I said with resignation. "They'll despise me. They'll call me a heretic and laugh me to scorn. They'll persecute and torment me. They'll try to destroy me. You know they will, don't you."

The radiant face saddened. And then God said softly, "O yes. I know. How well I know."

I heard his words and something irrevocable changed in me. I went numb. Now I knew. Now I understood. And it was as though large chunks of who I had been began falling away, tumbling through time and space into eternity. I just let them fall. No fear now. No resistance. No sense of loss. All that was dropping away was unnecessary now. Extraneous.

I began to feel light and warm. Energy began to surge through my whole being, enlivening me, as though I were a rusty old turbine that had been charged up and was starting to hum.

Then two strong, motherly arms reached out and drew me close to the bosom of all that is. And I was just there. Just being. Enveloped in being.

And we wept.

For joy.

An Excerpt from *Our Passion for Justice*
Carter Heyward

This excerpt may be presented by two or more readers.

Reader: Recalling my past, I can see now that coming out has been a long and puzzling journey out of the heterosexual box, in which I was no more comfortable at age five than I am now. The experience is hardly rare, as we are coming to know from testimonies of women and men who, when they were girls and boys, were continually reminded that anatomy is destiny and that sex-role expectations are not to be evaded. My own parents made no conscious attempt to teach me rigid sex roles, yet both they and I lived in the heterosexual box that was far larger, and more deeply formative, than either they or their children could realize. Accordingly, I experienced the larger social order as squeezing something out of me, pressing something in on me, and eventually depressing into me feelings of shame about wanting to do things and be things that "weren't for girls."

Reader: Why did I want to be Superman and not Lois Lane? Matt Dillon and not Miss Kitty? Because Superman and Matt Dillon were more interesting to me. They led exciting lives. They made things happen. They were confident, assertive, energetic. Somewhere inside I knew (and knew rightly) that unless I felt myself to be an interesting, confident, and assertive person, completely capable of exerting as much will and leadership as the next person, I could never really love, or allow myself to be loved, by anyone. Not mutually. Not really. I knew also that any effort I might make on behalf of justice would be triggered by my own lack of self-esteem and by the painful inclination to identify with the underdog, rather than by the human *and sexual* impulse to work for justice on the basis of a strong confidence both in myself and in the power of God to love.

For many women, and I am one, coming out means that we are beginning to value ourselves and our sisters as highly as we have been taught to value men. Coming out means loving women, not hating men. Coming out means beginning to feel the same attraction, warmth, tenderness, desire to touch and be touched by women as we have learned to feel in relation to men.

Reader: For many years I have been coming out sexually, experiencing my attraction to women as well as men to be a valuable dimension of myself—as friend, lover, Christian.

I am a teacher in a seminary in which both women and gay/lesbian people have to struggle fiercely to keep themselves from being squeezed into the heterosexual box in which women must submit, and gay/lesbian people must repent. I am a priest in a church which, like most churches, threatens to collapse under the weight of a perverse notion of a sexuality that is to be neither celebrated nor related to other issues of love and justice. I am a woman in a church and a society that patronize women with reminders of how far we have come and of how much we have been given. And I am a lesbian—a woman who has come out of the heterosexual box and into another box, which, as boxes go, is far superior for my life as a responsible person, a Christian woman, in this world at this time.

Coming out, I come into the realization of myself as best able to relate most intimately—to touch and be touched most deeply, to give and receive most naturally, to empower and be empowered most remarkably, to express everything I most value: God in human life, God in justice,

God in passion, God as love—in sexual relationship to a lover who is female.

Reader: Coming out, there are things lost: the likelihood of bearing my own children and learning how to live better with male lovers. But the gain outweighs the loss. Coming out, I begin to envision and embrace the children of the world as my own and the men of the world as my brothers, whom I can better learn to know and love as friends. Coming out involves a recognition of the co-creative power I have always experienced in relation to women. Coming out is a confession that I need and want intimacy with someone whose values and ways of being in the world can support and be supported by my own. Coming out means realizing and cherishing my parents' way of loving and being in the world, of valuing who they have been and who they are, and of knowing myself both as bound to them and separate from them in my journeying. Coming out means remembering my other relatives and early friends in the hope that they can trust and celebrate the parts we have played in the shaping of one another's values.

Reader: Coming out is a protest against social structures that are built on alienation between men and women, women and women, men and men. Coming out is the most radical, deeply personal and consciously political affirmation I can make on behalf of the possibilities of love and justice in the social order. Coming out is moving into relation with peers. It is not simply a way of being in bed, but rather a way of being in the world. To the extent that it invites voyeurism, coming out is an invitation to look and see and consider the value of mutuality in human life. Coming out is simultaneously a political movement and the mighty rush of God's Spirit carrying us on.

Coming out, I stake my sexual identity on the claim that I hold to be the gospel at its heart: that we are here to love God and our neighbors as ourselves. Each of us must find her or his own way to the realization of this claim. I have given you a glimpse into my way. Where the journey began, where it will end, I do not know.

Biblical Readings

From the Hebrew Bible

- Ruth 1:1-18: The story of Naomi and Ruth.

- Deuteronomy 6:4-9: The Shema.

- Isaiah 25:6-8: Salvation for all people.

- Isaiah 43:1-2, 4a: "When you pass through the waters, I shall be with you."

- Exodus 22:21 and Leviticus 19:33: "You shall not oppress the stranger."

From the New Testament

- Matthew 22:34-40, Mark 12:28-34, Luke 10:25-28: The great commandment.

- Matthew 25:34-40: "As you have done these for the least of my brethren, you have done it for me."

- Luke 10:29-37: The good Samaritan.

- Luke 12:57: "Why do you not judge for yourselves what is right?"

- John 4:7-29: The woman at the well.

- John 8:2-11: The woman caught in adultery.

- John 13:1-20: Washing of the disciples' feet.

- John 15:12-17: Love one another.

- Matthew 9:9-11, 10:3, 21:3, Mark 2:14-16, Luke 5:29-30, 7:34: Jesus, friend of the outcast.

- Acts 10:1-20: The conversion of Cornelius.

- Acts 8:26-39: Conversion of the Ethiopian eunuch and baptism.

- Galatians 3:28: "We are all one in Christ Jesus."

- 1st John 2:7-11: The test of love.

- 1st John 3:11-17: Love in action.

- 1st John 4:7-21: The source of love.

- Romans 8:34-39: "Nothing can separate us from the love of Christ."

Services

Communion Service

Exhortation

Dearly beloved, we have received it that Jesus, on the night before he died, as he supped with his disciples in an upper chamber, took bread and broke it, likening it unto his crucified body, and poured out wine as a visible parable of the shedding of his blood. As we repeat this act in remembrance of him, may the spirit which kept him steadfast, even unto death, be quickened in us. We remember also that the bread and wine have been to Christians in all ages a sign of their fellowship with him and with one another; a source of strength; a witness to the power of sacrificial love. Conscious of the weakness of our own hearts and of the needs of our fellow people, let us here renew our communion with him and with all faithful servants of God who have found strength and joy in doing the will of God upon the earth.

Invocation

Eternal and loving God, unto whom all hearts are open, all desires known, and from whom no secrets are hid, cleanse the thoughts of our hearts by the inspiration of thy holy Spirit, that we may perfectly love thee, and by loving one another, worthily magnify thy holy name.

Confession

We come not into thy presence, most holy God, trusting in our own righteousness, but in thy manifold and abiding mercies. Remembering this day the great heart and passion of a son of humanity of long ago, we are ashamed of our selfishness and our misdeeds. We would here be turned to the way of his brave and tender spirit, and find that wholeness of life which shall be at once a divine blessing for us and a divine ministry from us. Forgive our failures and shortcomings, and by thy grace strengthen our faint-hearted desires for goodness, that we may henceforth serve thee by following the example of Jesus with courage and without shame, all the days of our lives. Amen.

Minister: May God Almighty have mercy upon you, forgive your sins, and bring you to everlasting life.

People: Amen.

People: May God Almighty have mercy upon you, forgive your sins, and bring you to everlasting life.

Minister: Amen.

Blessing of the Bread and Wine

Minister: Blessed are you, O God, who brings forth bread from the good earth.

People: May it become for us the bread of life eternal.

Minister: Blessed are you, O God, who brings forth the fruit of the vine.

People: May it become in us the spirit of Jesus, the peace of God.

Minister: Bless and sanctify with your holy Spirit, O God, these people through the gifts of bread and wine, that the spirit of Jesus may live in us, and we in him, in communion with you. Amen.

Words of Institution

The same night in which he was betrayed, Jesus took bread; and when he had given thanks, he broke it, and said: "This is my body which is broken for you. Do this in remembrance of me."

(The bread is passed.)

Take and eat in remembrance of Jesus.

After the same manner also he took the cup, when he had supped, saying, "This cup is the new testament in my blood; do this as often as you drink it, in remembrance of me."

(The wine is passed.)

Drink this in remembrance of Jesus.

Let us join together in silent prayer that the spirit which was in Jesus may be in us also, enabling us to know the truth, to do the will of God, and to abide in God's peace.

(All join in silent prayer and meditation.)

Closing Prayer

O God, thou Fountain of Love, thy Spirit is in us as a well of water springing up into everlasting life. Let every thought and motive be cleansed by its life-giving stream. Let each high resolve and holy desire be quickened into larger life, that the hearts of thy children may bear the fruits of joyful service and grateful love. Amen.

Closing Hymn

Benediction

Go forth into the world in peace. Be strong and of good courage. Hold fast to that which is good; render to no one evil for evil; strengthen the faint-hearted; support the weak, help the afflicted, honor all women and men; love and serve God with gladness and singleness of heart, rejoicing in the power of the Holy Spirit.

Service of Healing for Those Affected by AIDS

This service was conducted at First Church Unitarian Universalist in Jamaica Plain, Massachusetts, on February 13, 1990. It may be adapted to suit the particular needs of your community.

Prelude

Lighting of Candles

Greetings

Invocation

Reading

- Isaiah 43:1-4a

Processional Hymn

Love divine, all loves excelling,
Joy of Heaven, to earth come down;
Fix in us thy humble dwelling,
All thy faithful mercies crown.
Shepherd, thou art all compassion,
Pure unbounded love thou art:

Visit us with thy salvation,
Enter ev'ry trembling heart.

Breathe, O breathe thy loving Spirit
Into every troubled breast;
Let us all in thee inherit,
Let us find thy promised rest.
Come, Almighty, to deliver,
Let us all thy life receive:
Graciously return, and never,
never more thy temples leave. Amen.

Prayer

Readings

- 2 Kings 5:1-14
- "Touching and Being Touched" by Robert Coles, M.D.

Anthem

Greetings and Announcements

Offering

(To support the First Church AIDS Project and its work with the Shattuck Hospital AIDS Unit in Jamaica Plain and the Boston City Hospital Children's AIDS Unit.)

Anthem

Homily

"The Common Touch"
Reverend Terry Burke

Tonight we gather as part of a common ministry of loving, healing touch. Our lessons contain two stories of healing. One is the story of Naaman the Syrian, who was to the people of Israel a stranger, a foreigner, a military enemy, and a person of a different faith, but who is still healed.

Naaman was a great general, but he had leprosy. Leprosy, like AIDS in our time, was falsely regarded by some as a sign of divine disfavor (the text points out that Naaman was highly regarded by God). During a raid, Naaman's soldiers captured a young Israelite woman, and she has been put to work in Naaman's household as a servant. She tells Naaman's wife that there is a prophet in

Israel (Elisha) who can heal her husband. The King of Syria sends a letter to the King of Israel asking him to heal the commander. The King of Israel is horrified, believing the letter to be a pretext for fighting. However, there *is* a prophet in Israel, and Elisha tells Naaman to dip his body seven times in that muddy little stream, the Jordan River. Naaman is enraged; he has expected some dramatic gesture befitting his great station in life. A servant calms him down, asking, "Wouldn't you have done something difficult if the prophet had asked it of you? Why not try the ordinary thing that he suggests?" Naaman bathes in the river, and his skin is healed like that of a child. He has brought rich gifts, but is healed for free as a gift from God.

In this story from Second Kings, the powerful rulers, the kings, are powerless to heal Naaman. His healing comes about through the efforts of more ordinary people: the captured servant who shows compassion for her captor; the wife who listens to a socially insignificant servant; the servant who risks his master's rage to give him sound advice. Naaman is healed not by the mighty rivers of Syria, but by the ordinary little Jordan.

In the second lesson, psychiatrist Robert Coles writes about a six-year-old black girl who, during a crisis of school desegregation, is healed from the effects of racial hatred and bigotry. She is healed by the loving touch of the ordinary hands of her mother and grandmother. The frightened child is hugged by her mother, who is in turn hugged by *her* mother, and so they are touched and healed by the hands of God.

Ours is an ordinary, common ministry tonight—to give the loving touch of God. We are *all* here to heal and be healed—we all have roles in the healing story. There are those from the laity and clergy who will lay on hands and have hands laid on them. They have featured roles, like Naaman and Elisha. There are many behind-the-scenes organizers and planners of this service, who are like the helpful and essential servants. Then there are those who will sit simply in the pews, who are like the countless anonymous characters in the story. All are a necessary part of the healing, all are a part of God's story, and all are a part of our common story.

Our common ministry of healing, loving touch involves embodying God's love. That ministry does not end with this service. It continues when we go to the reception and shake hands with a stranger or touch a friend on the arm. It continues next week when we greet a person with AIDS with a hug.

May we allow our hands to be God's ordinary and divine healing hands. May we allow ourselves to touch and be touched. May we allow ourselves to be healed.

Hymn

Make channels for the streams of love,
Where they may broadly run;
And love has overflowing streams,
To fill them ev'ry one.

But if at any time we cease
Such channels to provide,
The very founts of love for us
Will soon be parched and dried.

For we must share, if we would keep
That blessing from above:
Ceasing to give, we cease to have—
Such is the law of love. Amen.

Litany for Healing

Leader: O God of all creation, your people cry out to you in their suffering and pain.

O God of love, hear our prayers.

Leader: We remember the healing of your people in times past. Hear us too in our present afflictions, especially those suffering from acquired immune deficiency syndrome—men, women, children, straight and gay, nonbelievers and believers: all of them your children.

O God of love, hear our prayers.

Leader: We pray for all those who have lost loved ones to AIDS. We remember those who have died from this illness. I invite you to name, silently or out loud, your friends and loved ones who have died.

(Members of the congregation may name those whom they wish to remember.)

Leader: We give thanks for the gift of their lives. May perpetual light shine upon them.

O God of love, hear our prayers.

Leader: We pray for the families and friends of all who suffer from AIDS.

O God of love, hear our prayers.

Leader: We pray for their nurses, doctors, and social workers, and all those in the health-care profession, that they may be sensitive and compassionate.

O God of love, hear our prayers.

Leader: We pray for all those involved in medical research, as they struggle to find a cure for AIDS.

O God of love, hear our prayers.

Leader: We pray for ourselves when we are caught in anger, fear, and confusion, that we may be healed in body, mind, and spirit.

O God of love, hear our prayers.

Leader: O gracious God, may we feel your presence in your lives.

O God of love, hear our prayers.

Leader: Let the life-giving power of the Spirit fill us all.

O God of mercy, bless us and heal us. Make us whole. Amen.

Invitation to the Laying On of Hands

Four or five prayer groups will be stationed around the room to lay hands on those who seek healing of mind, body, or spirit, for themselves or for others. The front groups speak Spanish; the rear group speaks Haitian. Please line up by the nearest group, and when it is your turn, you may stand or kneel by the group, depending on your preference. One of the ministers of healing will ask you, "What would you like us to pray for?" You may answer as generally or as specifically as you wish. They will then place their hands upon your head and shoulders and pray. Please pray silently with them. After the prayer concludes, please return to your pew.

If you prefer to remain in your pew, please pray for those at the prayer stations, as well as for your own concerns and loved ones.

The Laying On of Hands

Prayer

Closing Hymn

Amazing Grace, how sweet the sound
That saved a soul like me!
I once was lost, but now am found,
Was blind, but now I see.

'Twas grace that taught my heart to fear
And grace my fears relieved;
How precious did that grace appear
The hour I first believed!

Through many dangers, toils, and snares,
I have already come;
'Tis grace that brought me safe thus far,
And grace will lead me home.

When we've been there ten thousand years,
Bright shining as the sun,
We've no less days to sing God's praise
Than when we'd first begun.

Benediction and Response

Postlude

Service of Union
Marianne McCarthy Power

Opening Words

Honored Guests, we are invited here today to witness a covenant of love. We have come to celebrate the love that has brought our friends, _____ and _____, to the decision to accept each other totally and permanently in holy union.

Into this estate these two persons come now to be united and blessed by their sacred words, by the recognition of this church, and by your abiding devotion to each of them and both of them.

If life has meaning to us at all, it possesses it because of love. It is one of life's richest gifts when a relationship grows into a permanent bond of love, which leads two life paths to become joined and to proceed together along a common path, as partners in holy union. It is this growth which brings us together today.

This union is a covenant of love involving both privilege and responsibility. It calls for mutual esteem and concern, for bearing each other's infirmities and weaknesses, for comfort in sickness and sorrow.

It is, therefore, not to be entered into unadvisedly, or lightly, but thoughtfully, and understanding of the commitment for which it calls, for the bonds of this holy union have been cherished in every generation.

Our presence today shows ____ and ____ that they take with them into their union not only their commitment to one another, but also our commitment and encouragement to them.

In mindfulness of this commitment, ____ and ____ have asked that the following New Testament passage from the First Letter of Paul to the Corinthians be shared among us.

Reading

• 1 Corinthians 13:1-13

Vows

Will you, ____, take ____, to love and to cherish, to honor and to comfort, in sorrow and in joy, in hardship and in ease, to have and to hold, forsaking all others, from this day forth?

(Response)

Will you, ____, take ____, to love and to cherish, to honor and to comfort, in sorrow and in joy, in hardship and in ease, to have and to hold, forsaking all others, from this day forth?

(Response)

Blessing of the Rings

May I have the rings please. . . . May your rings always be the symbol of the unbroken circle of love. Love freely given has no beginning and no end. Love freely given has no giver and no receiver. You are each the giver, and each the receiver. May your rings always call to mind the freedom and the power of this love.

Pronouncement

With this community who affirms and honors it, I say that ____ and ____ are joined in a holy union that is both recognized and cherished by God and by this community. Let all others respect the threshold of their home.

Prayer

Beloved God, may you look with favor upon ____ and ____, who have become one in holy union. Give them wisdom and devotion in the ordering of their life together, that each may be to the other a strength in need, a counselor in perplexity, a comfort in sorrow, and a companion in joy.

May they grow in love and peace together all the days of their lives. May their life together be a sign of God's love to a broken world, that unity may overcome estrangement and joy conquer despair. Give them such fulfillment of their mutual affections that they may reach out in love and concern for others. Amen.

Benediction

Remember the comfortable words which Jesus said: "Love one another as I have loved you." May the love in your hearts give you joy. May the greatness of life bring you peace. May your days be good and your lives be long upon the earth. Amen.

Family Worship Service
Reverend Lucinda S. Duncan

Family worship services are 15-minute, child-centered services that children attend with their parents, before or during the adult worship service. People of all ages are welcome. When planning such a service, you should focus on a general topic synthesized into *one main idea* with one or more concrete examples.

Think of the main idea as a sentence you'd like the *children* to say that the service was about when they are going home. Think simple, and think on the young side. For example, if you have children aged three to nine attending your service, phrase your main idea and pick your example(s) to fit the developmental level and the life situation of a five-year-old. If the age range is larger, say three to twelve, visualize an eight-year-old in the third grade, and pitch the service to that age. Keeping the theme to one main idea not only allows you to spiral from the simple to the semi-abstract, but also increases the likelihood that all the children will grasp the essential meaning.

The following example illustrates the planning sequence for a service aimed at five- to seven-year-olds.

General Topic

To affirm the validity of bisexual, gay, lesbian, and/or transgender parenting.

Main Idea

It's OK to have all different kinds of parents, as long as they love their kids.

Example

Bring in an armload of stuffed animals, making sure that you have some "same" pairing among them. Sit them up front on little chairs if you have them. Explain to the children that this is such a wonderful collection of stuffed animals that you'd like to play "family," and ask if anyone would like to come up and pick out two of these animals to be the "momma" and the "poppa."

Call on someone little, and spend a little time appreciating how hard it is to decide. When the two animals have been selected, say something like: "Oh, aren't these nice ones! Thank you! Could you tell me why you picked *this* one and *that* one, and not all the others?" You are looking for the child's reasoning. She or he will tell you something like, "Well, this one's the daddy because he's the biggest (or fattest, etc.) and this one's the mommy because she's not as big."

Listen, acknowledging the child's reasoning, but look puzzled and say, "Oh, I get it, to be a daddy you have to be big?" The child will probably agree with you. "And the reason that mommies are mommies is because they're littler, is that right?" The child will probably agree, but may begin to feel uncomfortable.

Turn to the rest of the kids who, by this time, may be thinking that this might not be the only category. "Gee, I'm wondering about that. Do any of the rest of you think there might be another way to pick out the mommy and the daddy?"

Select an older child with a bit more reasoning and articulation ability. (Be sure to thank your first helper as she/he returns to her/his seat.) Repeat the selection sequence and go through the reasons again, this time looking for the idea that maybe the most important thing about being a parent is not what you look like or even whether you're a boy or a girl, but the fact that you love your children. Ask the kids how that idea feels to them.

Homily

After the children have returned to their seats, quickly pair some animals in other combinations, saying something like, "Gee, then if the most important thing about being a parent is loving your children, then we could even pick two *brown* bears, or two *little* bunnies, or two *boy* animals or two *girl* animals, right? Parents can be all kinds of people, and every family is a little bit different. Some families have a mommy *and* a daddy, some families have a mommy *or* a daddy, and some families have *two mommies* or *two daddies*. Parents come in all sizes and shapes and kinds; what matters most of all is that parents love their children."

Benediction

God of love and kindness, we are so grateful that parents are people who try to love their children. Help us to know that every family is different but that every family is loving. Amen.

Religious Education Guidelines

In general, the range and variety of loving, human, life partnerships should be represented in religious education materials. These partnerships should be named, not merely implied. Inclusiveness should not be assumed in a culture which assumes heterosexuality and denies homosexuality and bisexuality by omission. Families do not necessarily mean two parents, one male and one female. Parents may include two partners of the same sex, either male or female. When love or marriage is discussed, same-sex relationships should be included and presented alongside different-sex relationships.

Curricula with a specifically Christian orientation should stress the message of welcome to those marginalized. Children should be encouraged to understand that those who are socially rejected in our society are those for whom Christianity holds a special message and a special invitation to community.

PROGRAM RESOURCES

Books

Some of the following resources on bisexual, gay, lesbian and transgender issues are available from the Unitarian Universalist Association Bookstore. For more information please call (617) 742-2100 ext. 101, 102, or 123. To place an order call (800) 215-9076. Or write to: UUA Bookstore, 25 Beacon St., Boston, MA 02108-2800. Visit the UUA Bookstore online at http://www.uua.org/bookstore/index.html.

Bisexuality

Hutchins, Loraine, and Lani Kaahumanu, editors. *Bi Any Other Name: Bisexual People Speak Out.* A good collection of thoughts, essays, narratives, and information about bisexuality and the lives of bisexual people. The book is divided into four areas: psychology, spirituality, community, and politics. (Alyson) 1991.

Family Issues

Benkov, Laura, PhD. *Reinventing the Family: The Emerging Story of Lesbian and Gay Parents.* Like the families who are its subject, *Reinventing the Family* breaks new ground. A landmark book about the changing American family, it points the way to a society that honors a multiplicity of families created out of commitment, care, and love. (Crown) 1995.

Martin, April, PhD. *The Lesbian and Gay Parenting Handbook: Creating and Raising Our Families.* A sensitive, thorough look at the many issues involved in forming a lesbian or gay family. Combines the author's expertise and professional perspective with first person stories from gay and lesbian parents and their children. (HarperCollins) 1993.

Stacey, Judith. *In the Name of the Family: Rethinking Family Values in the Postmodern Age.* A thoughtful, insightful book on all different kinds of families in an age where the definition of the word "family" is public debate. The analysis of recent history combined with ideas about what might be best for our future make for excellent reading. (Beacon) 1996.

Relationships

Ayers, Tess, and Paul Brown. *The Essential Guide to Lesbian and Gay Weddings.* The latest in wedding etiquette, witty anecdotes from many recent gay and lesbian union ceremonies, and unexpected historical trivia make this an indispensable and truly entertaining resource for same-sex couples who want to plan an unforgettable and perfectly orchestrated wedding. (HarperSanFrancisco) 1994.

Butler, Becky, editor. *Ceremonies of the Heart: Celebrating Lesbian Ceremonies of Union.* A celebration of love and lesbian pride, *Ceremonies of the Heart* takes us into the lives of twenty-seven couples who have affirmed their relationships with rituals—weddings, handfastings, holy unions and ceremonies of commitment. Each couple describes the sometimes thrilling, sometimes difficult months leading up to the day of celebration, the response from friends and family, and the transformative power of the ceremony itself. (Seal Press) 1990.

Curry, Hayden, and Denis Clifford. *Legal Guide for Lesbian and Gay Couples.* Laws designed to regulate and protect unmarried couples don't apply to lesbian and gay couples. This book shows you step-by-step how to write a living together contract, plan for medical emergencies, and plan your estates. Includes forms, sample agreements and lists of both national lesbian and gay legal organizations and AIDS organizations. (Nolo Press) 1991.

Personal Growth

Buxton, Amity Pierce, PhD. *The Other Side of the Closet: The Coming Out Crisis for Straight Spouses.* Based on the author's five years of research and interviews with hundreds of spouses, this book explores the major issues straight spouses confront when their partners declare their homosexuality or bisexuality and offers practical guidelines for resolving these conflicts in the direction of positive growth. (IBS Press) 1991.

O'Neill, Craig, and Kathleen Ritter. *Coming Out Within: Stages of Awakening for Lesbians and Gay Men.* "A compassionate guide to spiritual and psychological health for lesbians and gay men. A parable of the spiritual journey of all people, as they cope with loss of dreams and move toward an integrated self."—Rosemary Radford Ruether. (HarperCollins) 1992.

Roscoe, Will. *Queer Spirits.* In an inspiring and loving testimony to gay spirit, Will Roscoe offers gay men a way to discover the myths and heroes within themselves. "This vibrant collection . . . lights our way on the healing path toward wholeness."—Mark Thompson, author of *Gay Soul.* (Beacon) 1996.

Politics

Blumenfeld, Warren J., editor. *Homophobia: How We All Pay the Price.* In both personal and analytical essays, the contributors show how the fight to end homophobia is everyone's fight if we are to bring about a less oppressive and more productive society. Concrete suggestions for transforming attitudes, behaviors, and institutions. (Beacon) 1992.

Blumenfeld, Warren, and Diane Raymond. *Looking at Gay and Lesbian Life.* A wealth of well-researched, up-to-date information about every major aspect of gay and lesbian life. (Beacon) 1989.

Lewin, Ellen, editor. *Inventing Lesbian Cultures In America.* An excellent collection of essays regarding the lives of lesbians in the past and present. The eight essays are divided into three areas entitled: Inventions, Conventions, and Reinventions. Good reading on gender and sexual identity. (Beacon) 1996.

Mohr, Richard D. *A More Perfect Union: Why Straight America Must Stand Up for Gay Rights.* "Whenever we demean gays and lesbians, we diminish ourselves. Richard Mohr makes this point time and again, clearly and poignantly, reminding Americans who we are as citizens and human beings."—William Sloan Coffin. (Beacon) 1994. Cloth.

Pharr, Suzanne. *Homophobia as a Weapon of Sexism.* An analysis of how homophobia works in our society as it relates to sexism. Much of her work is included in this manual. Answers the question of why homophobia exists and discusses the various insidious avenues of oppression. (Chardon Press) 1988.

Roscoe, Will, editor. *Radically Gay: Gay Liberation in the Words of Its Founder Harry Hay.* In 1948 Harry Hay began pursuing his vision of forming an organization devoted to the welfare of gay people: the Mattachine Society. For the last fifty years, he has grappled with each new wave of cultural and political thought and synthesized agonizing contradictions, from spirituality to Marxism, from art to politics. This first collection of Hay's own words—speeches, papers, and interviews—offers valuable insight into the vision of one man who made it possible for millions to live in freedom and with self-respect. (Beacon)1996. Cloth.

Racism

Barndt, Joseph. *Dismantling Racism: The Continuing Challenge to White America.* Begins by analyzing racism as it is today and how it has changed over the past few decades. Focuses on the task of dismantling racism, how we can work to bring it to an end and build a racially just, multiracial, multicultural society. (Augsburg) 1992.

Dalton, Harlon L. *Racial Healing: Confronting the Fear between Blacks & Whites. Racial Healing* takes on the fear most people have of talking about racism. Dalton urges us as individuals to speak openly about our racial beliefs no matter how uncomfortable or awkward such talk may be. He writes that blacks and whites "should simply put everything on the table. Own up to the tension. Acknowledge the risks. When someone inevitably screws up, rather than beat a hasty retreat, we should seize the opportunity to deepen the dialog." (Doubleday) 1995.

Feagin, Joe R., and Melvin P. Sikes. *Living With Racism: The Black Middle-Class Experience.* Despite the prevalent white view that racism is diminishing, this groundbreaking study exposes the depth and relentlessness of the racism that middle-class black Americans face every day. From the supermarket to the office, the authors show, African Americans are routinely subjected to subtle humiliations and overt hostility across white America. (Beacon) 1994.

Kiel, Paul. *Uprooting Racism: How White People Can Work for Racial Justice.* Discusses racism without rhetoric or attack. Helps us understand the dynamics of racism in our society, institutions and daily lives, and shares stories, suggestions, advice, exercises and approaches for working together to fight racism. At once gentle and provocative, *Uprooting Racism* will help you intervene strategically wherever racism occurs in public policy, institutional settings, or interpersonal interactions. (New Society Publishers) 1996.

Simons, Dr. George F., et al. *Cultural Diversity Fieldbook: Fresh Visions & Breakthrough Strategies for Revitalizing the Workplace.* Brings together examples of the leading thought and best practices on one of the most talked about business topics: diversity in the workplace. More than 150 articles, interviews, essays, and activities are combined with hundreds of resource reviews to provide a rich picture of the complex and diverse culture in which business is conducted. (Peterson's/Pacesetter Books) 1996.

West, Cornel. *Race Matters.* Despite the increasing climate of racial hatred and violence in America, discussions of race seem to be mired in traditional liberal and conservative rhetoric. Cornel West provides a transformative voice willing to go to the heart of the issues and help begin the healing of our nation. (Beacon) 1993.

Religion

Cherry, Kittredge, and Zalmon Sherwood, editors. *Equal Rites: Lesbian and Gay Worship Ceremonies and Celebrations.* This much-needed collection of worship services, ceremonies and celebrations include liturgies of spiritual beginnings, healing, blessings, holy communion, pride and empowerment, funeral and memorial services, seasonal and holiday rites, and covenant rites for couples. Also

a reference book for creating unique and meaningful worship services that address significant aspects of lesbian and gay spirituality. (Westminster John Knox Press) 1995.

McNeill, John J. *The Church and the Homosexual.* The first edition of this now-classic book, published in 1976, convincingly established that the Bible does not condemn homosexuality. In this fourth edition, McNeill calls on the Vatican to make a public act of repentance for its homophobia. (Beacon) 1996.

McNeill, John J. *Taking a Chance on God.* Explores how lesbians and gay men can claim a positive gay identity and at the same time have a fulfilling spiritual life. "McNeill draws on the insights of the gay and lesbian liberation movement, his counseling experience with lesbian and gay people, and a variety of faith traditions—Catholic, mainstream Protestant, Evangelical and other world religions—to produce a unique, comprehensive, life-giving ethic."—Equal Time. (Beacon) 1996.

McNeill, John J. *Freedom, Glorious Freedom: The Spiritual Journey to the Fullness of Life for Gays, Lesbians, and Everybody Else.* "John McNeill writes of a glorious freedom he knows experientially: oneness with God through oneness with the authentic self. At the same time this therapist-theologian and beloved, gentle prophet paints a broad canvas. He connects personal and global liberation in a compelling way, describing the essential and special roles of gay and lesbian spiritualities in birthing something new in human history. This warm, personal book is also intellectually and spiritually bold."—James B. Nelson. (Beacon) 1996. Cloth.

Thompson, Mark. *Gay Soul: Finding the Heart of Gay Spirit and Nature with Sixteen Writers, Healers, Teachers, and Visionaries.* Longtime *Advocate* editor, Mark Thompson, has compiled black-and-white photographs with searching, provocative interviews with 16 renowned gay elders whose vision and leadership illuminate the spiritual dimension of gay life. (HarperSanFrancisco) 1995.

Transgender Concerns

Brown, Mildred L. and Chloe Ann Rounsley. *True Selves: Understanding Transsexualism.* "Millie Brown has made a tremendous contribution by sharing her extensive knowledge and personal experiences with other professionals, with transgender people themselves, their friends and families, and the very interested public in general." —Leah Cohan Schaefer, past president, The Harry Benjamin International Dysphoria Association.

Feinberg, Leslie. *Transgender Warriors.* "Feinberg's chronicle of transgender people throughout time and across cultures, woven into a fascinating personal narrative, is at once disarming and a call to arms. Men and women have had their histories. This is the history book for the rest of us."—Kate Bornstein, author of *Gender Outlaws.* (Beacon) 1997.

Feinberg, Leslie. *Trans Liberation: Beyond Pink or Blue.* A stirring call for tolerance and solidarity, this collection of inspiring speeches argues passionately for the acceptance of all trans people— and for the need to build coalitions between progressive political groups. (Beacon) 1998.

Youth

Bass, Ellen, and Kate Kaufman. *Free Your Mind.* The definitive practical guide for gay, lesbian, and bisexual youth and their families, teachers, counselors, and friends. Alive with the voices of more than fifty young people, rich with accurate information and positive practical advice, *Free Your Mind* talks about how to come out, deal with problems, make healthy choices about sex, connect with other gay youth and supportive adults, and take pride and participate in the gay and lesbian community. (HarperPerennial)1996.

Bauer, Marion Dane, editor. *Am I Blue?: Coming Out From the Silence.* Original short stories for young adults deal with growing up gay or lesbian, or with gay or lesbian friends or parents. Features stories by Lois Lowry, William Sleator, Jane Yolen, and more. (HarperCollins) 1994.

Herdt, Gilbert, and Andrew Boxer. *Children of Horizons: How Gay and Lesbian Teens Are Leading a New Way Out of the Closet.* With a new epilogue on teens and AIDS, this book provides the first indepth examination of the trials faced by gay and lesbian teens. "Refreshing . . . provides a wealth of inspiration and some practical suggestions for adults who would like to provide services for gay and lesbian youth, but who may not be sure how to begin."—Lambda Book Report. (Beacon) 1996.

Pollack, Rachel, and Cheryl Schwartz. *The Journey Out: A Guide for and about Lesbian, Gay, and Bisexual Teens.* Contains common sense advice on "coming out," dating, love, health, gay youth politics, homophobia, harassment, religion, and more. Personal stories and experiences of gay youth, lists of resources around the country, up-to-date information on gay youth issues, and practical strategies to prepare you for whatever may come on the journey out. (Puffin) 1995.

Videos

To rent from the Unitarian Universalist Association Video Loan Library, contact Kathy Rogers of The Etc. Co., 8080 Pierpont Road, Bloomfield, New York 14469. Phone: (716)229-5325. FAX: 716-229-2857. Email: uuavideo@juno.com. There is a $15 charge for each rental.

AIDS

Common Threads. Profiles of five individuals memorialized in the AIDS quilt. Powerful and moving. (79 minutes)

Sex, Drugs, and AIDS. While targeted for junior high through young adult, this video contains good information about HIV and AIDS for all adults. Strong section on homophobia.

Families/Youth

Always My Kid: A Family Guide to Understanding Homosexuality. Excellent information and narratives about parents and learning of their child's sexual orientation. (74 minutes)

Gay Lives and Culture Wars. Focuses on gay and lesbian youth and their families as they come to terms with being gay.

Pride and Prejudice. Toronto gay and lesbian youth group tells their story and reflects on life in the larger heterosexist society.

History

Before Stonewall. Powerful story of lives of bisexual, gay, lesbian, and transgender people prior to 1969. Excellent history. (87 minutes)

The Times of Harvey Milk. Academy Award winning documentary of the slain gay civil rights leader from San Francisco. (87 minutes)

Pink Triangles. Powerful movie of the history of discrimination against bisexual, gay, lesbian, and transgender people. (35 minutes)

Politics

Ballot Measure Nine. A moving account of how Oregon citizens fought for the rights of bisexual, gay, lesbian, and transgender people in 1992. (80 minutes)

It's Elementary: Talking About Gay Issues in Schools. Terrific video about how some schools have helped reduce homophobia through education. (77 minutes)

Teaching Respect for All. From the Gay, Lesbian, Straight Teachers' Network (GLSTN), this excellent resource explains why it is important to talk about sexual orientation issues in schools. Good for teacher training. (50 minutes)

Religion

Welcoming Congregation. The Unitarian Universalist Church of Rockford, IL, discusses the program based on their own experiences.

Sermons

Available through the Office of Bisexual, Gay, Lesbian, and Transgender Concerns at the Unitarian Universalist Association. OBGLTC, UUA, 25 Beacon St., Boston, MA 02108. (617)742-2100.

Services of Union

Available through the Office of Bisexual, Gay, Lesbian, and Transgender Concerns.

Pre-Marital Counseling Guide for Same-Gender Couples. A resource for those who perform commitment and marriage ceremonies for same-gender couples. (OBGLTC, 1997)

Planning Guide for Same-Sex Services of Union. An information packet on services of union. (OBGLTC, 1986)

Unitarian Universalist Pamphlets

The following pamphlets on bisexual, gay, and lesbian issues are available from the UUA Bookstore. For more information please call (617)742-2100, ext. 101, 102, or 123. To place an order call (800)215-9076. Or write to: UUA Bookstore, 25 Beacon St., Boston, MA 02108-2800. Visit the UUA Bookstore online at http://www.uua.org/bookstore/index.html. Please add $3.00 handling for all prepaid orders.

Unitarian Universalism: A Religious Home for Bisexual, Gay, Lesbian and Transgender People. Barbara Pescan.

Unitarian Universalism: A Welcoming Place for Bisexual, Gay, Lesbian and Transgender People. Scott W. Alexander.

Is Our Church Gay? Answering Children's Questions About Homophobia and Sexual Orientation. Meg Riley

These pamphlets are available through the Office of Bisexual, Gay, Lesbian, and Transgender Concerns.

Unitarian Universalism: A Serious Spiritual Alternative for the Gay & Lesbian Community. Office of Bisexual, Gay, Lesbian, and Transgender Concerns.

Welcoming Congregation. Office of Bisexual, Gay, Lesbian, and Transgender Concerns. And Interweave.

Young Religious Unitarian Universalists: A Loving Community. UUA Youth Office.

MEASURING YOUR PROGRESS

Once a congregation feels it has achieved all 16 action steps (see Guidelines, page 13) and has taken a congregational vote in affirmation of being recognized as a Welcoming Congregation, a brief description of how the action steps were met in the three major areas, along with the results of the congregational vote, should be sent to the Office of Bisexual, Gay, Lesbian, and Transgender Concerns. Upon receipt of this information, the Office will send the congregation a letter of congratulations, along with 2 posters that proclaim that they are a Welcoming Congregation.

Please note that the OBGLTC does not ask for this information in order to "rate" a congregation's work, but rather to keep ourselves informed of the good work being done in our congregations, and to provide ideas for other congregations involved in the Welcoming Congregation process.

When you are ready to be acknowledged as a Welcoming Congregation, send your information to: UUA-OBGLTC, 25 Beacon Street, Boston, MA 02108. Or, if you prefer, you may send it electronically to: obgltc@uua.org

The Welcoming Congregation

Please include the following information when you notify the OBGLTC of your status:

Name of your congregation:

City, state/province:

Your name:

Date:

An action summary or description of the work done in the areas of education, congregational life, and community outreach (refer to Guidelines on page 15).

Examples of advertisements, bylaws, speaker/worship guidelines, pamphlets, etc. that you have created.

Results of your congregational vote.

Plans for further congregational action in the area of bisexual, gay, lesbian, and/or transgender concerns.

Notes

Notes

Notes

Notes

Notes

Notes